Football
DYNAMO

Football DЦNAMO

Modern Russia and the People's Game

Marc Bennetts

Published by Virgin Books 2008

2 4 6 8 10 9 7 5 3 1

Copyright © Marc Bennetts 2008

Marc Bennetts has asserted his right under the Copyright, Designs and Patents Act 1988 to be identified as the author of this work

First published in Great Britain in 2008 by
Virgin Books
Random House
Thames Wharf Studios,
Rainville Road
London, W6 9HA

www.rbooks.co.uk

Addresses for companies within The Random House Group Limited can be found at: www.randomhouse.co.uk/offices.htm

The Random House Group Limited Reg. No. 954009

A CIP catalogue record for this book
is available from the British Library

ISBN 9780753513194

The Random House Group Limited supports The Forest Stewardship Council [FSC], the leading international forest certification organisation. All our titles that are printed on Greenpeace approved FSC certified paper carry the FSC logo. Our paper procurement policy can be found at www.rbooks.co.uk/environment

Mixed Sources
Product group from well-managed
forests and other controlled sources
www.fsc.org Cert no. TT-COC-2139
© 1996 Forest Stewardship Council

Typeset by TW Typesetting, Plymouth, Devon

Printed and bound in Great Britain by CPI Bookmarque, Croydon CR0 4TD

This book is dedicated with love and thanks to Bill and Jo Bennetts
(a.k.a. Mum and Dad)

Contents

Foreword

'The beautiful game,' writes Marc Bennetts in this remarkable book, 'was the anti-Enigma Machine through which Russia could be decoded.' If he's right, then watching the Russian Premier league could save the world's spies a lot of work. In fact, a subscription to the *Sovetski-Sport* newspaper could have shortened the Cold War. And yet Bennetts gets you to believe the claim. This book might not crack Russia's code – probably nothing can – but it does make the country a little bit less incomprehensible, and it's very funny along the way.

In 1992 I spent a month having the traditional foreign journalist's experience of bafflement while getting lost all over Moscow. The city's size, greyness and filth was reminiscent of South London circa 1973, but otherwise it all felt pretty alien. Then, one Sunday afternoon, I went with some Brits and Russians to the Spartak Moscow vs CSKA derby in the massive Luzhniki stadium with the statue of Lenin in front. It was a gorgeous sunny day in August, and I realized that this was the perfect Russian tourist event: it was an authentic Russian occasion, because the game wasn't being staged for our benefit, and in fact nobody even cared that we were there; the setting and the fans' behaviour were so familiar that we could barely recognize the differences between it and Britain.

Like many foreigners who spend any time in Russia, I found that there was something addictive about the country, an attraction that isn't obvious at first glance. Anyone can fall in love with Rome.

What attracts people to Russia may be the intensity of relation-ships, the joys people have despite everything, and – something that surprised me – the national sense of humour. The experience inspired me to go away and spend a year studying Russian every day. I never got far enough to have a simple conversation.

I was just a passing observer whose hopes for more were defeated. Bennetts has gone native. He came to Russia planning to stay for a year. That was a decade ago. Then he fell in love with a Russian woman, and much more bizarrely, with Russian football. In fact he may be the only person from outside the former Soviet Union with the latter affliction.

Like all foreigners, Bennetts began with the sense that Russia was unknowable: 'There was a certain *something*, inaccessible to the casual observer, at the core of the Russian game. This was encapsulated, for me at least, in the form of the terrace chant – "*Sudyu na milo*" – that the fans would invariably begin to shout whenever a decision went against their side.'

The chant literally meant 'Ref on soap', but that didn't seem to make sense. Eventually Bennetts cracked it: 'I found out that the idiomatic phrase was correctly translated as "Make soap out of the ref!" and referred to the Soviet practice of producing hygiene products from the fat of slaughtered stray dogs, a fate that the enraged supporters deemed only fit for the object of their righteous indignation.'

Having figured that out, Bennetts was away. Over the years he watched Moscow transform from post-communism to late-capitalism (the exact opposite of Marx's prophesy) while football made the same journey. When he first arrived, so few people cared about the game that you could walk into some matches off the street without paying; or as one Muscovite fan told me, during the years of chaos, 'So many matches are fixed that as a supporter all you can do is cheer on the odd player of quality who plays honestly.' By the time Bennetts finished his *Football Dynamo*, the oligarchs and state energy companies had turned the Russian game into 'one of the world's richest'.

Everything has changed, and yet the corruption and underperfor-mance of Russian football – hilariously documented in this book – have remained intact, as if these were facts of nature, impervious to any manmade influences. One thing Bennetts conveys is how miserable it must be to be a Russian professional footballer: if the Soviet-relic manager doesn't get you, the new mafia will.

This book is packed with brave and surprising interviews (conducted mostly in Russian), with everyone from humble fans to Russia's best players and its richest oligarchs. Getting those interviews must have been even more of a feat than it would have been in another country. The author, after all, is 'a foreign writer lacking official Russian press accreditation in a land where documents are accorded a particular reverence'. It's exhausting just to think about how much work went into this.

In one of his interviews, he asks Evgeni Giner, oligarch owner of CSKA, whether the team really fixes matches as everyone says. At the end of the interview Giner sees him out of the door, and tells him: ' "Your book should concentrate on the game itself, on the matches, not on the scandals. It's easy to write about that kind of stuff," he added. "Dostoevsky, Tolstoy, Dickens," he went on, throwing in a token English writer, "they didn't write about scandals, did they?" '

Most writers hearing this might get a touch concerned. In Russia, the ins and outs of football are considered a dangerous subject to discuss, like Chechnya, or sales of nuclear missile parts. Happily, Bennetts was naïve enough to ignore Giner's advice.

The 'matches' tend to lose something in the telling. The best football books therefore usually steer clear of them. The best books – and this one fits in the football-in-one-country tradition of David Winner's *Brilliant Orange*, Alex Bellos's *Futebol* and Phil Ball's *Morbo* – are always about a place as much as the game. Bennetts doesn't just know the history of Dynamo Moscow, gruesomely gripping as it is. He also knows about Dostoevsky and Gogol and the Bolshevik revolution and 'zapoi', the Russian word for 'bender', if a few drunken nights out in Britain can be said remotely to compare to an experience straight out of the Apocalypse. As a bonus, he gives us a marvellous cameo of Steve McClaren.

You'd think this book – packed with horrors – would do nothing to advance the cause of Anglo-Russian friendship. In fact it just might. Bennetts writes about the Russian game – and by extension, a large chunk of Russian daily life – with such love that the reader cannot help but be infected. Just look what happened to the Bennetts family. After Russia beats England in the crucial qualifier for Euro 2008 in Moscow, the author calls his mother-in-law to congratulate her. 'She sounded a touch bemused by my joy at Russia's victory,' he writes. (And having read the preceding 200-odd pages, you believe that his joy has to do with more than just hoping that a Russian qualification will help sell his book.)

But it turns out Bennetts is not the only convert:

Back in England, won over by my enthusiasm and their many trips to the country, . . . my father later told me than when Pavlyuchenko scored his second goal he and my mother had leapt around the room cheering so much that 'the neighbours must have thought we were Russian'.

If George Blake, the MI6 agent-turned-Russian 'superspy' now living out his last years in Moscow, reads this, as he should, you imagine his octogenarian eyes twinkling with recognition. But this book does more than just help you learn to love Russia. It even helps you learn to love Russian football.

Simon Kuper,
February 2008

Prologue

In July 2007, the month that Britain and Russia engaged in tit-for-tat expulsions of diplomats in connection with the murder of the ex-KGB officer Alexander Litvinenko, I went to watch Spartak Moscow take on Zenit St Petersburg in the Russian capital. The crowd of 50,000 was one of the season's biggest and the match itself a thrilling display of open football, as Spartak ran out 3–1 winners, showing no respect for their opponents' recent multimillion-dollar signings. Leaving the stadium after the match, I couldn't help thinking back to the first ever games I had attended in Russia over a decade before.

Back then, Russian football had been in a bad way, characterised by low attendances, crumbling stadiums and a severe image problem. This was hardly surprising. Russia itself was in the midst of a cataclysmic upheaval, the one-time superpower slowly being torn apart by almost total social and economic collapse, rampant corruption and brutal civil war in Chechnya. The rarely sober Boris Yeltsin was in the Kremlin, and the ideological emptiness caused by the collapse of communism had yet to be filled by the affluence that democracy and capitalism were supposed to bring. Life in Russia was a battle for survival and, naturally enough, football was furthest from most people's minds.

'I remember going to matches in the years immediately following the collapse of the USSR,' a long-time Dynamo Moscow fan,

Dmitri Dudenkov, told me recently. 'The gates were so low that they frequently used to open the turnstiles at half-time. Anyone who wanted to could just wander in. Tickets were really cheap, but, still, no one was at all interested in the game. People would casually stroll in off the street to catch the second half of games featuring the country's top sides and players. We had, you understand, other things to think about.'

A decade on, everything has changed. Yeltsin is long gone, and Russia has grown rich on oil dollars. This wealth has brought about a confrontational foreign policy, which has, in turn, sparked fears of a new Cold War.

These changes have not passed football by. Supported by the vast fortunes of the Kremlin-backed oligarchs and the gas and oil industries, the country's football industry has likewise been reborn, rapidly becoming one of the world's richest, the huge wages on offer tempting players and trainers from all over the world to Russia.

However, both on and off the field, Russia's rebirth is not without its dark side. Indeed, were the nation's recent improbable re-emergence as a world power to be represented as a football match, it would probably look something like this – 3–0 down at half-time, playing with ten men, the manager incapacitated by a drink problem, the second half sees the teetotaller assistant manager take control and the side, spurred on by the appearance of their new record signings, claw their way back into the match, scrambling home the winning goal in injury time. This miraculous comeback is not without scandal, however. There are rumours that wads of cash changed hands in the referee's dressing room during the break, and that the forced substitutions of two of the opposition's star players were the result of stomach cramps brought about by someone tampering with their half-time oranges . . .

Before I moved to Russia, I knew all about Lenin, Stalin and all those other guys. I had studied them, I could tell you all the facts and figures you wanted to know about the Great October Revolution. I'd read almost all the Russian classics, and I'd managed to force myself to stay awake through most of respected Soviet-era director Andrei Tarkovsky's films. What I wasn't so clued up on, though, was the country's football.

Of course, as a child, I knew even less about the beautiful game in Russia. Despite being brought up in Bristol, I was infatuated with Brian Clough's Nottingham Forest. My home town is a mere 120 miles away from Nottingham, although, on Saturday afternoons, forced to make do with Ashton Gate and Bristol City, those miles may as well have been light years.

If I thought of Russia at all, it was in terms of the Cold War, or as an excuse to annoy teachers by professing to being a Young Socialist and refusing to study on the days that Soviet General Secretaries passed away. And in the 1980s there were many such opportunities; three of them, Brezhnev, Andropov and Chernenko shuffling off to the great Party Congress in the sky between 1982 and 1985.

But – Russia and football? Why, even Liverpool, the mortal enemies, had never been drawn against a Soviet team, let alone Nottingham Forest. My footballing knowledge, garnered from televised away legs, stretched about as far as Bulgaria, or East Germany.

As I got older, Soviet football vaguely made itself known. There was Oleg Blokhin and his otherworldly dribbling, and the team's distinctive red shirts, but I had no real interest in the side. They were basically quarter-finalists and, in my mind, differed little from fellow underachievers such as Belgium or Yugoslavia. (Granted, the Soviet Union reached the 1988 European Championship Final but, as Khrushchev commented regarding the uncertainty over the exact number of victims of Stalin's purges in 1930s Russia, 'No one was keeping count.')

Later, in my early twenties, I began to cultivate a mild obsession with Russia, with its history and its writers. Eventually, in 1997, I decided to put my growing, yet unproven, love to the test and move to Moscow. I initially planned upon staying for a year, to get a taste of the place, and then to move on, perhaps to Vietnam or South America. That was more than a decade ago.

Upon arriving in the Russian capital, in the midst of the Yeltsin-era chaos, speaking little of the language and surrounded by a foreign way of life, I was immediately drawn to one of the things that was instantly familiar to a white, twenty-something male – football.

However, despite the seemingly homogeneous nature of the world's favourite sport, there was a certain *something*, inaccessible to the casual observer, at the core of the Russian game. This was encapsulated, for me at least, in the form of the terrace chant – '*Sudyu na milo!*' – that the fans would invariably begin to shout whenever a decision went against their side.

'*Sudyu*' – 'ref' – '*na*' – 'on' – '*milo*' – 'soap'. 'Ref on soap?' I slowly translated, struggling to fathom the expression. What could they possibly mean? Perhaps 'soap' here was slang for something? But what? Bribes? Steroids, maybe? But no, 'ref' was in the accusative case. Whatever was going on, it was happening *to* the man in black. Exactly what this was, I was unable to determine, although the fury in the fans' voices led me to suspect that it was something deeply unpleasant indeed.

Not having been in the city long, I was forced to go to my first games in Moscow alone, and I had no one to turn to for an explanation. It was only later that I found out the idiomatic phrase was correctly translated as 'Make soap out of the ref!' and referred to the Soviet practice of producing hygiene products from the fat of slaughtered stray dogs, a fate that the enraged supporters deemed only fit for the object of their righteous indignation.

The satisfaction I felt upon solving this riddle was immense. Life in Moscow can be frustrating, at times incomprehensible, and if I could crack the intricacies of the country's football then, or so I reasoned, everything else would follow. The beautiful game was the cipher, the anti-Enigma Machine through which Russia could be decoded.

Over the years, I gradually became a *fanat*, the names of Russian teams and players, once unpronounceable, becoming as familiar as those of friends and relatives.

Despite my growing interest in the Russian game, I was not always able to fully share my enthusiasm with friends and family back in the UK. Although the British media was increasingly full of Russian oligarchs and spies, Russia, and its football, remained the Great Unknown, isolated by geography and language, culture and history.

For me, though, no matter what has happened – the economic crisis of 1998, the Chechen War, the Abramovich/Chelsea story, the Beslan tragedy – through good times and bad, football has remained a constant; linked, invariably, to the events, yet at the same time providing a sometimes welcome distraction.

This book, then, is an attempt to convey something of my passion for football in the world's largest country. There have been many fine books on Soviet-era football, but this is the first devoted to the modern Russian game. Although it has proven neither possible nor desirable to totally ignore the Soviet period, the main focus is firmly and unapologetically on post-perestroika Russia.

For a foreign writer lacking official Russian press accreditation in a land where documents are accorded a particular reverence, collecting the interviews and information necessary for this book was a particularly daunting undertaking. At the time, I had never interviewed anyone in my life, and I was more than a touch apprehensive at the prospect. If Russian football is *terra incognita* for the world at large, then the country's top players are a mystery to their own people, their lavish lifestyles and gigantic salaries granting them a Brahman-like status in a land where, despite the wealth in Moscow and other major cities, the average standard of living still lags far behind European norms.

Nevertheless, I was not to be dissuaded, and I began contacting clubs, explaining my mission to press officers and the like. I arranged meetings with players and trainers, but also with journalists and hooligans, fans and businessmen – anyone, in fact, with the slightest connection to the game in Russia. From the great rivalry between CSKA and Spartak to the irresistible symbolism of a Chechen side lifting the Russian Cup, from the 'Dutch Revolution' transforming the national team to the Soviet-era curse on Dynamo Moscow, I travelled through Russia and its football. In the majority of cases, confounding my initial expectations, people were both helpful and ready to talk, if perhaps somewhat surprised that an Englishmen should be so taken with their national game.

A confession. The stories of corruption and the tales of bribery and violence that I heard while researching this book did nothing to lessen my fervour. My affection for football in my adopted homeland, like that for a lover with a scar, or a woman with an unpredictable nature, was undiminished and, in a way that remains tantalising and (perhaps rightly so) beyond analysis, somehow even enhanced.

CHAPTER ONE

Spartak is a religion

'Football is the ballet of the masses.'

Dmitri Shostakovich

It is 8 a.m. on a November morning in Moscow in 2006, and the first snows have just fallen. I am walking through the underpass at Smolenski Bulvar when I see the Spartak fan. Standing alone at the top of the concrete steps, face red from either alcohol or the cold, he is shouting with all his might: 'Spartak! Spartak! Come on! Come on!' the last syllable in 'Spartak' stretched out for an eternity. 'You can catch CSKA,' he finishes, but quieter now, as if he doesn't quite believe it himself, a random oath, directed at Spartak's perennial rivals, escaping his lips as his proclamations come to an end.

Unlike in Western Europe, the Russian season runs from March to November, and there are just two games left to play in the 2006 campaign. Spartak Moscow are in second place, trailing CSKA by three points, and while few people give them a chance of overtaking the 2005 UEFA Cup winners, hope, as the Russians are inordinately fond of pointing out, dies last.

Just as there are those who welcomed the end of Spartak Moscow's domination of the national game, there are as many who took the side's fall from grace as a personal insult. I look back at the fan once more before turning the corner, and he gives me the thumbs up, drawing breath before resuming his early morning declarations of faith.

Spartak Moscow were formed in 1922 as MKS. In 1935 they were renamed and reorganised by the club's acknowledged founders, the Starostin brothers, the elder brother, Nikolai, deriving the club's new name from Spartacus, the slave who led a revolt against Rome. Obsessively honest figures, the principles of fair play and sporting behaviour that the Starostins believed in remain, despite the manifest corruption in the Russian game today, an essential part of the Spartak ethos.

In the USSR, Spartak were the only side not directly affiliated with the Soviet regime. While the remaining teams were all exclusively connected with, and financed by, one of the many state organisations or industries, Spartak were sponsored by civilian organisations, by the trade unions; for many, supporting the 'Red and Whites' was seen as a way of covertly expressing dissatisfaction with life in the USSR. It was during this period that Spartak earned the moniker of the 'People's Team'.

This legend lives on today. Although now no more or no less attached to the prevailing system than the majority of other Russian sides, there is a romanticism about Spartak that most other teams simply do not possess.

Though one of the top clubs in the former Soviet Union, Spartak really came into their own in the 1990s, after perestroika. They dominated Russian football, winning the championship every year but one between 1992 and 2002, coasting to the title most seasons.

'Spartak – Champions!' was their supporters' chant, and at the time it sounded like a mere statement of fact rather than a boast or a promise. The side enjoyed such a grip on the Russian game in the 1990s that the shockwaves are still being felt today. Throughout my journey, I found that all, or practically all, roads led to Spartak, and I had little option but to make the club's offices my first port of call.

Sergei Dmitrievich Shavlo, Spartak Moscow's general director, sits in his office surrounded by cups, trophies and oversized, framed photographs. Directly behind his desk is the USSR Cup. He seems possessed by the room, by the history around him. The ceilings are impossibly high and, indeed, the entire building is a Kafkaesque sprawling maze of corridors and turnings, so much so that his secretary laughed when I told her I would find my own way out after the interview. In the nineteenth century the building was a military barracks, and then lay unused for many years, but now, like many things in the largest city in Europe, it belongs to LUKoil, one of Russia's biggest oil companies.

One of the first Soviet players to sign a contract with a foreign club, Shavlo played in Austria for more than a decade. Before this he was a striker with Spartak, playing for the team until 1985. He only became general director of Spartak Moscow in 2005, but gives the impression of being a man whose entire life has always revolved around the Red and Whites, or 'Meat', as they are affectionately known as by their fans, a reference to the side's supposed origins in the catering industry.

'Spartak is a religion,' is one of the first things he says, before offering me a plate of chocolate biscuits and calling for tea.

The collapse of the USSR in 1991 meant more than just the end of the world's first socialist state; it also signalled the disintegration of Soviet football. This was, to some, far more significant. The Soviet Union, while never having lifted the World Cup, had been one of the planet's most respected teams, producing players such as Lev Yashin, Oleg Blokhin, Andrei Kanchelskis and others. Overnight, the Soviet Union's players found themselves deprived of the centralised state system which had nurtured and encouraged them, and thrust into a new, exhilarating and sometimes frightening world.

The USSR Championship, a multi-ethnic league spanning fifteen republics, had been perhaps the most diverse national competition on earth: a complex spectrum of footballing styles and attitudes, from the brawn and bustle of the Baltic states to the technical, short-passing game of the Russians, from the eccentric, dribbling frenzy of the Caucasus to the pedantic, almost crude football played in Kazakhstan, Tajikistan and Uzbekistan. But, as each newly independent republic formed its own respective FA, the great inter-Soviet rivalries of the past were brought to an abrupt and premature end.

In 1992, the Russian Football Federation held its first league championship. Without the Ukrainian champions, Dynamo Kiev, the Georgians, Dynamo Tbilisi, and others, the new competition had a parochial feel about it. Gates were down, and money was tight.

'Around the time of perestroika,' began Shavlo, 'all the teams were strongly supported by the state, through industry and other governmental structures. Naturally, when problems began to arise in the country, this financial assistance was mostly cut off.'

Football does not exist in a vacuum, and I tried to imagine what would happen if the capitalist, secular Christian society that is Britain today suddenly buckled under its own weight, to be replaced with something initially indistinct, all the certainties stripped away. How, I wondered, would Rooney and co deal with that? In Russia, there occurred a football brain drain, with many of the country's top players leaving the country.

'It was a catastrophic period for Russian football,' continued Shavlo. 'The players who left, they saw the West as their saviour, but by leaving they in effect took their experience with them, and as a result were unable to pass this onto the next generation. For the majority of clubs, Spartak excluded, the early 1990s was a terrible time.'

So how did Spartak avoid this fate? How did they continue to attract top players and, in some cases, even hang onto them?

'Spartak were the richest side in Russia because they were the best. It was a blessed circle. Champions League football meant cash. And cash meant the best players, which, in turn, meant more titles, and more European football. We managed to collect the top footballers from the former republics, the best Ukrainians, Georgians, Uzbeks and others. We could offer them financial security at a time when half the country was starving.'

But now, in the second half of the first decade of the twenty-first century, with oil prices at an all-time high, and Russia producing around nine-and-a-half million barrels of black gold a day, Spartak are no longer the wealthiest team in Russia. The other clubs have found, or been found by, sugar daddies, super-rich individuals willing (directly or indirectly) to support them and their dreams of glory. Football is prestigious now in Russia, and the oligarchs, the men who carved up Russia's assets amongst themselves during the turmoil of the immediate post-Soviet period, want in. CSKA Moscow were sponsored by Roman Abramovich's Sibneft before signing a deal with the Russian Bank of Foreign Trade in 2005, while cross-town rivals Dynamo Moscow have been showered with cash by Alexei Fedorichev, the filthy-rich owner of Fedcom, and Zenit St Petersburg are owned by Gazprom, the gas giant with bottomless pockets.

This new reality has made it hard for Spartak. The country's new wealth, or rather the affluence of its minuscule upper class, has brought about a democracy in Russian football. Now, other teams can offer the kind of wages that only Spartak could once afford. The ceiling has, in fact, been raised, and the top Russian clubs can now contend financially with their Western counterparts and, in many cases, outstrip them.

Following the end of more than seventy years of Soviet rule, for the first time in history, foreign footballers began to sign contracts with Russian sides. In the first few seasons after perestroika, the quality of these imports was low to say the least, but as Russia's economic clout has grown, footballers of genuine ability have begun arriving in Mother Russia.

'A real problem for us a few years ago,' recalled Shavlo, 'was that players would come from Africa, from Latin America, sign contracts, and then not perform. Start hanging out in nightclubs, and so on. Now we are a lot more careful with our transfer policy. The professionalism of the footballers we buy has to be of the highest standards.'

As Egor Titov, the only player left in the side from the glory days of the 1990s, would later tell me, 'In the early days after the break-up of the Soviet Union, clubs would just pick up foreign players, "legionaries", as we call them, from anywhere. We had Brazilians in the team who had been, literally, spotted playing on the Copacabana, or wherever,' he said, laughing at the memory, 'and they didn't really have any interest in fitting in with the rest of us. They paid them well, much better than us, simply because it was prestigious to have foreigners, especially South Americans, in the side.'

In 2000, Spartak signed a sponsorship deal with LUKoil. The resulting oil dollars have kept Spartak near the top of the pile in financial terms, but the success to which they were once accustomed has been slow in coming. Spartak fans were shocked by their team's third-place showing in the 2002 Championship, and then horrified as the side came in eighth and tenth the following two seasons. From 2005 to 2007, they exhibited signs of a revival, and finished second three years in a row. However, while the fans welcomed this relative turnaround in fortunes, there was no hiding from the fact that the days when Spartak were assured of the championship before a ball had even been kicked were long gone.

But then, so was Oleg Romantsev.

Anyone who watched European or international football in the 1990s will be familiar with Oleg Romantsev, if not by name then as the morose figure who sat puffing away on cigarettes as Spartak, or the Russian national side, did battle. A stern man, hailing from Krasnoyarsk in Siberia, Romantsev ruled Spartak supreme. He was not a man given to levity, or euphoric outbursts of joy, despite the team's monopoly on success.

Romantsev, a former Spartak player and Soviet international, was the manager of the side during the glory years, as well as being the club's president. This last fact, according to my already fading copy of the 2000 football yearbook *Moscow Clubs*, is what made Spartak so successful. Romantsev was in a unique position in European football. The only man who could fire Romantsev the manager was Romantsev the president, and he was hardly likely to give himself the axe just because a few results failed to go his way. With the freedom this gave him, Romantsev was able to experiment; to build arguably the greatest club side Russian football has ever seen.

Oleg Romantsev all but disappeared from Russian football in 2005, after brief unsuccessful spells, post-Spartak, at Dynamo Moscow and Saturn FC. This chain-smoking symbol of the Russian game has retired to the countryside, rarely in contact with journalists and the world of football. Technically, he is still involved in the sport. He is a consultant at Nika, a side from the third echelon of Russian football, but in reality the most successful club manager in Russian history has retired from the game.

Naturally, I wanted to speak to him.

'He's living his own life now, he rarely answers the phone,' Shavlo told me, dampening my hopes of an interview.

'Even if I could contact him, he wouldn't agree to an interview. Especially with a foreigner,' was the response from the editor at the Russian daily sports newspaper *Sport-Express*.

I took a rickety electric train out of Moscow to Spartak's Tarasovka sports complex in the autumn of 2006. The out-of-town training camp was enclosed behind a high fence, and were it not for the gigantic 'Spartak' emblem on the gates, it would have resembled nothing so much as a military training camp or a hush-hush scientific research institute.

I was there to attend a Spartak training session and to speak to Egor Titov, the club's captain. In 2003, after a Euro 2004 play-off against Wales that Russia won 1–0, Titov tested positive for bromantan, an attention-enhancing substance produced for Soviet soldiers in Afghanistan. He maintains his innocence to this day, claiming that the club doctor had simply failed to properly check his diet. He was, however, banned from football for a year, during which time he became a regular on Russian chat and reality shows. The club doctor was subsequently fired, and a special commission was set up by the Russian Football Federation to investigate. However, commissions have a funny way of dragging on in Russia, and this one is no exception. The commission members have yet to announce their results, and it seems unlikely they ever will.

Egor Titov is now back in the Spartak side and playing as well as ever. He smiled wryly when I asked him about his former manager, the man who had made him one of the most successful players in Russian football.

'Oleg Romantsev was extremely hard to please,' he said, in what turned out to be something of an understatement. 'For example, if we were winning 5–0, and then conceded a goal in the last minute, he wouldn't say anything about the five we had scored, just go on and on, yelling at us about the one we had let in. But that wasn't all. Once, we had to get a point at home to become champions for the third or fourth time in a row, and we won 1–0, but almost gave away a goal at the end. We played badly, but we won the title that day. We looked around for Romantsev to do a lap of honour with him, to, you know, throw him up in the air in celebration as is the tradition here, but he was nowhere to be seen. We eventually found him in the dressing room, face as black as thunder.

' "What are you lot so happy about?" he shouted, as we came in, looking for the champagne. "You going to play like that all the time? You have a Champions League match against Bayern Munich on Tuesday, and that kind of football won't get you anywhere!" '

Was it, I wondered, an effective way to manage?

'Absolutely,' said Titov. 'You could never let yourself relax. There was no euphoria, no danger of underestimating your opponents.'

Curious, I asked Titov why he had never played abroad. Bayern Munich, I knew, had been interested in him, and he had also had enquiries from English clubs.

'Honestly? I was afraid to go to Oleg Romantsev's office and tell him I was leaving. At that time, Romantsev was looking to keep the side together. Up until the mid-nineties, he had had a develop-and-sell policy, but after this period he craved success not only at home, but also in the Champions League. He didn't look kindly upon players deserting his team. Dmitri Alenichev (a member of the victorious 2003 UEFA Cup and 2004 Champions League Porto side managed by Jose Mourinho) did it when he left for Roma, but he had already signed the contract before he plucked up the courage and walked into the boss's office. Romantsev was angry about it for a few years, but finally forgave him.'

In 1995, during their 3–0 Champions League defeat to Spartak, Graeme Le Saux and David Batty of Blackburn Rovers came to blows on the snowy touchline of the Luzhniki Olympic arena. It is one of my earliest memories of Russian club football, and I asked Titov if he remembered the incident. The Spartak captain laughed. 'Yeah, I was on the bench for that game, but I remember we all cracked up. I'd never seen anything like that before, and I still haven't. It was still the first half, the score was 0–0, but Romantsev said that we would win easily after that and, well, he was right.'

Ultimately, the pressure of combining posts got to Romantsev, and both his health and Spartak's results worsened as the twentieth century drew to a close. It was around this time that rumours of a drink problem began to circulate.

Drink problem or no drink problem, the Spartak manager's behaviour had always been erratic – as one story has it, after a friendly between Belarus and Russia, a *Sport-Express* journalist went up to Romantsev, who was standing alone next to the team bus, puffing away on a cigarette, and requested an interview.

'What? Can't you see I'm talking to the doctor?' yelled the Spartak manager in reply.

In 2003 Oleg Romantsev was fired from Spartak. Problems had begun with the death of Nikolai Starostin seven years earlier. Romantsev inherited the entire Spartak enterprise from the club's founder, but sold on his stock in 2000 to the LUKoil executive

Andrei Chervichenko, a man who had made his fortune in the early 1990s during the country's 'bandit capitalism' phase.

'I brought Chervichenko to Spartak,' Romantsev stated at the time, 'and I am glad that the right investor has been found.'

However, the two men's relationship soon began to deteriorate. Romantsev started to give interviews criticising Chervichenko's policies, accusing him of lacking respect for the 'Spartak tradition'. The final straw came when Romantsev gathered a group of journalists together on the eve of the 2003 Russian Cup Final and claimed that Chervichenko had been attempting to sell the following day's match. The day after the game, which Spartak won, Chervichenko, who had promised not to comment on the Spartak manager's comments until after the final, fired Romantsev.

I went to visit Andrei Chervichenko at his offices not far from Bakunin Street, named after the revolutionary Russian anarchist. Chervichenko had long given up the Spartak presidency, cutting all ties with the club, yet the team's emblem still adorned the gates to his business premises.

'I just got sick of football,' he told me, after I had been ushered through to his office by a chunky, monosyllabic bodyguard. 'I got tired of paying inflated wages. Russian football doesn't invest enough in the grass roots. Everyone is obsessed with the search for stars who aren't going to perform even if they can be persuaded to come to Russia in the first place. We have a different way of life here, not at all European, and it is hard for foreign players, no matter how much you can afford to pay them. Russia's infrastructure simply isn't conducive to getting the best out of world stars.

'I got tired of hearing that Spartak under my control transformed into an evil empire. But look, when I took over the club, for example, all the financial records of the team had simply been wiped clean from the computers. As for the cup claims, well, we won, didn't we? Romantsev even named the price I was supposed to have been asking. One and a half million dollars. Complete nonsense.'

Despite all the bad things I had read about him, Chervichenko cut a sympathetic figure, and I couldn't help feeling that he had been used as a scapegoat for all the side's troubles. His name remains a dirty word amongst Spartak supporters to this day.

It was during Chervichenko's reign that Egor Titov was suspended for failing a doping test, and the ex-Spartak owner explained how this had come about. 'That,' he said, 'was one of the club doctors' fault. I always used to moan that our players were too slow, that they didn't move around the pitch fast enough. After my complaints, it seems that they got together and decided to solve the problem in their own unique way.'

Chervichenko, for all his claims to be sick of the sport, is a man obviously still in love with football. On the wall of his office hangs a CSKA pennant. I recalled the theory put about by Spartak fans, enraged by Romantsev's sacking and by the decline of the undisputed 1990s Russian champions, that Chervichenko had been sent to them by their rivals, CSKA. His mission? Destroy Spartak from within. The proof, they claimed, is that he now openly roots for CSKA, even allegedly draping himself in the ex-Red Army team's flag whenever they take on Spartak.

'I don't support CSKA,' countered Chervichenko, obviously weary of the accusation. 'It's just that, well, my memories of Spartak are not all entirely good. To be honest, I'm glad I'm out of the game. Now Russian football is simply a war between oligarchs, between businessmen. They don't care about money, because all Russian sides make a loss. It's all about prestige, about one-upmanship. And they are ready to use any means necessary to achieve their goals. Football in Russia has become a lot dirtier in the last few years, that's for sure.'

We spoke again of Romantsev, and Chervichenko's expression changed, becoming suddenly morose. 'He was a great manager, the best of his generation in Russia, but he just lost it with the drinking. To be honest, I felt sorry for him.'

Shortly after Chervichenko's takeover of the club, Romantsev's alcohol problem become an open secret, as the once genius trainer descended into an alcoholic haze, detached from reality and the players around him. During a Champions League match against Liverpool at Anfield in 2002, Romantsev's son reportedly sought out Chervichenko in the VIP Box. 'Papa wants vodka', he said. 'If he doesn't get it, he can't guarantee the result.'

History remains murky as to whether or not Romantsev got his dose, but Spartak lost 5–0 that day, the side showing no spirit or fight as Liverpool scored almost at will. For a side that had once won six group games out of six in the tournament, this was unforgivable.

Russians have always been famed for their drinking, so much so that Mikhail Gorbachev felt obliged to introduce prohibition in the Soviet Union in May 1985 in an attempt to put a halt to the rampant alcoholism that was already taking its toll on the nation's economy and health system. His efforts to steer the Soviets to abstinence were ultimately unsuccessful, however, and the illicit production of moonshine – 'samogon' – rocketed, not to mention a sudden rise in sales of medicinal and industrial spirit. The never-popular policy of prohibition was later quietly dropped.

However, deprived of the safety nets that socialism provided, the New Russia quickly found itself engulfed in an epidemic of alcoholism of catastrophic proportions, as what was already a serious social and health problem transformed into something on an apocalyptic scale.

According to the Russian Ministry of Health, the per capita consumption of pure alcohol in 2007 was around four gallons per person. Around 50,000 Russians die of alcohol poisoning every year, compared with, say, the US, which has a population almost twice as large, but where the number of deaths from alcohol poisoning remains stable at around 300 every year.

In the mid-1990s, breweries began pumping out super-strength versions of their beers, and it is a common sight to see secretaries, builders and businessmen swigging down these concoctions first thing in the morning. Until relatively recently, beer was considered, both from a legal and social point of view, a soft drink.

The Russian word for 'a bender' – as in the sustained consumption of alcohol – is 'zapoi', yet the English word struggles to fully describe either the proportions or the commonness of its Russian counterpart. '*Zapoi*' is the plague of the Russian provinces, where whole months are routinely lost in alcohol-induced mists. Romantsev's poison, it was said, was vodka with champagne chasers.

Another figure springs to mind. Another legendary manager cut down by drink, another manager not afraid to speak out of turn, similarly obsessed with success in Europe. As far as I know, Oleg Romantsev and Brian Clough never met, yet if they had, they would undoubtedly have had much to discuss.

'Romantsev used to read five books a day,' claimed Titov, out of the blue.

'Five?'

At first I thought I had misheard, but Titov nodded in confirmation. 'He slept a maximum of four hours a night.'

Still hoping for an interview, I asked the Spartak playmaker if he was still in touch with the bookworm genius of Russian football.

Titov looked genuinely sad when he replied, 'To tell you the truth, I haven't spoken to him for quite some time.'

The image comes of its own accord . . .

Oleg Romantsev in some tiny, remote Russian village, sitting by the river, incessantly smoking. Gone from football. He focuses on the water, the ripples, and sees the crowds, the human waves, the days of title after title. But he cannot allow himself to return. His health will not bear it. And besides, football is different now in Russia. Now, half the teams are made up of foreigners, and he doesn't know how to communicate with them. How can he be an Iron Fist to a player if he cannot speak his language? That was why he never trained abroad. The offers were there, from Spain, Italy, but he never went. What would he have done there? Away from Russia? He lights another cigarette.

'The Russian people need an Iron Fist!'

Anyone who lives in Russia for any amount of time is bound to hear this sentiment expressed. Russians, or so supporters of the idea would have it, are too undisciplined, too prone to drinking and other vices to be suited to the democratic, relatively liberal systems of government favoured by the West.

As Vladimir Zhirinovsky, the leader of one of the largest political parties in Russian today, said in 2003 when attacking liberal opposition figures, 'Russia wants and needs authoritarianism. So calm down and go and give lectures abroad. We are not the West. We have our own civilisation. You are all subjects of his majesty in the Kremlin. You should accept that for all time. There will be no democracy in Russia. No independent courts. No press freedom. Either accept it or leave.'

This longing for order imposed from above is the reason why Stalin remains popular in Russia today. In a recent survey, one quarter of Russians said that, were he still alive, they would definitely or probably vote for the former dictator, the man responsible for the deaths of twenty million of their compatriots in the Gulag.

Stalin's popularity shows no signs of slipping, either. In 2007 the Russian *Nezavisimaya Gazeta* newspaper reported that Russian educational authorities were set to introduce a new textbook for Russian schools that described Stalin's reign as 'effective'.

The Russian desire for an Iron Fist is also undoubtedly the reason behind the continued popularity of Vladimir Putin, the ex-KGB man who came to power in 2000. Upon taking office, Putin subsequently tightened state control over every aspect of life in his attempt to roll back the disastrous effects of the country's mid-1990s experiment with Western-style democracy. Despite almost immediately closing down the majority of the country's independent mass media, Putin's no-nonsense manner won favour with the majority of Russians, and in 2004 the former security-service chief was re-elected for a second term with some 70 per cent of the vote.

'He stands, above all, for stability – stability before freedom, stability before choice,' wrote Richard Stengel, managing editor of the US *Time* magazine at the end of 2007 after naming Putin their Man of the Year. The description sounded a lot to me like Romantsev's man-management style.

'Russian footballers,' said Ruslan Nigmatulin, a former Spartak goalkeeper and a member of the national side under Romantsev, 'need to be constantly screamed at. Even if they win, they need to be shouted at.'

The confession was a little odd, I thought, coming from a one-time player, but Nigmatulin was adamant, and he was not the only Russian footballer to say such things. We were talking in a European-style patisserie off Tverskaya, in the centre of Moscow, a few steps away from the former Museum of the Revolution.

'They need to be yelled at, kept on their toes,' he continued. 'Foreign trainers who work in Russia, they just don't understand. They try to explain things in a civilised manner, to do their best to be polite. But with Russian players it is impossible to be so mild. Oleg Romantsev understood this well. He knew that if you don't keep at Russian footballers they just relax, satisfied with their contracts and their lives, and they won't give 100 per cent on the pitch.'

Vlastimil Petrzhela, the former Czech manager of Zenit St Petersburg, echoed this opinion. In an interview recently printed in the Russian press he recalled that when he took over the team in 2002 he was shocked by the players' attitudes. They had, he said, no desire to improve their skills or to try to win trophies. Their salaries were all they were concerned with and 'they had no devotion to the game'. They were so badly motivated, Petrzhela claimed, that even the lure of lucrative contracts could do little to jolt them out of their deeply ingrained lethargy.

As a result of this real or perceived laziness, Russian players are cursed with possibly the strictest training regime in the entire world. Indeed, almost all the players I spoke to on my travels rolled their eyes and groaned when I asked them about the infamous '*sbori*', or training camps, which they are forced to attend.

These camps are held during the close season, and each lasts between two and six weeks. In the four-month gap between seasons, players are almost constantly away from home. They are more than often held abroad, but sometimes in the Russian south, in Black Sea resorts like Sochi and Adler. Separated from their families, the players are subject to strict diets and heavy training sessions. Footballers in Russia are also obliged to stay at the club's out-of-town training camps before games, including home matches, with the result that if a team has two matches a week they are, again, never at home. As the former Spartak striker, Vladimir Beschastnykh, commented, 'Sometimes I feel like they are training us for the Special Forces.'

'The *sbori* really are unbearable,' Nikolai Roganov, the editor of *Total Football*, Russia's first glossy football magazine, told me in early 2007. 'I went on one once with Spartak, and they are intensely claustrophobic. The players, after a long season, are stuck in a hotel in the middle of nowhere, and there is really nothing at all for them to do there except train, read, watch films, and so on. When you've been stuck together with the same bunch of guys for nine months, and then you have to spend another three months in a hotel with them . . .' Roganov left his sentence unfinished, yet a sudden image of a crazed Jack Nicholson roaming the corridors of the Overlook Hotel in *The Shining* flashed in front of my eyes. 'They miss their families,' continued Roganov, 'have to train every day, and come back to Russia in time for the start of the season, completely sick of football.'

Although discipline and firebrand managers are not uncommon in the West, there is clearly not such a deeply institutionalised harshness. For example, in England, it is hypothetically possible for a player to be late for a match. This would be impossible in Russia, for the players are driven to the stadium straight from the training camp.

'The whole system of *sbori* comes from Soviet times, from away matches,' said Dmitri Kotov, archivist of Soviet football, when we met in his north Moscow flat. 'The players would be kept in the training camps prior to international fixtures to ensure they were in top form before representing the USSR. They had the country's honour to uphold, after all. After this, it just became standard practice for club sides as well.'

Did he agree that Russians needed an Iron Fist?

'Perhaps not Russians as whole,' he commented, 'but the players, certainly.'

Post-Romantsev, following a series of largely unsuccessful appointments, including the Italian Nevio Scala, formerly of Borussia Dortmund and Parma, Spartak turned to Vladimir Fedotov, a long-term club insider. He was one of their own, and under his command the team immediately began to perform, just in time for the 2006/07 Champions League.

A squat, gruff man, he is of the Soviet school of management, muttering inaudible monosyllabic commands as much to himself as to his players. In fact, he seemed a lot, character wise, like a sober Romantsev.

The son of Grigori Fedotov, the famous Stalin-era centre forward, the Spartak manager still recalls childhood visits to the dictator's country home with his father. The young Fedotov would be plumped down in front of a TV to watch Disney cartoons (forbidden at that time in the USSR) while his father and the man who transformed the Soviet Union into a superpower went off to play billiards.

With the 2006 season more than halfway through, and Spartak running head to head with CSKA, I attended one of the club's training sessions, and observed as Fedotov watched proceedings from the side of the pitch, his face bare of emotion. A German TV crew was filming a report about Spartak, and asked Fedotov to 'say a few words to the camera about the upcoming match'. (Spartak had been drawn with Bayern Munich in the Champions League group stage.) Fedotov considered this request for approximately half a second. 'Let's do it next time,' he snapped before stomping off to grunt at his players. 'Next time?' wondered the Germans, aloud. The next time the two teams were drawn together in European football? They left without their interview.

'Faster, stop messing about, what's that?' grunted Fedotov, striding over to cajole the Spartak first team as they went through a series of exercises. The effect, as their manager's words reached them, was instantaneous. The players responded, stretching that bit more, jumping that centimetre higher, noticeably increasing their speed.

Fedotov allowed himself a smile.

The Iron Fist was back.

There then occurred a moment that will haunt me all my life. The ball bounced up, over the net surrounding the training field, and down, down towards me. Everyone, or so it seemed, turned to stare. Titov and his team-mates, Fedotov himself. 'This is it,' I thought, 'I'll trap the ball, knock it up and volley it back.' Dreams of a Spartak first-team place raced through my head. Fernando Cavenaghi, Spartak's Argentinian forward and record signing, hadn't been performing lately, and his place in the team was surely up for grabs.

What can I say? The ball landed awkwardly, hit a tuft of grass, and rolled away. My moment was gone. My chance of a glistening career stillborn.

The weekend after the training session in which I failed to secure a Spartak first-team place, Fedotov's charges were due to take on CSKA, the reigning league champions.

Football rivalries exist all over the world. Every nation has those games that contain that extra something, a tension born of history and mutual loathing. In Russia, there are no derbies more keenly anticipated, no matches with more of an edge than those between CSKA and Spartak Moscow.

'I realised the second I joined the club that CSKA were the main rivals,' said Denis Boyarintsev, the Spartak midfielder, as the players wound down after the training session. 'There is even a special clause in the contract that says we are obliged to defeat them,' he joked.

'A lot of people walk around saying CSKA are the enemy, but that's not really right. I mean, they're just people as well,' said Egor Titov, tactfully. So CSKA aren't the enemy? 'Well, in a sense they are, of course,' confessed the Spartak captain, his true feelings finally breaking through his diplomacy.

Amongst Spartak fans, CSKA are known as GVK, '*Giner Vsyo Kupil*' or 'Giner bought everything', a reference to Evgeni Giner, CSKA's baseball-hat-wearing, cigar-smoking president, and his side's alleged practice of match-fixing.

Since becoming president of CSKA in 2001, Giner has acquired a Godfather-like status within the world of Russian football. As a source close to Spartak Moscow said, 'All of our referees are under his influence. He enjoys good relations with them all. One he can help get a flat, the other, his wife find work. As for new referees, well, they are of the impression that Giner is omnipotent, and he himself does everything he can to perpetuate this myth.' Giner denies the claims.

As the 2006 season reached its climax, with CSKA in first place, Leonid Fedun, LUKoil vice president and Spartak's owner, said, 'CSKA will become champions because they have used their administrative resources well.'

Aside from the, as yet unproven, existence of the outright buying of games, it is an open secret that Russian football teams regularly offer cash incentives to their rivals' opponents to encourage them to put in good performances. While not strictly forbidden, no clubs have yet admitted to making or receiving payments. In Russia, this practice is known as 'stimulation'. 'Everywhere we go, an armoured bank truck is sure to follow,' said Egor Titov, commenting on the issue, getting in his customary dig at CSKA.

Spartak themselves were not above suspicion though, a rumour spreading towards the end of the season that they had taken part in the very same practice of 'stimulation' that they had accused CSKA of. A million dollars was the sum mentioned, although the allegations remained unproven.

If the charges were true, though, then it would be more proof, if any were needed, of the funds available to Russian club owners.

Immensely wealthy men, the financial rewards the Russian Premier League can offer are irrelevant, as are any potential payments by UEFA for, say, participation in the Champions League or UEFA Cup.

Igor Rabiner is the author of one of the few books in Russia to deal with the side of football that is not exclusively devoted to statistics and facts, the first work about the national sport to be written with real passion and wit. In that sense, perhaps it would not be too unfair to think of him as the Russian Nick Hornby.

Rabiner's *Kak Ubivali Spartak* – or *How they Killed Spartak* – chronicles the fall of the Red and Whites, and the author spoke to me in late 2007 about his resentment of the businessmen who had taken control of his beloved Spartak.

For many club owners, he told me, the teams are 'just ways to open doors, both political and economic. Big business is responsible for destroying the principles and spirit that made Spartak special,' he told me.

As Rabiner was speaking, I recalled an incident that he had described in his book; a poignant example of how I imagined a real 'People's Team' should behave, both on and off the field.

The story concerned the deciding match for the 1983 Soviet championship, when Spartak faced the Ukrainian side, Dnepr. With the Moscow club needing a victory to claim the title, and the scores still level in the second half, Dnepr's centre forward had broken for goal. The Spartak defender, Bazulev, had the chance to save his side with a 'professional foul', but he refused to foul his opponent and Dnepr scored, denying the Muscovites the championship.

'After the game,' Rabiner told me when I brought up the topic, 'Bazulev started to regret his honesty, his adherence to the principles of fair play, but the manager told him not to worry, saying that he had done the right thing.'

'That match encapsulated everything that Spartak stood for until the businessmen came in,' he concluded. The club's current owners, he went on, 'are against the fans expressing their opinions, bringing banners to the match and so on. What's more, they see the players as, well, mere employees,' he said, almost spitting out the last word. 'No respect,' he concluded.

There were many Spartak fans, however, who still clung to the concept of the side as the 'People's Team', supporters who refused to believe that an honest club would simply be unable to function in the cynical world of modern Russian football.

'When I look at Spartak, I feel real pride,' a member of the Spartak fan club told me the day before the derby with CSKA. 'The club was built on the foundations of truth and fairness. Spartak has always been famed for its sporting principles.

'It was our founder who once said, "Everything is lost, except honour". That has kept us going through the last few years, when success has been hard to come by. But, you know, clubs like CSKA, with their desire to win at any cost, will never understand that. They just don't speak the same language.'

The subsequent Spartak–CSKA encounter ended in a 2–2 draw, Spartak snatching a point with nine minutes remaining on the clock. As is par for the course whenever the two teams meet, passions spilled over from the field to the terraces, and to the streets around the stadium, mass brawls breaking out all over the city.

Despite being the most successful Russian club side ever, Spartak Moscow are without a stadium of their own, and play their home matches at the Luzhniki, the gargantuan 80,000-capacity arena reconstructed for the 1980 Moscow Olympic Games, and the proud owner of a five-star rating from UEFA. The Luzhniki also boasts an impressively large statue of Lenin. Once found everywhere in Russia, they are now fairly rare. I wasn't certain why this one had survived the craze for tearing them down, and no one else seemed to be sure either.

In truth, the Luzhniki is an abomination: a soulless, Soviet folly with a running track around the field that affords matches about as much atmosphere as a preseason training session. Granted, when the stadium is full, when all the seats are taken, the mood is something special, but this is a rare occurrence, especially now that the national team has all but abandoned it in favour of the recently built Cherkizovo, in the northeast of the city. In 2009, even Spartak will desert the Luzhniki, moving to a new ground in the Tushino district of Moscow, and the Olympic sports arena will become, in effect, a ghost stadium, home only to the extremely poorly supported First Division side, Torpedo Moscow. Despite being chosen by UEFA to host the 2007/08 Champions League final, the Luzhniki is in reality a stadium condemned, surplus to requirements in the New Russia.

I had arranged to meet Vladimir Shevchenko, press attaché for Spartak, before attending a Friday evening game in which Spartak would be taking on Saturn, or the 'Extraterrestrials' as they are commonly known, from just outside of Moscow.

Vladimir was courteous enough, meeting me outside the press centre at the Luzhniki, More than courteous in fact, considering that I had managed to address him as Alexander three times during our initial correspondence, confusing him with the press attaché from Lokomotiv, Spartak's cross-town rivals. Still, he hadn't held it against me. 'This is Marc, he's an English journalist. He's writing a book about Russian football,' he informed the guard, taking me past security, and gifting me the phrase that would open many doors for me.

I recalled my first ever visit to the stadium, back in 1997, during the 'bad old days' of Russian football. There had been a little over a thousand fans in attendance, swallowed up by the vastness of the arena, their chants echoing oddly in the overwhelming emptiness. The sound was, in a way, slightly disturbing, like some malevolent, malefic ritual chant, or a scene from a Hammer Horror adaptation of a Dennis Wheatley novel. Goosebumps ran up and down my arms, and the game ended goalless.

Back in the future, before the game against Saturn, the voice of LUKoil, in the form of a recorded announcement stating that the oil company was Spartak's main sponsor, boomed out across the stadium with Charlton Heston-like authority. Oil money had dragged Russia into the twenty-first century, carrying the country's football with it, and no one was going to be allowed to forget it.

The game ended 1–1, Saturn equalising in the last minute, but you could sense that Spartak had other things on their mind. Specifically, their forthcoming 2006/07 Champions League second-round qualifying fixture against yet another comically named team, Sheriff, the champions of Moldova.

As the Russia season runs from March to November, teams qualify for Europe some nine months in advance, and Spartak would be taking up the Champions League spot they had earned with their second-place finish in the 2005 campaign. In case you hadn't figured it out, Russia's footballing calendar differs from mainstream Europe's due to the simple fact that the minus-thirty temperatures that are far from uncommon from November to March make football a logistic and physical impossibility during the winter months.

Spartak snuck through the subsequent qualifying rounds, drawing 1–1 away, and 0–0 at home against Sheriff, and then defeating Slovan Liberets of the Czech Republic to claim a place in the Champions League group stage, returning to the competition proper after an absence of three years. Their last appearance, in 2003, had been catastrophic. With the team in the midst of the death throes of Romantsev's reign, Spartak had been hopelessly outclassed, losing all six of their group matches, finishing the tournament with a shameful goal difference of scored one, conceded eighteen.

Back in his office at the centre of LUKoil's labyrinth, Sergei Shavlo was in no mood to reflect on the past. As a man who had lived and played in Europe, he possibly valued European football just that extra bit more. 'The Champions League,' he said, a look of satisfaction spreading across his face, 'is where Spartak belong.'

However, Europe's major club tournament, despite Shavlo's enthusiasm for the competition, was to hold no great joy for the club. In 2006 the side finished third in their Champions League group, subsequently going out tamely to Celta de Vigo of Spain in the UEFA Cup, while in September 2007 the 'People's Team' fell in the third qualifying round, losing on penalties to Celtic after a tie that the Scottish club's manager, Gordon Strachan, described as 'having everything'.

'I've had some good nights as a player and a manager,' the *Guardian* reported the effusive Scottish trainer as saying after the match, 'but this will be one of the ones that I'll still be telling people about in the golf club in twenty-five years.'

'Spartak are much better than half the teams who have made it through to the Champions League,' a relieved Celtic fan wrote on the club's website forum. Indeed, as if proving the point, the Muscovites subsequently eased through their 2007/08 UEFA Cup group with a game to spare, confirming themselves as one of the favourites to lift the trophy. Nevertheless, with the 2008 Champions League final due to be played at the Luzhniki, it was difficult not to reflect on what might have been had the club been a touch more fortunate in the penalty shootout in Glasgow.

Before I left him, Shavlo showed me some of the cups and trophies that he kept in his office. Apart from the USSR League Championship trophy, there were Russian FA Cups, and a strange little plaque that Leeds United had presented to the side on the occasion of their 1999 UEFA Cup tie, a match that had to be transferred to Bulgaria due to the freezing conditions in Moscow.

My interview over, Sergei Shavlo saw me out. I sat and waited for the press attaché to come and lead me through the twisting corridors to the exit.

'Do you like our building?' asked the secretary. I nodded that I did. And did she like football, perhaps support Spartak?

'Well,' she replied, 'when I first started work here, a few months ago, I hated the sport. But now, well, I've fallen in love with the club.'

Or, as Igor Rabiner – author, sports journalist, but above all, Spartak fan – put it, 'Millions of people believe in Spartak; they have no right to let us down.'

CHAPTER TWO

National traumas and orders from above

'We hoped for something better, but things turned out like they always do.'
Viktor Chernomyrdin, ex-Russian Prime Minister, August 1998

Despite the bitter rivalry between CSKA and Spartak, there were times, I knew, when players from the two clubs called an uneasy truce for the sake of Russian national pride. For a foreigner undergoing a crash course in life in Russia, the events that shook the country in the Yeltsin and Putin years were inextricably linked to football, the troubles and woes of the nation reflected in the missed chances, soft goals, harsh decisions and dropped points that, with few exceptions, characterised the Russian national side's performances.

Sport in the former Soviet Union, as in many other communist and totalitarian states, was considered hugely significant for international prestige. Victory heralded the wonders of socialism; defeat was a calamity, a disgrace to the ideals of Lenin and Marx.

Accordingly, colossal amounts of resources were pumped into the USSR's sporting infrastructure, and talented youngsters were encouraged, nurtured and provided with the very best in terms of equipment and facilities.

However, this care and attention, while more than bearing fruit in other fields such as athletics and gymnastics, just failed to turn the Soviet football team into world-beaters. The team came close to immortality, but although the national side enjoyed a great deal more respect, both at home and abroad, than its post-perestroika Russian counterpart, its only triumph at a major tournament came a lifetime ago, at the 1960 European Championships.

Russians are, understandably, proud of this victory, imagining it as pointing to a one-time dominance of European football. However, even though the Soviets had and would produce some truly world-class footballers, the inaugural European Championships had been weak to say the least, the facts somewhat diminishing the misty-eyed remembrances of Russian football fans old enough to remember the only time the USSR managed to bring any silverware home.

For starters, the tournament, which had no qualifying rounds, included only seventeen teams. The competition had a heavy East European feel to it, and neither West Germany nor England were involved. The Soviets would defeat Hungary and Czechoslovakia on their way to the final, their passage being considerably eased by a walkover against Spain in the quarter-finals, General Franco having personally pulled the side out of the competition due to civil unrest at home.

The final was a showdown against Tito's Yugoslavia in Paris, and the Soviets ran out 2–1 winners, the deciding goal scored by Viktor Ponedelnik, whose surname translates as 'Monday'. Accordingly, the Soviet state newspaper *Pravda* ran a headline the next morning, on the Tuesday, with the headline, 'Monday scores on a Monday'.

The USSR came close to successfully defending their title four years later, losing 2–1 in the final to the 1964 European Championship hosts, Spain. Two years on, the side reached the semi-finals of the 1966 World Cup in England, losing by the same score to West

Germany at Goodison Park, the Soviet keeper Lev Yashin, clad all in black, winning over the English crowds with his displays of goalkeeping virtuosity.

As a result of these near misses, much as 1966 would later do in England, 1960 subsequently gained a mythical status in the USSR, providing inspiration for generations of Soviet athletes to come. A few years before the world's first socialist state finally tore itself apart, the Soviets had a chance to lay the memories of 1960 to rest when they took on Holland in the final of the 1988 European Championships in West Germany. However, 24 years on from their loss to Spain, they were to taste defeat in a final for the second time, the side going down 2–0 to a Dutch team inspired by the genius of Ruud Gullit and Marco van Basten.

Post-perestroika, the Russian national team struggled. Even when the side did make the final stages of tournaments, they failed miserably on each occasion to get out of their group, cracking up under the pressure and weight of expectation. Rare highlights included Oleg Salenko's record-breaking five goals during a 6–1 victory against Cameroon in the 1994 World Cup in the USA. Mirroring the national side's tendency to flatter to deceive, Salenko would go on to score only one more goal for his country in his career, gaining a mere eight caps. Typically for Russia, the performance meant nothing, the side already having been eliminated from the tournament following losses to Sweden and Brazil in their first two group matches.

Russia failed to qualify for both the 1998 World Cup and Euro 2000. Although they made it to the 2002 World Cup, the side once again failed to make progress from their group, losing 1–0 to Japan and 3–2 to Belgium after beating Tunisia 2–0 in the opening match. The Japanese defeat was accompanied by an orgy of violence in Moscow as crowds of drunken fans set ablaze cars and attacked 'Asian-looking' passers-by, the incident one of the first manifestations of the growing nationalism that would characterise President Putin's reign.

Georgi Yartsev, a one-time Spartak Moscow manager, took the team to the finals of Euro 2004, but once there Russia simply fell apart. A series of semi-public squabbles after the opening 1–0 defeat to Spain demoralised the team before the next match against the hosts, Portugal. Russia were outclassed and out-thought by Figo and co, and were lucky to only lose 2–0. The side picked up a consolation victory against the tournament's eventual champions Greece in the last game, but it was, as usual, too little, too late.

Yartsev, an unassuming, quiet man, had a fairly undistinguished CV at the time of his appointment to the post of national team manager. He had, it was true, won the league title with Spartak in 1996, but he had been, in reality, nothing more than a stopgap as Oleg Romantsev took a brief hiatus to lead the national side to that year's European Championship in England. (Even Romantsev's Iron Fist was unable to help the national side, however, Russia gaining only one point and going out at the group stage, again.)

Yartsev had favoured the much-trumpeted 'Spartak style' that had seen the club do so well in Europe in the late 1980s and early 1990s. In the hands (or feet) of talented, quick players, the aforementioned style is somewhat similar to the 'Total Football' played by the Dutch in the 1970s: short, accurate passes, lots of running off the ball. The problem was, when he tried to carry it out with the players he had chosen, a mixture of ageing stars and unreliable youngsters, it simply degenerated into a series of off-target, telegraphed passes and a defensive line that was unable to react to anything even approaching originality and spontaneity from the opposing forwards.

There was speculation that one of the reasons Yartsev had got the job was because he was a member of the pro-Kremlin 'United Russia' party. President Putin, they said, liked to have a hand in everything. Even if he wasn't actually that great a football fan, he still wanted to make sure 'his people' were in place. It was, after all, Putin who had muttered during his first few months in power, 'Those who aren't with us are against us.'

Daniel Kalder, the Scottish author of two fine books, *Lost Cosmonaut* and *Strange Telescopes*, devoted to the bleaker sides of Russia and the Russian character, lived in Moscow for many years in the 1990s and mid-2000s, and recalls that 'Russia in the late nineties was a post-apocalyptic nightmare. The cynical, barely concealed criminality of the ruling elite created a sense of despair among ordinary people that was impossible to avoid in any conversation. Perhaps because I came from a country with an equally shitty national side, I regularly found myself getting dragged into conversations lamenting the state of Russian football, even though I personally had no interest in the sport. The collapse of their sporting prowess was a source of shame and humiliation. I remember once I started rubbing it in – at least Scotland was small. What was Russia's excuse? A string of defensive justifications followed: "Russia is too big" or "The weather is too cold", etc. – but there was no conviction in these statements. Both I and the guy making the excuses knew that Russia, a vast country with enormous reserves of potential could and should be doing much better.'

The simple truth may be that very large nations do not necessarily make for successful football teams. China, India, the USA – none of these countries have particularly good sides, although, admittedly, they do not have the tradition of football that Russia has.

Brazil, it is true, is a large country with no lack of success, but then football in Brazil is more than mere sport – it is a way of life, the beating pulse of the nation, and for Brazil failure in football is unthinkable, a national catastrophe when it occurs.

Perhaps Russia is just too massive, still too disorganised, to make the best of its players. Or, possibly, there is something in the temperament of Slavs, some sluggishness, an apathy that prevents them achieving glory. How many times have I heard Russians complaining about the national team, grumbling that, 'They don't care, they just don't care!'

Elke Klusmann, a German dramatic arts teacher who has worked with Russian children, suggested to me that this lack of competitiveness is visible from an early age. 'The Russian kids hug each other at kindergarten, help each other out. German children, on the other hand, mostly fight and scratch. That's why they even had to ban football in some German schools.'

While this may be a case of extreme stereotyping, considering the relative success in football that the two nations have enjoyed – the Germans even managing to reach the 2002 World Cup Final with their weakest side for years – she may well have had something there.

Pavel Baev, a Russian national and research professor at the International Peace Research Institute in Oslo, commented that, 'At the core of its national identity, Russia is neither a nuclear super-power nor a spoiled petro-state, but a country of hopeless football fans.'

Russian football, however, he went on to say, 'has been traditionally too strongly dominated by coaches, bosses of all sorts – and that suppressed the individual freedom of the players, denied them the panache and joy of free choice. *"Zaorganizovannost"*, as we say in Russian – overmanagement.'

Or perhaps the reason runs deeper? It has become something of a cliché in Russia itself to speak of the national side's appetite for self-destruction, the team's habit of throwing everything away with one moment of madness. It is a very Slavic trait, and one that Fyodor Dostoevsky never tired of examining. His *Crime and Punishment*, first published in 1866, contains perhaps the most famous example of the Russians' predilection for last-minute, turnabouts and twists, invariably to their disadvantage. As the novel comes to an end, the story's anti-hero, Raskolnikov, has apparently gotten away with the murder of a pawnbroker at the start of the book, but instead of going on to live 'happily ever after', he makes a sudden and unforced confession, condemning himself to exile to Siberia. (There are, of course, also issues of the Christian concept of redemption here.) Dostoevsky's classic existential work *Notes from the Underground* also explores the desire for pain and suffering, the book's narrator seeking out misfortune in order to experience unhappiness, satisfying in the process some deep and mysterious need for loss and humiliation.

Although no Russian side has as yet been exiled to the snowy wastes of Siberia for losing a game, a fondness for last-second defeat and subsequent misery has dogged the team throughout its history. The most recent example of this was the side's November 2007 2–1 defeat in Israel that handed Steve McClaren's England a lifeline in their Euro 2008 qualification bid. At 1–1, and needing a victory to place themselves in prime position to pip England for a European Championship spot, Russia had looked to be in control, and were launching attack after attack. It seemed to be only a matter of time before the second goal went in. And then, as injury time approached, Dmitri Sychev of Lokomotiv Moscow hit the post, the ball was cleared, and CSKA's Sergei Ignashevich, usually one of the team's most reliable defenders, stumbled, allowing Omer Golan to race through to score Israel's second and winning goal with almost the last kick of the night.

Happily for both Ignashevich and Russia, however, England had their own unresolved complexes, and went down 3–2 at home to Croatia four days later, allowing Hiddink's men to progress to the final stages of Euro 2008 after their 1–0 victory over minnows Andorra.

Almost a decade before the Israel match, there had been another game, and another late goal. Unlike in 2007, however, there was no late reprieve, no Croatians to rescue Russia from a catastrophe of their own (subconscious) making.

On 9 October 1999, Russia faced their Slavic neighbours and kin, the Ukrainians, in a Euro 2000 qualifying match that would decide both side's fates. After Russia had lost their first three games in Group Four, including a humiliating 1–0 defeat in Reykjavik to Iceland in the autumn of 1998, Oleg Romantsev agreed to take control of the team for the second time in his career. The Russians subsequently performed rare heroics to win the next six ties, including a glorious 3–2 victory in Paris over France, the then-reigning world champions. Everything was perfectly set for the side's final qualifying fixture against Ukraine.

The situation in the group was particularly tight. With one game remaining, Ukraine were top with 19 points, and Russia and France were level on 18. Russia, however, had a superior goal difference to both the French and the Ukrainians. The deciding match was to be played at the Luzhniki Olympic arena. A sell-out crowd was expected.

Besides the small matter of qualification for the European Championships, the Russia–Ukraine match had extra significance as a meeting between the two main republics of the former USSR In the first match between the two sides in Kiev, in September 1998, Ukraine had triumphed 3–2, and this was Russia's chance to get revenge.

Until the 2004 Orange Revolution that brought the Western-leaning Viktor Yushchenko to power, the state of affairs in which Ukraine existed as a separate country was considered to be a ludicrous, temporary phenomenon by many Russians (and not an inconsiderable number of Ukrainians). In fact, Ukraine's very name means, roughly, 'On the edge (of Russia)'.

There are hundreds of thousands of Ukrainian migrant workers in Russia at any given moment, not to mention the large permanent ethnic group within the country, many with Russian citizenship. Intermarriage is extremely common, as you would expect, and the line between 'Russian' and 'Ukrainian' is a thin one at best. To confuse matters even more, the language spoken in the east of Ukraine is Russian, and many 'Ukrainians' living in that part of the country speak nothing else.

This schizophrenia is captured perfectly in the Russian 'Goblin' translation of the film version of *The Lord of the Rings*. Goblin is a 'translator' who, bored with the Peter Jackson blockbusters, decided to make up his own versions. His interpretations bear no resemblance to the original plots, using slang and street humour to tell entirely different stories, complete with swearing cops, Russian politicians, and more. They are on sale everywhere in Russia, in flagrant disregard of any copyright laws, and are at least as popular as the originals.

In the scene where Gollum is grappling with the 'good' and 'bad' sides of his personality, Goblin has the Russian and Ukrainian parts of his character battling it out for supremacy.

'But our Spartak Moscow will do your Dynamo Kiev any day!' grunts the 'Russian' half of Gollum, only to be met by a stream of curses from his 'Ukrainian' side.

Another aspect to Russian–Ukrainian relations, though receding further and further into the collective memory with each passing year, is the Ukrainian famine, the 'Great Hunger' of 1932–33. It is estimated that anything between three and five million people died in Soviet Ukraine during enforced collectivisation, when grain and other foodstuffs were taken from the villages to the cities, and peasants could be shot for breaking the rules and holding back grain. Storehouses full of supplies were kept locked throughout the darkest days of the famine, guarded by well-fed and well-armed party members.

In his book *Harvest of Sorrow*, British historian Robert Conquest puts forward the widely accepted theory that Stalin was fully aware that collectivisation would bring famine, and that he persisted with the strategy in order to eliminate the anti-Communist intelligentsia and rising Ukrainian nationalism.

Nevertheless, it would be inaccurate to suggest that the Great Hunger had made the Ukrainians resent their Russian neighbours. The fact was that in Soviet times no one spoke about it, and by the late 1990s there was a steadily increasing number of people who were, astonishingly, not even aware that such a thing had ever taken place.

At half-time in the most important match to have been played in Moscow since the birth of the Russian Federation, the score was 0–0. Russia had gone close, but had been unable to break down the tough Ukrainian defence. In Paris, France were leading 2–0 against Iceland. If results stayed as they were, France would be top, Ukraine second and into a play-off, and Russia out.

Russia had no choice. They had to win. But first they had to score. They tried to build, playing the short-passing game that

Romantsev's teams favoured, but nothing was getting through the stubborn Ukrainian defence. And then – news from France. Astoundingly, Iceland had drawn level. It was now 2–2. This was enough to put Ukraine through in first place, with Russia into the play-offs. And France, the world champions no less, would be knocked out by the combined might of the two former Soviet republics.

A sudden downpour began, and then, seconds later, it was announced that France had retaken the lead. Russia were on their way out again. Stung into action, the Russians launched attack after attack, but the Ukrainians were resolute. With seventeen minutes to go, Russia got a free kick just outside the box. Valeri Karpin, despite his girl's name and flowing blond locks, stepped up and blasted the ball with exceedingly unfeminine power past the wall and into the net.

It was the 87th minute, and Russia still led by virtue of Karpin's goal, when Andrei Shevchenko swung in an apparently harmless free kick. The Russian defenders had harried him all night, and he was tired – it was all he had the strength left to do. Even superstars wear out, and, anyway, this was before the height of his fame, when he was still a mere mortal.

Now, when I think about that moment, I see it all in slow motion, in freeze-frames moving towards the inevitable. The crowd knew it too. They could sense the ball heading for the net; sense the inevitable weight of history and tradition guiding that sphere into the Russian goal. The Russian keeper, Alexander Filimonov, went up for the cross . . . and stumbled . . . punching the ball into his own net.

Filimonov was on his knees now, disgusted with himself. The Ukrainians were, understandably, ecstatic. I remembered the words spoken by the Russian footballer commentator on the state-run First Channel when the Spartak defender Yuri Kovtun had scored an own goal in the last moment in Reykjavik, dooming Russia to an inglorious defeat in only their second game of that very same qualifying group. 'People get shot for things like that,' he had said, referring to Andres Escobar, the Colombian defender gunned down in 1994, supposedly for his own goal against the USA in that year's World Cup. I wondered what fate they would dream up for Filimonov.

The Russians poured forward, but everyone knew it was all over. There was to be no last-minute reprieve. Oleg Romantsev stormed off to the dressing rooms, leaving an ashtray full of cigarette butts behind him. The final whistle blew, and Russia were out. France had won 3–2, and took first place, and Ukraine would go into the play-offs.

A long, deep silence settled upon the stands around us. It was a tangible thing, that shock. You could feel it, enshrouding the stadium, ghosting through us all as we made our way to the Metro. The supporters around me were numb. Russia had succumbed to the Slavic fondness for unhappy endings, Filimonov throwing away progress to Euro 2000 with a grand suicidal gesture worthy of the finest works in the Russian literary canon.

While the players and the coach were quick to deny any hard feelings towards Filimonov, he would never play for the national team again. Strangely enough, he went on to play for Dynamo Kiev for a short time, his blunder obviously having been forgotten in the Ukraine at least. Although he is back in Russia now, no one will let him forget that slip-up. 'Aren't you guys ever going to stop asking me if I've got over it yet?' he pleaded to *Sovetski-Sport* in 2005.

'That was one of the most disappointing nights of my career,' said Vladimir Beschastnykh, the Russian centre forward that night, when I asked him about the game.

Several years had passed since the match, but it was still obviously fresh in his mind. 'We had done everything, even beaten the French in Paris. We'd lost the first three games, I remember, but then we'd won the next six. We were seconds away from qualifying. In first place, too.'

There wasn't much I could say, and I began to feel a touch ashamed at having brought up the subject, digging up old traumas. 'And then Shevchenko's cross . . .'

'That was no cross,' Shevchenko commented years later in an interview, going on to claim that he had fully intended to place the ball in the back of Filimonov's net.

After the match, the Russian media were quick to quote the country's former prime minister Viktor Chernomyrdin and the words he had uttered after the Russian economic crisis of 1998, during which the rouble had been devalued, wiping out at a stroke a large section of the population's savings.

'We hoped for something better, but things turned out like they always do,' he had said, striking a chord with the deeply fatalistic Russian psyche. The phrase seemed to sum up both Russia and its national football team, and was used for many years to report on the latest disaster to befall the national side.

Even Russia's unlikely political and economic revival under President Putin could, initially at least, do little to lift the side. Oleg Romantsev had tried his hand (twice), as had CSKA's Valeri Gazzayev and Yuri Syomin of Lokomotiv Moscow, but none of them had been able to turn the fortunes of the Russian side around.

In the 1990s, in the decade following the break-up of the USSR, Russia was in real danger of ceasing to exist as a fully functioning state, as a brutal separatist war in Chechnya, an unheralded crime wave, and the sheer incompetence and corruption of the Yeltsin regime ripped the world's largest state apart at the seams. It seemed no small wonder, then, that if Russia could not manage to pay wages on time to state employees, if it could not ensure the safety of its citizens from criminal groups or guarantee that savings would not be rendered worthless overnight, that its football team should be so utterly unsuccessful in its attempts to make a mark on the world scene.

However, as the fruits of record-high world oil prices trickled down to the general population, the standard of living rose, the threat of social meltdown retreated, and for the first time since perestroika the country's football fans had the luxury of devoting themselves to the game. Criticism soon became widespread and bitter as the country's stars repeatedly failed to meet the expectations of the New Russia.

The biggest film of the twenty-first century so far in Russia, more successful than any Hollywood blockbuster, is *Nochnoi Dozor*, or *Night Watch*, a film about supernatural beings who have divided Moscow amongst them, one side ruling at night, the other during the day.

In October 2004, after Russia were thrashed 7–1 by Portugal during a 2006 World Cup qualifier, the match having started at midnight Moscow time, Russian fans labelled the inglorious defeat '*Nochnoi Pozor*', cunningly changing one letter to obtain the new meaning 'Night Disgrace'. It's an extremely flexible thing, the Russian language. Which was more than could be said for the rigid, flat Russian back four that October night in Lisbon.

At the time of Russia's humiliation at the hands of Portugal, I was living on the thirteenth floor of a fifteen-storey tower block in the north of Moscow. The vast majority of Russians live in such tower blocks. Affluent, well to do, struggling to make ends meet, dirt poor – the only thing that separates the people is the condition of their actual flat. Tower blocks in Russia are the ultimate egalitarian statement, the lasting triumph of the sunken communist system. Your neighbour might be anyone, from a granny with her dog that barks all night, to a seven-person family of Azerbaijanis, to a westernised twentysomething couple whose flat is crammed full of stylish furniture from some Swedish hypermarket.

The main disadvantage of living in a tower block is that, obviously, you have no garden. Most Russians have access to dachas, small houses in the countryside, but these are not so convenient for when you feel like a quick kickabout. Of course, there are the streets, but for honing those essential 'keepie-up' skills and so on, there is nothing like a back garden, away from the eyes of the world, a place where a footballer can develop, hone those feints and little tricks that give him his character.

Perhaps this is why the Russian footballer is so pragmatic, so downright unadventurous. He has never had the opportunity to learn any tricks. Of course, it could also be something to do with the training system, the scientific emphasis on team play and systematically planned set moves inherited from Soviet times, when individual initiative was actively discouraged in all fields of life.

Things had begun promisingly enough in Lisbon, Russia even pushing deep into Portugal's half in the opening minutes. But then, just as it was looking as if Russia might be able to get a foothold, Portugal had the ball in the net, Pedro Pauleta meeting a cross with an outstretched leg. Russia stirred, Dmitri Bulikin and Alexei Smertin missing chances, before in the 39th minute the Manchester United star Cristiano Ronaldo deflected a Pauleta shot into Vyacheslav Malafeev's net for Portugal's second goal.

On the stroke of half time the Brazilian-born Deco hammered a shot past Malafeev from 20 metres– 3–0. The second half came, and the humiliation went on as Portugal added a fourth. Russia got one back, but it was a mere consolation goal. There were no hopes of a comeback. Then 5–1, Then 6–1. And finally, taking the score into the realms of disgrace, the seventh!

The final whistle sounded, mercifully signalling the end of the rout.

All over Russia, in the tower blocks, in the bars, in the villages with their flickering TV sets, a silence fell – more than shock, the void itself, engulfing the country – the Portuguese onslaught had left Russia numb. Russians were used to losing, since the split-up of the USSR they had had little to cheer about, but this . . . this was something else. This was a humiliation, a mortifying dishonour that transcended football.

'*Nochnoi Pozor*'.

7–1.

'Seven–one,' said my neighbour, a pensioner, as we were waiting for the lift the next morning. 'It would never have happened in the Soviet Union.' This is a fairly common response to misfortune amongst those Russians nostalgic for life in the USSR but, for once, it had some grounds in reality. In 1983 the Soviet national team had beaten Portugal 5–0, Oleg Blokhin and co running rings around the hapless Portuguese defenders, scoring almost at will.

The hammering that Russia took that night quickly entered the ranks of Russian urban folklore. Apart from the '*Nochnoi Pozor*' pun, it inspired TV comedians for months to come.

There is also a famous Russian rock song, by the group Chaif, the chorus of which is 'Argentina–Jamaica, 5–0', in honour of the 1998 World Cup match of the said result. It is a song about the loss of hope, about shattered dreams, and there were those who suggested Chaif should do a follow-up; a remix maybe, with this time the unfortunate and much derided Russian football team in the role of the Reggae Boys.

One of the most popular jokes at that time went as follows:

Brazil are playing a match against Russia. 'Ah, I can handle this lot on my own,' says Ronaldo, 'you guys take a rest.' Half-time comes and goes, and Russia are 3–0 down. However, the side make a spirited comeback in the second half, and almost snatch a draw, pulling two goals back after Ronaldo is sent off in the 75th minute.

Even taking into account the almost complete control that the Russian authorities enjoyed over the mass media, there was no way the Lisbon result, which reflected badly on President Putin's pledge that Russia would eventually 'catch up with Portugal' (in terms of GDP), could be hushed up.

Heads would roll after the Portugal match. Putin had apparently been enraged and, not so long after, the long-serving Russian Football Federation President, Vyacheslav Koloskov, would resign his post, reportedly having come under pressure from government officials to do so.

'He didn't go voluntarily,' said Viktor Ponedelnik, hero of Russia's 1960 European Championship victory.

'You know,' a fan wrote on an Internet forum after the game, 'in the USSR they said there was no sex, but we had football. Now, we have plenty of sex, but no football. Maybe we should abstain for a while?'

Whatever the relative merits of the logic behind this train of thought, it was clear to everyone that the Russian football team needed much more than a prolonged period of national celibacy to lift it out of its footballing gloom. In its darkest days, there was only one thing that could restore confidence and belief to the team – Russia needed, in short, a saviour.

A few weeks before the Dutch trainer Guus Hiddink took over the side in the summer of 2006, I travelled to Lokomotiv Moscow's out-of-town training camp to speak to the national team's young striker, Dmitri Sychev. After I had been waiting for more than an hour in the (admittedly comfortable) lobby at the club's training camp, Sychev came out to give me the lowdown on Russia's inability to develop a national side worthy of a nation whose vast territory stretches from Finland to China, from Iran to the Arctic Ocean.

'You know,' he began, 'in the Soviet Union there were more players to choose from,' said Sychev. 'We had Ukraine, Georgia, the Baltic States, etc.,' he went on. 'They all had very talented players. Maybe we miss them?'

True as this may have been, the population of post-USSR Russia is still 141 million. When you compare this with, say, Portugal's 10 million, it becomes clear that the problem lies deeper than mere demographics.

Sychev thought again. 'People don't relate to football in the same way in Russia as in, say, England. There it's a national obsession. Here, people have other interests.'

I let the (intended or not) sarcasm slide.

'That doesn't mean that we don't feel pride when we play for Russia. Everyone wants to help the motherland out,' Sychev added. A touch defensively, I thought.

A pause.

'To be honest,' the young forward concluded, 'I don't know why Russia has had such bad results since the break-up of the USSR.'

Russia's all-time top scorer Vladimir Beschastnykh was no more the wiser, telling me around the same time as I spoke to Sychev,

'Maybe we eat the wrong food, take the wrong vitamins. I don't know. Foreigners, generally, jump higher, run faster than us. It's a real mystery to me.'

President Putin, in a traditional question-and-answer session with the public in 2006, had his own opinion. 'There are far too many foreigners in Russian football,' he declared, 'and this is bad for the development of the national game.'

However, as a keen motorist and football fan pointed out to me, getting rid of, or imposing strict quotas on, foreign footballers would not necessarily lead to an increase in the quality of home-grown players. Drawing an analogy with the strict controls and high taxes placed on foreign cars, he noted that Russian vehicles had not improved as a result of the artificial limits, but that, rather, they had simply become more expensive due to the lack of competition. Russian players were already receiving some of the highest salaries in Europe, and placing restrictions on foreigners would, he suggested, simply serve to push up these wages even more.

Pavel Baev at the International Peace Research Institute in Oslo: 'For the Kremlin in Putin's second term it was sort of important to make sure that the oligarchs were investing not only in Chelsea but also in the domestic game, and that it should be entertaining enough to regain massive attention. However, this sort of financial support can secure the import of half-decent stars and coaches – but not the cultivation of home-grown talent. The production of great players has been discontinued.'

In late 2005, with Russia's World Cup qualification hopes all but dead, President Putin, still furious at the way Russia had been torn apart in Portugal, contacted the new president of the Russian Football Federation, Vitali Mutko, and instructed him to build up the national side, to look for sponsors and investors.

Putin, naturally enough as a former KGB officer, had inherited the Soviet leaders' belief that sport was intimately connected to prestige on the international scene, and spineless and incompetent displays like the one in Lisbon were hindering his attempts to restore Russian greatness and world influence. Oil money was transforming Russia into a potential superpower, and states that aspire to regional, and even global, leadership simply do not get beaten 7–1 at football by tiny south European nations.

Mutko, in turn, contacted the oil oligarch and Chelsea FC owner Roman Abramovich, and the sixteenth-richest man in the world, doing his part to rescue Russian national pride, promptly conjured up Guus Hiddink, who immediately set about rebuilding the demoralised Russian team.

Every cloud, they say, has a silver lining or, as the equivalent Russian proverb has it, 'Happiness wouldn't exist, if misfortune wasn't around to help it along'.

CHAPTER THREE

CSKA Moscow – all that glitters

'We are not responsible for your loss.'
English-language sign in a Moscow shopping centre.

While Spartak Moscow claim to be the 'People's Team', CSKA have long been seen as the face of Russian business, golden boys of the country's national sport, their 2005 UEFA Cup triumph making them the first Russian (as opposed to Soviet) side to lift a European trophy.

As Russia has changed, emerging from the wildness and uncertainty of the 1990s, then so, accordingly, has the nature of its champions. If Spartak Moscow were the side of the nineties, their domination over the Russian game (much like the Yeltsin administration's simultaneous grip on power) chaotic, yet absolute, then CSKA are the team that most characterises the cold efficiency of the Putin era – cynical, professional, utterly ruthless and masters of the 1–0 victory.

CSKA is a sports club, a complex organisation devoted to a diverse number of sporting activities, including basketball and ice hockey. Founded in 1911 by a group of skiing enthusiasts, the club was transformed in the 1920s into the team of the Soviet Army. After going through a number of name changes, the side settled on its present moniker in 1960. CSKA stands for *Tsentralni Sportivni Klub Armii*, or The Central Sports Club of the Army, and its original function was to assist with the physical health of Soviet soldiers.

Today, although their main sponsor is the Russian Bank of Foreign Trade, CSKA retains its association with the armed forces. Indeed, the club are still semi-owned by the Ministry of Defence and, after one recent memorable victory over the Italian side Parma, the then-defence minister Sergei Ivanov went into the CSKA dressing room to congratulate the team. He also reportedly joked that they would now be safe from the draft.

Despite its obvious affluence, the CSKA set-up is an odd mix of old-school Soviet and hard-edged capitalism. Attempting to get accreditation for the 2006 Champions League match against Arsenal, I sometimes had the impression that I was trying to prise military secrets out of Sergei, the club's press attaché. Arranging an interview with CSKA's president was tortuous, necessitating weeks of phone calls and laser-precision planning, not to mention a touch of cunningness on my behalf.

As the 2006 title race heated up, CSKA travelled to Rostov, some 450 miles to the south of Moscow, for a potentially tricky fixture. After the match, which CSKA won 2–1, a report by TV presenter Vasili Utkin on the Moscow-based NTV Plus TV channel claimed that the game had been fixed in favour of the champions. The evidence presented was damning. CSKA's first goal was scored with four of the Army players left completely free in the penalty area, only one Rostov defender, Miguni Kanenda, from Mali, attempting to resist. This could perhaps have been explained away as extremely sloppy defending, but there was more to come.

The same player, Kanenda, later earned a penalty. The spot kick was put weakly to the keeper's right and was parried, but the resulting rebound somehow ended up in the back of the net.

Immediately after the goal, the Rostov players' faces were studies in despair. Having equalised against the reigning champions, instead of leaping for joy, or any other of the things that footballers are prone to doing after hitting the back of their opponent's net, the goalscorer, Kalachev, from whose leg the ball had ricocheted over the line, shook his head and walked slowly back to the centre circle. CSKA scored the winning goal shortly afterwards, Rostov's players, as Utkin pointed out, seemingly helping the ball over their own goal-line.

After the match, it was announced that Kanenda, Rostov's man-of-the-match, would miss the next fixture because of head injuries that he had somehow mysteriously incurred in the dressing room. The Malian international, however, refused to comment on rumours that his team-mates, furious at his 'betrayal', had attacked him following the final whistle.

'I always seem to get lucky in Rostov,' said Ivica Olic, CSKA's two-goal hero, after the game. CSKA did not take the accusations lying down though, and following an Utkin article in *Sovetski Sport* that elaborated on the Rostov fix claims, the club took the newspaper to court for slander. CSKA won the initial trial, and *Sovetski Sport* was ordered to print a retraction. However, an appeal court later overturned this decision, and a further court action by CSKA against Utkin was also dismissed. No retraction was ever printed.

Everywhere I went I heard accusations against CSKA, from the media, from Spartak, from ordinary fans. However, despite CSKA's failure to defend their name in court, I wasn't sure that I entirely bought it. Nothing, I reasoned, could be that corrupt. Even Russian football.

I would, I realised in a flash, have to meet with the object of the allegations. To talk to, and look into the eyes of CSKA's president Evgeni Giner, a close friend of Roman Abramovich, and the man accused by many of cynically and knowingly destroying the beautiful game in Russia.

Walking through the large compound that is CSKA's north Moscow headquarters, I stumbled upon the club's Alley of Glory, dedicated to the side's sporting heroes, and paused to read the inscriptions on the bases of the bronze busts. As I was doing so, a jeep full of soldiers drove past, a couple of them glancing at me suspiciously.

There were, I was surprised to note, no members of CSKA's UEFA Cup winning team among the two dozen or so busts. Perhaps the club just hadn't got around to casting them yet? Having finished with the Alley of Glory, and still puzzling over this omission, I took a wrong turn and walked right into the officers' clubhouse. Upon realising I was in the wrong place, I asked for directions to the press centre. The two soldiers on guard duty hesitated for a second, and then relented, pointing me in the right direction.

I arrived early for my interview with Evgeni Giner. Whilst waiting in reception, flicking through a copy of that morning's *Sovetski-Sport*, a club secretary brought me tea and biscuits. Spartak Moscow had also given me tea and biscuits and, in keeping with the great rivalry between the two sides, I couldn't help but compare their offerings. CSKA's biscuits, if you are interested, were of a far superior class.

I had been trying to organise my interview with Giner for months, and had got used to being asked to call back in a week, or to hearing that the CSKA president was out of the country, at a business meeting or a UEFA conference. Things would, in all likelihood, have continued like this interminably, had I not taken a risk. Coming to the end of my researches, and still not having had an opportunity to quiz Giner, I resorted to telling the press attaché that I had heard a lot of terrible, compromising things about CSKA, and that if the club president continued to deny me an interview, if he had no interest in defending his side's honour, then I would have no choice but to simply repeat all of these verbatim. If CSKA did not wish to see their good name damaged throughout the green and pleasant land of my birth, then it would be a good idea for Giner to spare me half an hour or so.

Although I had no desire to blackmail the club, I was counting on the fact that CSKA cared enough about their reputation in England to grant me an interview. This was around the time of the Alexander Litvinenko polonium-poisoning scandal that rocked the UK in late 2006, and my father joked that 'they will either agree, or have you shot'. While, obviously, CSKA are in no way connected with the recent violence perpetrated against certain members of the media in Russia, it was indicative of the worsening image that the country was enjoying in the West. The day after my call, CSKA's spokesman rang and invited me to visit Giner at the club the following afternoon. My bluff had paid off.

Evgeni Giner, who has consistently described himself as a 'simple Soviet man', didn't appear that pleased to see me when I walked into his office, and I wondered if this was a reaction to my not-so-veiled threat or, as the victim of an extremely bad press of late, he was simply ill-disposed to journalists per se. I began with a pleasant question, reminding Giner, as he lit up a fat cigar, of Arsène Wenger's recent prediction that a Russian team would win the Champions League within the next decade.

'I agree wholeheartedly,' replied the CSKA president. 'Perhaps even sooner. Russian football is on the rise, a huge amount of money is currently being invested in it, and the infrastructure of the sport is being rapidly developed.'

While Russian football may have a glorious present, compared with the low point of the 1990s, I enquired as to why the country's oligarchs and businessmen had only recently begun to invest heavily in the sport. 'I think that any clever businessmen tries to invest money when the prices are low, be it in real estate or a football team,' answered Giner. 'The asking prices for Russian teams are extremely attractive at the moment. There is a lot of interest in the game in Russia right now, and as the sport develops, the costs will undoubtedly rise. Now is simply a good time to invest in clubs.'

'For me, though,' Giner said, expounding, 'CSKA is a hobby, not a business. It's something I can afford to do, something I get – most of the time – satisfaction from. My real businesses are connected with the energy and hotel sectors. I've been offered Italian, Spanish and even English teams, but CSKA is my first and last club.'

Having got the pleasantries out of the way, I asked Giner straight out, or as the Russians say, 'to the forehead', if fixed games existed in Russia.

'You know,' replied Giner, 'I've never been able to figure out exactly what a fixed game is.' He sat back in his chair.

I defined the matter under discussion as when 'two teams have agreed beforehand on the result of a game'. Giner sighed, and launched into a long explanation, taking in the recent World Cup, various Champions League fixtures, motivation, and a number of other topics, displaying the verbal gymnastics you would expect of a successful Russian businessman, but not actually answering my question. I posed it a different way. Was, I enquired, Russian football 'clean' of corruption?

'I'm not in a position to confirm that one way or the other. Anyone can say anything they want, but without proof, it's meaningless.' Why then were CSKA so often the object of accusations?

'No one likes the rich or the powerful. No one likes our success. If some games might appear strange, that does not mean we bribed our opponents. You have, it appears, been paying too much attention to Spartak's outbursts. And look,' he went on, his voice rising now the conversation had taken a not-so-agreeable turn, 'we've been playing well in the UEFA Cup and Champions League for three years now. Does that mean we fixed games there? Against Benfica, Sporting, Arsenal? Other sides simply envy us.'

Giner had recently given an interview, widely reported abroad and seeming to confirm Spartak's 'stimulation' claims, in which he appeared to admit that CSKA paid out cash bonuses to their rivals' opponents.

'That was just badly translated,' said Giner. 'I personally don't see anything wrong with such "stimulation", but we don't take part in it, because it's a legal grey area. If UEFA ever expressly permit it, then we will certainly begin. And, I might add, all the money will be, naturally, above board, and all taxes paid.'

In Russia, where until recently the tax police wore ski masks and carried Kalashnikovs, it is an extremely good idea to keep on the right side of the tax inspectorate. As the Russian saying goes, 'Pay your taxes and sleep well'. In Russia, there are some organisations even more powerful than well-connected football clubs.

That same morning, Spartak's owner Leonid Fedun, prolonging his three-year-long battle of words with CSKA, had declared that he was in possession of certain documents that proved the existence of corruption in Russian football. However, he said he would not be making the said papers public. 'Fedun says he has proof, some documents. Why doesn't he show them?' said Giner, taking a long drag on his cigar, and glancing at his watch.

I was reminded of Andrei Chervichenko, and his opinion that Russian football was now nothing more than a battle between oligarchs, a mere matter of prestige. I repeated this to the CSKA president, along with the former Spartak owner's statement that Russian football had become a lot more corrupt in the last few years, to which Giner broke in with perfect comic timing, saying, 'Yeah, well, since Andrei left the game, of course it's become a lot dirtier. Maybe we should invite him back to clean it up?'

My time almost up, I posed what I had imagined to be one of the more innocuous questions on my list, asking Giner to clarify the club's one-time relationship with Roman Abramovich. 'Roman Abramovich has never had any relationship with CSKA,' replied the CSKA president, clearly irritated. I reminded him, although I was certain he hadn't forgotten, that Abramovich's former company, Sibneft, had been CSKA's sponsors until 2005.

'And?' asked Giner, raising his voice. 'That means nothing. Roman, I am sure, didn't decide to sponsor CSKA. There exist such things as advertising departments. The decision was made there. Companies decide where to invest money, where it will be the most advantageous for them, in terms of publicity. My personal friendship with Roman Abramovich had absolutely nothing to do with it,' Giner concluded, his face red with anger. I got the feeling he had been asked about this a lot.

You will not be surprised to learn that I decided against posing the most provocative of the questions on my list, dealing with recent rumours to the affirmative: 'Does Roman Abramovich continue to fund CSKA in any way whatsoever?' Somehow, I got the feeling that it wouldn't be well received.

Whatever the truth behind the match-fixing allegations, there is no denying that there is an element of resentment at the success Giner has brought to CSKA. As Alexei Smertin, the former Chelsea midfielder, pointed out to me, Russians have a great capacity for envy. Indeed, there is an old Soviet saying, 'Real happiness is when your neighbour's house burns down'.

The editor of *Sport-Express* was equally sceptical, telling me that he considered Spartak's accusations and outbursts to be 'ugly'. 'If you have proof, then let's see it,' he said, 'but to make comments like that in the heat of the moment isn't very helpful, to say the least. In Italy they had real evidence – phone conversations were recorded and so on, but Spartak have nothing to back up their accusations.'

'I simply don't hold with the theory that Giner is involved in buying matches,' said Nikolai Roganov, at *Total Football*, when I spoke to him at the end of the 2006 season. 'He is a phenomenal businessman, a superb manager in the wider sense of the word, and we should be thankful that he has decided to bring his expertise to Russian football. As for all the rumours, all the stories, well, I believe in facts, and they speak for themselves. After all, you can't buy the UEFA Cup.'

As Leonid Vorokhovski of the St Petersburg magazine *Smena* put it, 'It is just not fair to consider Giner and CSKA as symbols of evil in Russian football. Are the other clubs in the Premier League all saints? Alas, they are not.'

'Judge not, that ye not be judged,' in other words.

In October 2006 I attended the Champions League match between CSKA and Arsenal. When the draw for the group stage had been made, the English press had been dismissive of the Russians' prospects. The majority of newspapers predicted that Arsenal would top the group and CSKA would finish last.

After the club's UEFA Cup victory, CSKA's manager Valeri Gazzayev had spoken of Russians' tendency to see themselves as 'second rate', yet it appeared the English media was also suffering from the same affliction. With six Russian national side regulars in the team, and three Brazilian international newcomers, plus the twelfth man of fanatical home support, it looked like lazy journalism, at best, to write off the Muscovites' chances so early.

Before the Arsenal game, CSKA had drawn their first group fixture and won their second, while Arsenal had yet to drop a point. It was cold, but not yet freezing, the mercury hovering around plus one. The match was to be held at Lokomotiv's Cherkizovo stadium, as CSKA, though the 2003, 2005 and 2006 Russian champions, lack an adequate ground of their own and are a nomadic side, moving from stadium to stadium as the occasion demands. Construction work has begun on their new ground, but the club are not expected to play there for another couple of years at least. For Russian Premier League fixtures, they rent out Dynamo's Petrovsky Park, but for big European occasions, they relocate to Cherkizovo, Russia's finest stadium.

Cherkizovo, unlike many Russian grounds, has no running track, and the fans are pressed right up to the side of the pitch, making it one of the few stadiums in the country that has real atmosphere. The ground was packed that night, full of huge banners, the crowd performing well-rehearsed chants. Up in a small sector in the South End, the tiny contingent of Arsenal fans who had made the trip to Moscow looked lost.

I had managed to get a press-box ticket for the game, and found myself next to a talkative middle-aged English reporter. 'I cover all of Arsenal's matches abroad,' he told me. 'This is the third time I've been to Moscow, and I've yet to see them win.'

Previous trips to the Russian capital had seen the Gunners beaten 4–1 by Spartak in 2000, and a dull 0–0 draw with Lokomotiv in 2003. Moscow, it seemed, was not a lucky city for Arsène Wenger's side.

In their Champions League games against Chelsea in 2004, CSKA had been apologetic and hesitant on the ball, wary of their more illustrious opponents. But now, brimming with the confidence that their 2005 UEFA Cup victory had given them, they passed the ball around amongst themselves, taking time on the ball, making regular forays into Arsenal's penalty area. Against Chelsea, Vagner Love had been so nervous he had sent a penalty flying high over the bar, but now he was running at the Arsenal defence as if they were just another Russian provincial side there for the taking.

CSKA's new confidence was symbolic of the power that Russia as a whole, and not only its football, was experiencing. With massive reserves of natural resources, Russia was, for the first time since the break-up of the USSR, able to exert genuine political and economic influence over its neighbours. The very same month that CSKA took on Arsenal as equals, President Putin was being fawned over by European heads of state, desperate to ensure that winter's uninterrupted flow of gas, at an EU meeting in Helsinki.

In the 24th minute, CSKA gained a free kick. Daniel Carvalho, one of CSKA's Brazilians, stepped up and, after some discussion with his team-mates, blasted the ball into the net. 1–0! CSKA were firmly in control.

'I remember the first time I came to Moscow,' the fantastically named Vagner Love recalled in an interview with the Russian press. 'It was summer, and twenty degrees when I stepped off the plane. I thought, "Who would have thought it?" Not much colder than Brazil.'

The striker's initial warm feelings for Russia didn't last long, however. Even after CSKA's UEFA Cup victory, the Brazilian team members, Love especially, had been rumoured to be unhappy in Moscow. Back in 2005, he had said, 'I would prefer to leave Russia and go back to Brazil. It will be extremely difficult to get into the Brazilian national side whilst I'm here, as the coach just doesn't have the opportunity to see me in action.'

The deadlocked striker regularly went AWOL, jetting back to Brazil on the slightest excuse, and his compatriot Carvalho was said to be setting up a deal with a top European side. The weather was, perhaps understandably, getting to them and, as Carvalho explained, the Russians themselves were making a somewhat less than favourable impression. The grimaces and sighs that pass for normal on the streets of Moscow were making them pine for the sun-kissed beaches of Brazil.

However, in September 2006 Love, Carvalho and Dudu earned call-ups to the Brazilian national side, their country's new coach, the legendary Dunga, using them extensively in the five-time World Cup winners' autumn tour. The Russian-based Brazilians took their chances, with both Carvalho and Love getting on the score sheet, returning to Moscow with smiles on their faces. The Russian media marvelled at what a difference a few caps could make.

'The call-up of Vagner Love, Carvalho and Dudu to the Brazilian team is a great honour for CSKA,' said Valeri Gazzayev. Indeed, the whole of Russian football hoped it would prove to other top players, so far reluctant to make the move to Russia, that it was possible to remain in the limelight whilst playing for one of the country's leading clubs.

There was a twist, however, to the inclusion of Vagner Love and co in the Brazilian squad that autumn. The Brazil–Argentina friendly in London in September 2006 was partly organised by Renova, a Russian company run by Victor Vekselberg, Russia's third-richest man. Renova had recently acquired the rights to stage the Argentinians' next eighteen friendlies, paying around $1,000,000 a game, in a move which led the president of one Buenos Aires club to call the deal the 'privatisation of our country's football'.

After the deal, Vladimir Abramov of Sovintersport, a Russian agency involved with the sale of Russian players to foreign teams, commented in the Moscow-based *Novaya Gazeta* newspaper that Vekselberg was no football fan, and that he and the other oligarchs were turning not only Russian football but also the world game into mere 'show business'.

'There may well come a time,' he said, 'when the line-ups of the

Argentinian and Brazilian sides are decided in Russia! Do you think that our CSKA and Spartak legionnaires got into the Brazilian and Argentinian sides just like that?'

'It's the first rule of show business,' he went on. 'Set everything up, so that everything is yours. We [Russia] are getting ready to buy up all the world's best sportsmen, and of course Europe is afraid of that.'

There was no clear proof that any pressure had been brought to bear on either coach to include Russian-based players, yet it was an unsettling thought.

'For me,' commented Uli Hoeness, Bayern Munich's general manager, in an interview with the German newspaper *Kieler Nachrichten*, 'this is the beginning of the end for football. It is absolutely crazy that the Argentinians have sold the rights to their games to a Russian investor.'

Indeed, the circumstances surrounding the Brazil–Argentina match were deeply symbolic for the future of world football. Apart from the Renova connection, and the CSKA and Spartak Moscow players who graced the Emirates Stadium that day, the Argentine side could boast Carlos Tévez and Javier Mascherano, recently transferred to West Ham from Corinthians with the help of Media Sports Investment, a company with links to the London-based Russian oligarch Boris Berezovsky. The final part of the symbolism was the stadium itself, or more accurately its owners Arsenal, who were the subject of a takeover bid by a consortium of Russian businessmen. As a statement of Russia's growing influence within the planet's favourite sport, it was downright impressive.

Against Arsenal, CSKA hung on for another 1–0 victory, Thierry Henry having a late goal disallowed for offside. After the match Arsène Wenger, while complimenting the Russian champions, complained about the state of the pitch, saying that Champions League football, and CSKA, deserved better. When asked if Arsenal had underestimated CSKA, Wenger smiled wryly and said that maybe CSKA had overestimated Arsenal.

Before the return match in London, referring to Henry's disallowed 'goal', Wenger stated that, for him, the first game had finished 1–1.

'Yeah, right,' retorted Gazzayev at the press conference, and proceeded to tell a joke to illustrate the difference between reality and hypothesis. 'A girl goes up to her father,' began the CSKA manager, 'and asks, "Dad, what's the difference between the virtual world and reality?" The father replies, "I'll show you. Go and ask your mother and brother if they would sleep with someone for a million dollars." She does so and, having received affirmative replies, the father says, "See, that's the difference. In the virtual world, our family has two million dollars, but in reality your mother is a whore and your brother is a rent boy."

The joke went unreported in the English press.

Valeri Gazzayev is one of Russia's best-known managers, his large, black, drooping moustache something of a Russian celebrity in its own right. When CSKA reached the quarter-finals of the 2005 UEFA Cup, Gazzayev promised to shave off the said facial adornment if the team were to win the trophy. After doing so, he went back on his word, and pledged to do so only in the event of the side lifting the Champions League.

He is also known for shooting at firing ranges before matches, using a gun presented to him by then-Russian defence minister Sergei Ivanov on the occasion of CSKA's UEFA Cup success. 'Shooting helps me settle my nerves,' said Gazzayev, when questioned about his hobby.

'Training sessions are great with Gazzayev,' said Carvalho, 'we can joke with him, have fun, and it makes the whole club set-up very relaxed. He really helped me and the other Brazilians settle in.'

Gazzayev hails from North Ossetia, in Russia's mountainous North Caucasus region. As is the custom there, when he first began to crawl, his mother put objects on the floor in front of him symbolising his possible future directions in life. Little Valeri, as his mother tells it, ignoring all the other items, made his way straight to the ball, clutching on to it tightly.

In his playing days Gazzayev turned out for Dynamo Moscow, Lokomotiv Moscow and Dynamo Tbilisi, as well as the national side. A prolific striker, he finished his career in 1986 and immediately went into management, coaching the Dynamo Moscow youth team, before eventually taking over the first team in 1991. After two spells at Dynamo, with a five-year period at Alania Vladikavkaz in between, he accepted an offer to manage CSKA in 2001.

The most successful manager of the post-Romantsev era, Gazzayev's career looked to have come to a premature end in 2003. Having accepted, and then resigned from, the post of national team manager while remaining at the helm at CSKA, Gazzayev was sacked by the club after failing to get them to the lucrative Champions League group stages, defeated by the Macedonian outsiders FK Vardar. 'That was a catastrophe for the side,' a long-time CSKA fan told me. 'Giner had invested heavily in the club, everything was set for this bright European future, and then, boom, they were out of the Champions League.'

Despite the obvious setback, many people were still shocked when Gazzayev, despite winning the Russian championship for CSKA that year, was dismissed by Evgeni Giner and replaced by the Portuguese manager Artur Jorge. However, eight months later, with Jorge struggling to adapt to life and football in Russia, Giner brought Gazzayev back to the club. Obviously not a man to hold grudges, the moustached Ossetian immediately went on to lift the Russian Premier League title, the Russian Cup and the UEFA Cup.

'I found out that there are interesting things aside from football,' said Gazzayev. 'I was involved in business, and happily spent eight months without the game.'

Prior to winning the UEFA Cup, Gazzayev's efforts in European competitions had often ended in complete humiliation. This tradition began during his time at Dynamo Moscow – the Muscovites losing 6–0 at home to Eintracht Frankfurt in a UEFA Cup game in 1993. It remains the heaviest defeat in the history of Soviet and Russian clubs in Europe.

Three years later, it was Glasgow Rangers' turn to humble Gazzayev. Having broken, for one season at least, Spartak Moscow's grip on the Russian title while managing his home-town team, Alania Vladikavkaz, the new Russian champions lost 3–1 in Scotland, and then went down 7–2 at home to complete a 10–3 aggregate defeat. Under Gazzayev, Alania also lost 4–0 to RSC Anderlecht and 3–0 to MTK Hungária FC.

Gazzayev, however, came back to CSKA with a slightly different way of looking at the game. Prior to his return to football, his teams had been renowned for their attack-minded style, but upon taking the helm at CSKA for the second time, his tactics became more mature and more pragmatic. The results duly followed.

After CSKA's UEFA Cup triumph, President Putin invited the victorious side to his private residence in Novo-Ogaryovo, just outside Moscow. As a former member of the KGB, Putin would make a natural Dynamo supporter (the former team of the security services) but, despite attending matches regularly in his first year of the presidency, he has long stopped pretending to show any real interest in the game. Despite this lack of enthusiasm for the sport, the CSKA photo call was clearly too good an opportunity to pass up.

CSKA had brought along a gold top with 'Putin' emblazoned on the back. 'It's an outstanding achievement,' said the president, referring to the UEFA Cup victory. 'I'm not an expert in football, nor an experienced fan of the game, but nevertheless I saw the match and enjoyed your performance, and was excited by your skills.'

Putin also praised Valeri Gazzayev, saying that the coach had managed to unite the players from different countries, who played different styles, into a strong and skilled unit. All in all, the speechwriter had done well.

'Who scored the third goal? When you tricked the keeper?' asked Putin, suddenly.

Silence.

Everyone turned to look at Vagner Love, who was staring straight ahead, oblivious to the turn the conversation had taken.

'He did,' said Gazzayev.

'*Ne ponimayu*' (I don't understand), muttered Love, sensing at last that the President of the Russian Federation was talking about him.

'Ah, he understands everything. He's always saying that. Whenever there's hard training to be done, it's, "*Ne ponimayu, ne ponimayu*,"' grinned Gazzayev.

Then the president was given a ball and began bouncing it, before Love, through a translator, commented that CSKA were a football, not basketball, team. President Putin attempted a few keepie-ups, but he only managed a couple, the players applauding his valiant efforts nevertheless, the Brazilians smirking as the leader of the largest country on Earth demonstrated skills that a five-year-old girl would be ashamed of on the beaches back home.

After the CSKA–Arsenal game, I wandered through to the Mixed Zone, the area that players are obliged to pass through before leaving the stadium. There was a barrier separating the footballers from the journalists, and the majority of players strolled past with mobile phones stuck to their ears, engaged in imaginary conversations, ignoring the journalists' pleas for quotes. The CSKA players were the first to come out, and a middle-aged drunk, having clambered around the barrier, bear-hugged Vagner Love with great enthusiasm.

After posing with Love, the drunk spied Thierry Henry. The Frenchman was giving an interview to the English dailies. I was impressed by how good his English was. 'I'm fuming,' repeated Henry a few times, referring to the disallowed goal, pursing his lips to illustrate exactly how 'fuming' he was. The drunk was eying Henry. 'I wanna photo with him,' he said to his mate, a CSKA security man. 'No, no,' came the reply. 'That's Henry, he's not one of ours, he won't understand.'

Vagner Love, admittedly, has an extremely limited command of Russian, but the security man was referring to more than mere linguistic comprehension. What he was saying was that Love was used to life in Moscow, to being grabbed by inebriated strangers with gold teeth and dodgy moustaches; in other words, to the unpredictable nature of things in the Russian Federation. Thierry Henry, in his crisp, pristine Arsenal tracksuit, obviously wasn't. But the drunk wasn't having it. 'I want to have a photo with him.' His mate laid down the law. 'Yuri,' he said, holding up his hand, 'that's enough!' Henry walked by, still fuming, lips still pursed, and straight onto the Arsenal bus that would take him away from Moscow.

2007 was the year that the CSKA machine, for so long seen as infallible and all-powerful, faltered, Valeri Gazzayev's men finishing third in the league and failing to win a game in the Champions League. CSKA had six Brazilians in their team that season, and the Russian media was full of speculation that 'Brazilian power' had sown discontent in the ranks of the Army side. Indeed, just days before the club's final 2007/08 Champions League match against Fenerbahce in Turkey on 12 December, Vagner Love reportedly left the club's training base, allegedly vowing to quit the side. CSKA lost the subsequent match in Istanbul 3–1, ending Group G in last place with just a single point.

The club was also plagued by injuries, with both the side's number-one goalkeeper, Igor Akinfeev, and Daniel Carvalho sidelined for months right at the start of the campaign, only making a comeback when the title had already slipped away. 'Please God, let that be the worst season we ever have,' Gazzayev told the *Noviye Izvestiya* newspaper at the end of the year.

The side's 2007/08 European flop was even more disappointing in light of their previous Champions League adventure. Up until the fifth match in the 2006/07 tournament, a home game against Porto, CSKA had yet to concede a goal, and were in first place in Group G, the 1–0 home victory against the Gunners having put them in prime position for qualification.

However, the Moscow fixture against Porto would prove to be vital. Needing a win to make sure of progress to the play-off stages, a listless CSKA went down 2–0. Having just returned from claiming the domestic title in the port of Vladivostok, four thousand miles to the east, the Russian side's players looked shadows of themselves. To their credit, though, they refused to blame the sixteen-hour return flight that they had undertaken a couple of days before the game.

The last match saw Arsenal and Porto play each other, both needing a point to go through at CSKA's expense. The irony was obvious – having been accused of match-fixing all season, CSKA were in danger of becoming the victims of an 'arranged' result themselves. Arsenal and Porto duly played out a 0–0 draw, and CSKA were out.

'Your book,' said Evgeni Giner, seeing me out after the interview, 'should concentrate on the game itself, on the matches, not on the scandals. It's easy to write about that kind of stuff,' he added. 'Dostoevsky, Tolstoy, Dickens,' he went on, throwing in a token English writer, 'they didn't write about scandals, did they?'

I assured him that I would be writing about the actual football as well, but that my book was concerned with the entire spectrum of the Russian game, and that I was obliged to write about allegations of corruption. Football mirrors society, I told him, just as society mirrors football. He appeared less than impressed by my catchphrase, and we went our separate ways, Giner to a meeting with some suited officials, I to the nearest Metro station.

CHAPTER FOUR

The cursed team

'Sins cannot be undone, only forgiven.'

Igor Stravinsky

Despite its recent economic rebirth, Russia still possesses a great many reminders of the Soviet era. From the architectural motifs of its buildings to the country's national anthem, the USSR may be dead, but it is anything but forgotten.

While Spartak and CSKA are Russia's most successful post-perestroika sides, there are others, with equally distinguished histories, that have been unable to live up to their Soviet-era reputations. While many of these clubs' woes can be explained away by a simple lack of finances, leaving them powerless to compete with the buying power of the top sides, there are others whose problems have their roots in Russia's troubled – and often brutal – history. Teams haunted by the ghosts of the USSR, unable to shake off the legacy of more than seventy years of totalitarianism.

Although they have not won the league title since 1976, Dynamo Moscow are undoubtedly one of Russia's most famous teams. They have their roots in a factory club, founded in 1897 by an expatriate Englishman, Clement Charnock. A Blackburn Rovers supporter, Charnock's side likewise turned out in blue and white, colours Dynamo continue to wear to this day.

In 1903 that team became OKS Moskva, and in 1923, after the Bolshevik Revolution, the side was officially renamed Dynamo Moscow and was incorporated into the Dynamo Sports Society, set up by one of Russia's original Iron Fists, Felix Dzerzhinsky, the head of the notorious *Cheka*, forerunners to the KGB.

After World War II, just before the Cold War began in earnest, Dynamo were sent on a tour of Britain, playing four games, beating Cardiff and Arsenal and drawing with Chelsea and Rangers. The games attracted much attention both at home and in Britain, and were watched by a total of 270,000 fans. This tour was immortalised in the Soviet Union in a play, *19–9*, referring to the side's goals for and against, portraying the Dynamo players as paragons of socialist virtue in an evil capitalist land. There was talk of Britain sending a team on a reciprocal tour to the USSR, before the Cold War intervened, putting paid to the plans. George Orwell, for one, had been against the idea, writing in *Tribune* in 1945 that 'sport is an unfailing cause of ill-will, and that if such a visit as this were to have any effect at all on Anglo-Soviet relations, it could only be to make them slightly worse than before'.

In 1972, Dynamo almost became the first Russian team to lift a European trophy, losing 3–2 to Glasgow Rangers in the final of the European Cup Winners' Cup.

On 18 March 2006, in their very first game of the new season, Dynamo Moscow were forced to abandon plans to kick off their campaign at their home ground, Petrovsky Park. The seventysomething-year-old stadium was in urgent need of repairs, and so Dynamo were forced to play at the Luzhniki, a stadium where they had not won for a quarter of a century.

While the workmen hammered away at Petrovsky Park, Dynamo's 'home' match against Shinnik ended 1–1, the Moscow club squandering a host of chances.

The continuation of the side's 25-year run of bad luck at the Luzhniki is not the only misfortune to have befallen the team in recent years, however. In 2005, Dynamo Moscow underwent a dramatic overhaul, financed by their then-president Alexei Fedorichev and a sponsorship deal with Xerox, going on a spending spree which would see them part with more than $100 million; nine Portuguese players arrived at the club, most of them internationals, including recent Champions League winners Maniche and Costinha from Porto.

As Dima, a friend of mine and a lifelong Dynamo fan, said at the time, 'A hundred million dollars! He could have bought himself a fleet of tanks for that, and done something more constructive, like invade Georgia, for example.' He was obviously joking in his suggestion that Russia seize control of the tiny former-Soviet Caucasus republic, but still, the nagging doubt that Fedorichev could have put his money to better use persisted.

Dynamo was effectively transformed, in the space of six months, into a Moscow-based Portuguese side. A Brazilian manager, Ivo Wortman, was even brought in to aid communication problems, and the few remaining Russians in the side were ordered to learn Portuguese. Not long after, a rumour went around that Dmitri Bulikin, the club's unsettled centre forward, had been placed on the transfer list for refusing to do so. Seeing as how he was later brought back into the team, this was either a malicious lie or he had been doing some frantic cramming on the language of Pele and Ronaldinho.

Despite the absurdity of the situation, expectations were sky-high: there was talk that Fedorichev was forming a second Chelsea in the Russian capital, buying the best for any price, and success along with it. But things soon started to go wrong. Midway through the season, the increasingly unsettled Maniche gave an interview to a Portuguese newspaper in which he claimed that he didn't like 'the Russian Championship, the weather, or even the country itself'.

Once back in the Dynamo ranks, however, Maniche, falling back on the excuse popular all over the world, claimed that he had been 'mistranslated', and that he was simply 'missing his family'. Nevertheless, before the end of the season he was gone, first to Chelsea and then to Germany, to the 2006 World Cup, where he turned in the kind of performances that must have made the Dynamo directors wonder if they might not have been somehow tricked into buying a Maniche lookalike.

The remaining Portuguese contingent had similar problems adapting to Moscow, and the team, instead of battling for a Champions League place, finished mid-table, not even gaining a UEFA Cup slot.

Before the start of the 2006 season, with most of the Portuguese SuperLiga players having departed for warmer climes, Fedorichev decided to build a team that would have no problems with adaptation. He moved for experienced Russian internationals, bringing the then-national team captain Alexei Smertin back from England, and poaching the Russian national goalkeeper Sergei Ovchinnikov and former national manager Yuri Syomin from Lokomotiv Moscow, among other deals. Everything, it seemed, would be fine this time. These were Russians, not unpredictable foreigners, many of them having played together at international level.

But things did not gone to plan – Dynamo struggled from the start of the season, and with ten games to play, were just one place above the relegation zone. Smertin was sidelined with injury, Ovchinnikov had left the side and Yuri Syomin had resigned, stating ominously that 'an evil fate hangs over this club.' Anything that could go wrong had, and Dynamo were staring relegation in the face for the first time in their long and illustrious history.

But if Dynamo were indeed a side playing under a bad sign, then what was the root of their trouble, of their misfortune? After all, curses must come from somewhere, they do not just pop up out of thin air.

Early one autumn morning in 2006, I was sitting in the offices of *Sport-Express*, discussing Dynamo Moscow's recent run of misfortune. Vladimir Konstantinov, editor of the paper's football department, and a man with a breathtaking knowledge of and enthusiasm for the Russian game, looked thoughtful. 'I've heard the idea of a curse mentioned,' he said. 'I don't know, it seems to me as if there is something else involved. Some dark force, perhaps.' He shook his head, indicating that such things were best left unspoken.

Lavrenty Beria, Stalin's sadistic secret police chief, fellow Georgian, and the man who almost took over the USSR after the dictator's death, was a fanatical supporter of Dynamo. Originally from the Soviet republic of Georgia, he had been a fan of the local team, Dynamo Tbilisi, but upon arriving in the capital in 1938 he switched loyalties to their Muscovite namesakes. Once in Moscow, he routinely used his influence to fix matches in favour of Dynamo, sending footballers and referees who were impertinent enough to score goals or give decisions against them to the Gulag.

Beria was also known for cruising the streets of Moscow late at night, ordering his personal security guards to drag off girls he took a fancy to. Once home, he would order the girls to crawl around his flat in a circle while he decided which one to rape. He called this 'The Flower Game'.

There are also claims that Beria was responsible for Stalin's death, indirectly at least, by depriving him of the necessary medical treatment after the dictator had a stroke at his dacha in 1953. The theory is given some credence by the memoirs of the late Soviet Foreign Minister Molotov, published in the 1990s, who claimed that Beria had boasted about 'taking out' Stalin.

Following Stalin's death, Beria set himself the aim of becoming leader of the USSR. Unfortunately for the bespectacled rapist, however, although undoubtedly fortunate for the rest of the human race, the country's new leader, Nikita Khrushchev, had him executed some nine months after Stalin's passing, scuppering the sadistic Georgian's plans to take over the reins of the fledgling nuclear state.

A few years ago, the Tunisian embassy, housed in Beria's former Moscow residence, decided to carry out extensive renovations. The repairs took a lot longer than anyone had figured, mainly due to the fact that the workmen kept coming across skeletons. In the gardens, in the foundations of walls, everywhere they dug they found human remains.

Could it be that some of those unfortunates had had their fate decided in the VIP box at Petrovsky Park? Perhaps Beria had resolved to do away with them whilst watching Dynamo launch a counterattack, his beady eyes flickering briefly as the decision to end a life registered in the part of his brain set aside for such matters.

Were the gods paying Dynamo back for their sins of their one-time patron?

'We are cursed,' said Dmitri, a long-time Dynamo fan, as we sat drinking tea in his flat, 'and it is all down to Beria. You see, during World War Two, Beria sent Nikolai Starostin, the founder of Spartak Moscow, to the Gulag for ten years. He could only have done it at that time because there would have been an outcry otherwise. He accused Starostin of attempting to assassinate Stalin during an exhibition match on Red Square in which Spartak had taken part. It was ludicrous, of course, but a lot of people were sent to the Gulag on trumped-up charges at that time, as I'm sure you know. But just look, Spartak have had the most success of any Russian side ever, and fortune has turned away from Dynamo. It's a curse, payback for the crimes of the past. I'm utterly convinced of it,' he concluded.

Open any Russian tabloid and you'll find page after page of adverts for clairvoyants, magicians and other occult masters offering to help you find love, earn money and generally become a success in life. The collapse of the Soviet Union, and its strict control over information and religion, saw Russia submerged in a tidal wave of spiritualism and New Age philosophies. In the early 1990s, national TV was often turned over to purported psychics and telepaths, the entire nation Omming away in front of cheap TV sets, wishing for imported jeans and the repair of everyday household items.

Russians have always been superstitious. Like most Europeans they were once rural pagans but, unlike in Western Europe, Russia has only experienced large-scale urbanisation since the 1930s, and these rustic superstitions have simply been transferred from the village to the city, from the huts and swamps of pre-industrialisation to the tower blocks and shopping centres of modern Russia. There exists in Russia today a significant section of the population – 'village urbanites' – uneasy with life in a modern urban setting.

'Never shake hands over the threshold.'
'Never give an even number of flowers.'
'Don't show your baby to anyone for the first forty days of its life.'
'Unmarried people should never sit at the corner of a table if they don't want to remain single.'
'Never give knives as presents.'

The list goes on and on, the beliefs and superstitions worming their way into everyday life.

There was also, on a more mundane level, entirely unconnected with the occult or 'dark forces', the issue of Costinha, the Portuguese international, and his boots. 'Costinha, one fine day, said that he couldn't train, that he didn't have any clean boots,' recalled Vladimir Konstantinov, back at *Sport-Express*, after a brief break in which he had broken into Portuguese to answer a call from a newly arrived Brazilian player, to help him out with some of the problems that can arise in Moscow for a foreigner who speaks not a word of Russian. ' "No, no," they told him, "here in Russia players clean their own boots." Costinha refused, and there was a great scandal, which, eventually, led to him quitting the side.'

And thus Dynamo bid farewell to one more multi-million-pound signing from the Portuguese SuperLiga – one of the players that their bid for eminence, their rise to first the top of the Russian football hierarchy, and then the European, was supposed to have rested on. For the lack of clean boots, a kingdom was lost.

'Of course,' continued Vladimir, 'this wasn't the only problem Costinha had at Dynamo, but it was indicative of the entire situation.'

How, I wondered, could the problem have been solved?

'Well, when I was working as a press attaché at Krilya Sovetov in Samara, we also had a problem. Then it was with a Brazilian who refused to clean his boots, but we managed to solve this quite easily. Instead of letting the whole thing blow up, we found a local guy, a long-time supporter of the team, and paid him four hundred dollars a month to clean boots. Given that the average wage in Samara was around three hundred, he was more than happy.'

Why then couldn't Dynamo have done this?

Vladimir shrugged. 'That's just not the way they do things there,' he said.

The thought occurred to me that perhaps the root of all Dynamo's troubles might lie not in some cosmic payback being visited upon them for the sins of the past century, but a simple lack of man-management skills.

Or, as Vasili Utkin, the Russian TV commentator, put it to me, 'Dynamo is utterly disorganised. You know what, for example, they feed the footballers at the training camp? Buckwheat and porridge – the kind of stuff I was given as a child at Pioneer (the Soviet-era Scouts) summer camp. International footballers are fed crap I wouldn't give my dog.'

I had been trying to arrange an interview with the former Chelsea player Alexei Smertin for more than two months, but the club's press attaché had failed to nail down the midfielder, and he had become a shadowy figure in my imagination; distant, unreal, a symbol of the misfortune at the heart of Dynamo.

During those two months, every time I called the club, Andrei, the club's press attaché, seemed to have become more and more depressed. He would answer the phone, let out a sigh that got longer and more pronounced as the team sunk lower and lower down the table, and say 'Dynamo Football Club' with all the enthusiasm of one pronouncing the name of a clinic for the fatally ill. Andrei eventually set up a meeting with Smertin for 13 September 2006, and we arranged to meet in the car park at Dynamo's stadium on the day of the interview. From there we would drive to the training camp.

After some confusion, I found Andrei standing next to the monument dedicated to the legendary Soviet goalkeeper Lev Yashin, the only goalkeeper ever to have won the European Player of the Year Award (1963) and who spent his whole career, from 1949 to 1971, at Dynamo. Sculpted in mid-air pose, ball in his hands, Yashin – or 'The Black Spider', as he was referred to throughout Europe – eternally defends the bronze goalposts behind him.

Andrei was a small man with a drooping moustache; his lugubrious expression reminded me of nothing so much as a greatly disheartened Deputy Dawg. We strolled in near silence to the press office. There was an unbearable unhappiness about the club. Everywhere there were photos of Lev Yashin and other legendary Dynamo players. They looked on disapprovingly as we walked down the long corridor to the pressroom. A quote from Yashin hung on the wall. It read, 'The trainer said to me, "You are playing for the best team in Russia, give it all you've got" . . . Well, I tried my best.'

Actually, during my first year in Moscow I thought that I had stumbled upon another monument to the Black Spider. Outside Rizhskaya Metro station in the north of Moscow, not far from the main station for trains to Latvia, there is a statue of a man, arms aloft, reaching for what I had assumed to be a ball (albeit an odd ball, with weird spikes sticking out of it – and, admittedly, the man wasn't dressed in a goalie's strip). 'Ah, Lev Yashin,' I thought, nevertheless, pleased to see a familiar face, and went closer to try to make out the inscription, which read: 'In honour of the creators of the world's first satellite.'

Dynamo rent out their stadium to the currently homeless CSKA, and there were posters scattered around the ground grudgingly advertising their illustrious tenant's forthcoming fixtures. We sat and waited in the pressroom for the driver to arrive. The wait was, without doubt, one of the longest twenty minutes of my life. There were three people working in the office, all of them with drawn faces, all of them given to the same sighing as Andrei. I felt uncomfortable. It was like being at a stranger's funeral.

Alexei Smertin left Russia in 2000 for the French club Bordeaux. In 2003 Claudio Ranieri brought him to Chelsea, where he was immediately loaned out to Portsmouth in order to adapt to life in England away from the media circus at Stamford Bridge. He returned to Chelsea the next season, with the side now managed by Jose Mourinho, and although not a regular he picked up a Championship medal. The following season, with Chelsea's midfield packed with stars, Smertin was again loaned out, this time to Charlton, for the start of the 2005/06 campaign, and in January 2006 he returned to Russia, signing a four-year contract with Dynamo Moscow.

The first time I saw Alexei Smertin play was for Lokomotiv, in Moscow, back in the Yeltsin era. Smertin's name is derived for the Russian word 'smert', meaning 'death', and because of this he is for ever, in what may well be a unique association, linked in my mind with Steve Death, the former West Ham and Reading goalkeeper.

I arrived for my meeting with Smertin at Dynamo's out-of-town training camp in early September, 2006 a few days before Dynamo were due to play Amkar, fellow candidates for the drop.

We were sitting on a low wall outside the canteen that the side were, for some reason not fully clear to me, forced to share with young pre-teen gymnasts from the Russian Olympic training programme. I got the hard question out of the way first. The curse. Dark forces. Did Alexei believe in them?

The Dynamo captain sucked on his odd-looking lollipop and looked thoughtful. 'Sure, I've heard the talk,' he replied, 'but I don't know, I don't want to think about it. I just try to keep myself from considering such things.' He laughed nervously, obviously having no desire to dwell on such matters.

Then what was the explanation for the run of bad luck?

The club captain lowered his voice to a conspiratorial tone. 'Dynamo has problems on an organisational level,' he confided. 'Every level of the team is in chaos.'

Vladimir Konstantinov at *Sport-Express* had offered the same opinion, saying that Dynamo was controlled by various factions with no single aim, no common language. I myself had encountered this. Aside from Andrei, the Deputy Dawg lookalike, Dynamo had three other press attachés, yet were the least effective at handling the media of all the sides I contacted. They also had, bewilderingly, six goalkeepers in the squad, suggesting that the club's transfer policy had gone haywire somewhere.

Having got the matter of the curse out of the way, we turned to other things. How, I wanted to know, had football changed in Russia during the six years he had been away?

'There are more foreigners now. When I left, there weren't so many, and the ones there were, were of pretty dubious quality. Now the players signing contracts are of a noticeably higher class.'

And Russia itself? Had it changed?

'Of course. Oil has transformed Russia. For the better.'

Smertin is an articulate speaker, able to spin together words and sentences in a manner most unlike a professional footballer. He confesses that he wants to counter the image, popular all over the world, that most people have of footballers. Which is to say, not too bright. Occasionally this comes across as slightly forced but, nevertheless, it was a real pleasure to speak to a footballer about matters other than 'The Beautiful Game'. Apart from this, Smertin was also unusual in that he, unlike the majority of Russian players who have played for foreign teams, had enjoyed his time abroad. Of all the players I spoke to, only Andrei Kanchelskis could be said to have taken as much pleasure in the experience of playing, and living, outside of Russia.

'Most people,' Smertin admitted, 'think that footballers are thick. And rightly so. In England, I tried to learn the language, but it was extremely hard when you are surrounded by guys whose vocabulary is limited to "fuck", and who make mistakes with grammatical tenses,' he complained, breaking into English to voice the oath. 'I noticed that after spending a lot of time with them and their "what the fuck you doing geezer?" take on the language of Shakespeare and Dickens, I found it quite hard to communicate with English people in a non-football environment.'

'Russian footballers read a lot more than most English players,' he went on, 'and not just glossy magazines.'

Ask (as I did) almost any Russian footballer what his favourite book is, and he is extremely likely to answer *The Master and Margarita* by Mikhail Bulgakov, a novel that revolves around the devil's visit to 1930s Moscow. Banned by Stalin, it was finally published in limited form in Russia in the 1960s, and is now one of the country's best-loved books. It is a story full of shadows and dark humour, and perfectly suited the atmosphere around Dynamo that year. I often took it to read with me while waiting for interviews, or travelling on the Moscow Metro.

Smertin, I had heard, was a book fiend, and whilst playing for Portsmouth had met John Fowles, the author of *The Collector*, *The Magus* and other classics of English post-war literature, just before the writer's death.

'I was introduced by a friend of mine,' he said. 'It was incredible to meet such a man. He was in a pretty bad way, but it was fascinating to actually get acquainted with him. His wife, Sarah, still keeps in touch.'

What other writers did the midfielder admire?

'Nabokov, Balzac,' he replied, without hesitation. 'And P.G. Wodehouse.'

This last reference would have seemed a touch incongruous had I not been more than familiar with the fondness that Russians have for Jeeves and Wooster. It would not be too much of an exaggeration to say that this, along with Sherlock Holmes, is the defining image most Russians have of England.

Although Smertin had obviously spent long enough in the country to realise that it was hardly a land of cunning servants and dim-witted gents, there was a great amount of idealisation in his reminisces. After he had recounted a visit to the Sherlock Holmes museum, he began telling me that 'English football was the best' for him, that it was 'a country where fair play was the norm, where the referee was never noticed, and very rarely discussed'.

Smertin constantly interjected English phrases into his Russian, and while he seemed to have a good enough grip of the language, I couldn't help feel that he had somehow not fully grasped everything that had been going on around him during his stay in Britain. When he admitted that he read poorly in English, the picture suddenly became clear. The dynamic midfielder had lived in a semi-fictional England of his own imagining, a world of idyllic football, unblemished by media scandal, by accusation and counter-accusation. For him, the English were, and remained, 'good sorts', and their fans the best in the world. It was a picture that had been, in all probability, formed before he left Russia, and nothing was going to contradict it, not even the constant squabbling and outbursts by Mourinho, Ferguson, Wenger and co.

In Russia, the discrepancy between the money earned by top footballers and the rest of the working population is greater than perhaps anywhere in the world. The gulf is unbridgeable, the millions paid out by oil-wealthy clubs to their stars elevating the defenders, midfielders and strikers of the leading Russian sides to godlike status within the country.

The economic boom sweeping through Russia may be in the process of transforming the country, but it is also exaggerating social differences, splitting the population into 'the wealthy' and 'the poor', with the spaces in between looking increasingly sparse.

The monthly wage for a star player in the Russian Premier League is around £70,000, meaning that a top professional footballer earns around 250 times more than the average Russian provincial factory worker.

Granted, the very top stars in the English Premier League earn far more than their Russian counterparts, yet while the salaries enjoyed by John Terry and co are unquestionably obscene, they are not, I would suggest, contributing to a rapidly widening, and potentially catastrophic, division at the heart of British society.

Many of the Russian Premier League's top players live in or around Rublevskoe Shosse, an out-of-town elite district also home to the late Boris Yeltsin's dacha. The area is a bustle of Mercedes and BMWs, of politicians and other celebrities speeding through the narrow streets, sirens flashing. In a city where psychoanalysis and private lawns are largely unknown, Rublevskoe Shosse is flanked by gigantic billboards for personal analysts and mole exterminators.

Although the question was provocative, and slightly obvious, I put it to Smertin, by far the most eloquent of the players I had met, that there was something wrong with this. It wasn't so much that I was looking for him to turn his salary over to charity, or to suddenly declare that the system was corrupt and to lead a players' revolt with the aim of reducing wage levels, more that I was simply curious as to how he would answer.

'My mother gets that all the time,' he began. 'Her friends say, "Your son gets all that cash for running around in the fresh air twice a week, and my son gets a pittance for working in the factory".' He shrugged. 'What can she say? What can I say? My opinion is a subjective one. Of course, I'd like people to earn more. I absolutely understand the negative feelings that people have towards footballers, and I relate to them with sympathy. But there's nothing I can do about it. I'm not going to have a go at the system. It wouldn't be, you understand, in my interests.'

I asked Smertin about his time at Chelsea and his days at the club owned by the Russian billionaire oligarch, Roman Abramovich.

'Roman Abramovich often attended training sessions. He came into the dressing room after every game. He was really involved in the whole set-up. I can't say that he is an expert on the game, but he's learning, and doesn't hesitate to ask if there are certain nuances he doesn't get. He mixes with the team, comes to the canteen, and really worries if things aren't going right.

'Why didn't you come to our training session?' Smertin enquired, keeping loosely on topic. I replied that I hadn't been allowed in, that the trainer had forbidden my presence. Smertin simply shook his head in bewilderment. He was, it appeared, long used to the incomprehensibility of life at Dynamo.

We were some way from Moscow, and I was thinking about the long bus ride home. (My delivery to the training ground hadn't included a return trip.) Smertin seemed to read my mind, and offered me a lift, which I accepted. We got into his sparkling new Mercedes. 'Do you like Led Zeppelin?' he asked, beginning a long conversation about rock music, English and Russian.

'I grew up on English rock,' said Smertin, before turning on the car sound system. 'I really envy musicians, they have a chance to express themselves. I mean, yeah, I can do that on the field, but no one except the most devoted supporters of the game is likely to notice.' As a defensive midfield player whose goals were as rare as an honest Russian traffic cop, I could see his point.

It was autumn, and all around us shadows had begun to fall, the sun receding further and further with each passing day, the city preparing for another winter. The last had been one of the harshest on record, temperatures dropping to minus-35 degrees. All around us, Stalinist buildings flashed by, interspersed by new boutiques and building sites. I still couldn't shake the idea of a curse on Dynamo. As Smertin changed CDs, putting on an album by Kino, the Russian new-wave group of the late 1980s, I recalled the etymological roots of the ex-Chelsea midfielder's surname. My mood was getting darker. We pulled up outside my Metro station, and I got out of the Mercedes.

'Good luck,' I said, by way of parting. Riding down the escalator, I had the very distinct impression that both Smertin and Dynamo were going to need it.

The following Sunday saw the home match against Amkar, from the ridiculously named Siberian town of Perm. With both teams perilously close to the relegation zone, it was, as the expression has it, a 'six-pointer'. In order to attract the maximum amount of fans to the ground, Dynamo had drastically lowered ticket prices, conspired to get the game pulled from the list of matches to be shown live on national TV, and put out a series of adverts in the sports press featuring Dynamo stars, both past and present, extolling all 'true Dynamo fans' to come and support the side.

Repairs had long been completed at Petrovsky Park, and so Dynamo would at least be spared the misfortune of playing such a vital game at the 'unlucky' Luzhniki.

The world's only constructivist-designed stadium, Petrovsky Park was built in 1928 and is currently the second-largest stadium in Moscow, with a capacity of almost 40,000. In 1941 it was used as a training centre for Russian troops preparing to defend Moscow from Nazi attack. Despite its historical importance, the overwhelming impression that the casual visitor to the Dynamo stadium is likely to take away is one of concrete, concrete and more concrete. Although the ground has a certain atmosphere about it, whatever constructivist intentions the architects may have had have been lost over the years, and the stadium is by far the most uncomfortable in the Russian capital.

The Soviet poet Lev Oshanin wrote an untitled poem about the stadium that was later used as a basis for the popular 1960s 'Football Song' and included the lines, 'The whole of Moscow rides stubbornly to Dynamo, forgetting about the rain.' It is quoted whenever there is a sell-out at Petrovsky Park, which, these days at least, isn't often.

The advertising and price slash for the Amtar match worked to an extent, and there were about 10,000 fans in attendance, a good 5,000 up on an average Dynamo gate. The game began at an infuriated tempo, both sides hoping for an early goal. A tiny contingent of Amkar fans had made the long journey from Siberia, and although my sympathies were lying more Dynamo's way, I couldn't help feeling admiration for these hardcore supporters.

The first half came and went. No goals. Midway through the second half, Derlei, one of the few Portuguese players to have remained at the club, lashed out an Amkar player and was sent off. The team's top scorer, he was hardly a player they could afford to lose.

As the club's results worsened that season, Dynamo became

possessed by a great fury. Halfway through the season, Sergei Ovchinnikov, the side's experienced goalkeeper, was shown red for attacking a referee, and would not play for the club again. In the match before the Amkar fixture another Portuguese player, Danni, had also been dismissed, for spitting at the man in black. And now Derlei. I was glad I had already spoken to Smertin, and that I wouldn't have to call Andrei the following day. I could only imagine the depths of despair to which Dynamo's press attaché would fall, and his melancholy would be contagious. The final whistle blew. o–o. Dynamo were now one place and two points clear of the relegation zone.

The Dynamo fans, like the players, had also begun to express their dissatisfaction, to demonstrate the depths of their wrath. At a recent game they had turned their backs to the pitch in protest, and a banner, directed at the players, had been held up. 'We will come to 1st Division games,' it had read, 'but will you?'

The question was a good one. How many of the internationals in Dynamo's team would be willing to play in the marathon that is the Russian First Division, flying across the country to away games, two matches a week, getting lumps kicked out of them by cynical, ageing defenders?

Relationships between the team and its supporters were rapidly worsening. At one home match Dynamo fans had unfurled yet another banner, featuring the image of the club's notorious patron, Lavrenty Beria. 'He sees everything', said the banner, the sadistic killer's eyes seemingly possessed of a life of their own, gazing into the soul of Dynamo.

'The "support" we got was incredible,' midfielder Igor Semshov recalled at the end of the season. 'I went over to the touchline during one match, and the fans were yelling stuff like, "Come on, you bastards, you cretins".' Indeed, one Dynamo player, Alexander Shirko, was unable to turn a deaf ear, launching himself, Eric Cantona-style, into the terraces after one game, coming to blows with an abusive fan.

Alexei Smertin, having recovered from an injury that had kept him sidelined of late, had played in the match, performing his usual low-profile holding role, but according to the club's website he had only been selected at the last moment. There were disagreements regarding his contract, and he had been on the point of quitting the side. However, at the last moment, a compromise had been reached. The exact details of the contract disagreement later became clear; Smertin had not been paid for five months. Suddenly, all the negative comments about Dynamo he had made during our interview made sense.

There was a time in Russia when the whole country went without wages for months on end, surviving on a kind of barter system, or being paid with the very products they were producing: wallpaper, condoms, gravestones, anything. Happily, that period is largely now over, except, oddly enough, for the country's footballers. This was not the first case of a Dynamo player complaining about the non-payment of wages. For a club able to splash out massive amounts of money on new signings, this seemed a little strange. Even odder is the fact that Russian footballers are one of the only groups of professional players in the world without an active and organised trade union to represent their interests.

'It really is bizarre,' said Vladimir Konstantinov, referring to Dynamo's salary problems. 'Dynamo buy new players, go abroad to luxury training camps, and so on, yet they can't pay their players on time. It's just another indication of the chaos reigning at Petrovsky Park.'

Dynamo had, not long before this conversation, claimed that they were in the race to sign the apparently unsettled Cristiano Ronaldo from Manchester United, but it is hard to see, even if they had managed to sign the Portuguese wunderkind, exactly how they would have been able to explain such matters as the non-payment of salaries to Wayne Rooney's 'friend'.

Dynamo's head, it seemed, just didn't know what its body was doing. A spastic hydra, flailing blindly on the fringes of the relegation zone.

Dynamo's inability to carry out the most elementary of functions reminded me of nothing so much as a short story by the Russian absurdist writer, Daniil Kharms, persecuted by Stalin in the 1930s for his downright oddness. In the untitled tale, the main character forgets how to count, namely, is unable to recall what comes first in the sequence of numbers – six or seven?

Dynamo were the same – unfocused, chaotic, incapable of making the simplest connections.

When Alexei Fedorichev, Dynamo's owner, gave up his controlling stake in the club during the autumn of 2006, Dynamo's results, miraculously, began to improve. By the end of the season, following a couple of hard-fought victories, the club were safe, and their status as the only side never to have been relegated was intact.

And then the rumours began. The story went like this. Frightened by Fedorichev's riches, by the businessman's intention to build a Russian 'Super Side', the other owners of the Premier League sides had made a pact to ensure that Dynamo went down. When Fedorichev left the club, however, the alleged pact was broken, and Dynamo were allowed to climb up the table.

In the conspiracy-ridden world of Russian football, it is sometimes difficult to separate fantasy from fact, myth from reality, and the anti-Dynamo pact story was just one more example of this. As a member of the Dynamo fan club put it, 'We've bought so many great players, even if there was a conspiracy against us, it doesn't stand to reason that we should have fallen so low.'

Conspiracy, curse, or just plain bad form, it was clear that, despite the late rescue act, there was something deeply wrong at the core of Dynamo. The failure of the Moscow side to achieve success, despite the millions invested in it, was indicative of the problems central to the ills of many a Russian club.

In Russia, the oligarchs want success now, and they are not prepared to wait. Fedorichev's buying up of what seemed like half of the Porto team, while extreme, was just one example of this. The money that companies such as Sibneft, LUKoil and Gazprom have invested into football has gone to pay wages and the transfer fees of foreigners, rather than promote the game as a spectator sport at grassroots level.

As Igor Rabiner at *Sport-Express* told me in late 2007, 'The main problem in Russian football is that the teams are not self-sufficient, they mainly just exist as the playthings of wealthy individuals. They pay little or no attention to the kids in their youth teams, to the fans, to the people essential for the future of the game.'

Money, as the saying has it, can buy you neither happiness nor love, and, cursed or not, Dynamo had found out the hard way that it is likewise unable to ensure success on the football field. This is undoubtedly one of football's eternal attractions. Although it is, admittedly, becoming a rarer and rarer phenomenon, a side with a tiny budget can sometimes perform better than a team packed full of multi-million-pound signings, turning tables, and providing the world of football with one of its cherished upsets. It is a simple and refreshing fact that the teams with the biggest budgets do not always win. For proof of that, just ask Real Madrid. Or indeed, Alexei Fedorichev and Dynamo Moscow.

Alexei Smertin left Dynamo for Fulham in February 2007, returning to the country whose football he admired so much after just a one-year break. His first three games for the side saw the Cottagers beaten as many times, including a 4–0 home defeat to Tottenham Hotspur in the FA Cup.

Dynamo, meanwhile, suffered a player shortage as the team's stars quit the side in quick succession: at one point the Muscovites had a mere sixteen players on their books – not even enough for full-scale training matches. In early 2007 they played out an ominous 1–1 draw with Ireland's Derry City in a pre-season friendly. The club's long-suffering fans steeled themselves for another season of discontent as the half-century curse continued to wreak havoc at Petrovsky Park and beyond.

Amazingly, however, with the odds stacked against them, Dynamo had their best season in years, even looking like title contenders at one point. They slipped away in the second half of the campaign to eventually finish in sixth place, but even that was better than anything any of the various million-dollar line-ups had ever managed at Petrovsky Park.

I didn't speak to Andrei, the terminally depressed press attaché at Petrovsky Park, again, but I hoped that the side's rebirth had gone some way to improving his mood. I was pleased too for Dynamo: despite its less than pure past, the club is a Moscow institution, and their small base of fans among the most loyal in Russia.

But what of the curse, of the eternal misfortune that Dynamo were supposedly afflicted with?

'These things come and go,' said Dmitri, the fan who had explained his theory of the curse to me. 'Curses can miss a generation, a season. It's far too early to relax.'

CHAPTER FIVE

Foreign affairs

'In Russia you can only believe.'
Fyodor Tyutchev, nineteenth-century Russian poet

In December 2007, President Putin was announced *Time* magazine's Person of the Year. The world's media took the opportunity to declare that Russia's long climb from the abyss it had fallen into after the disintegration of the Soviet Union was now at an end. President Putin had provided Russia with the Iron Fist it needed, and the country had responded. Freedom, the newspapers and TV stations said, had been swapped for security, democracy exchanged for a growing prosperity.

At the time I had been living in the country for over a decade. Moscow, in particular, bore only a passing resemblance to the Russia I had arrived in. The streets were full of flashy cars and teenagers grooving to their MP3 players, and the rouble was stronger than it had ever been.

There was, however, a growing sense of isolationism. With oil prices at an all-time high, and the country having paid off its billion-dollar foreign debts, Russia no longer had to kowtow to the

West, and the West, for its part, saw no real sense in engaging with Russia.

Tourism remained critically underdeveloped and foreign investment, despite the country's vast potential, was low, some two and a half times less than in neighbouring China, investors scared off by corruption and murky business practices.

Coupled with this, there was also an undeniable sense of moral superiority, something that is never far from the surface of the Russian psyche. It was the nineteenth-century poet Fyodor Tyutchev who wrote the following lines, lines which are still, smugly in many cases, quoted by Russians today to confused foreigners.

Russia can't be understood with the mind,
And can't be measured with a common yardstick:
It has a peculiar character –
In Russia you can only believe.

While Russians were travelling abroad in greater and greater numbers, their desire to live beyond its borders was rapidly receding. Many Russians, having emigrated from the USSR, were returning, setting up businesses, and busy becoming born-again patriots.

If the national side had qualified for the 2006 World Cup, Russia would have been the only team apart from Saudi Arabia unable to boast a single squad member playing outside of their home country.

Two years on, as Russia prepared for Euro 2008, the situation had hardly improved much, the midfielder Ivan Saenko at German club Nürnberg the team's only foreign-based player.

The majority of the footballers I spoke to, both those who had played abroad and those who had never left, claimed that they couldn't face life outside of Mother Russia, that foreign life was a mystery to them, and that Russians had a unique mindset, incomprehensible to outsiders.

'It's really hard for foreigners to understand the Russian

mentality, and for us to relate to them,' said Spartak's Egor Titov, explaining the unease he claimed he felt at being away from Russia for more than a week at a time.

After Russia had failed to qualify for the 2006 World Cup, orders came from high-up to rectify the situation, to provide the Russian Federation with a team it could be proud of, a side to match the nation's resurgent ambition. Accordingly, the Russian Football Federation set out to find a new manager. The country had money to spare and, for the first time, there was talk of appointing a foreigner. There were, in reality, no realistic options left within Russia itself.

'We've tried all the Russians, and not much has come out of it,' shrugged Dmitri Sychev, Lokomotiv Moscow's young striker, when I asked him about his feelings on the appointment of a foreign coach.

It was into this atmosphere of political intrigue and increasing isolation that Dutchman Guus Hiddink arrived. Initially a candidate to succeed Sven-Goran Eriksson in the England post, Hiddink had signed a contract with the Russian Football Federation before the 2006 World Cup, where his Australian team's gutsy performance was seen as something that Russian players would do well to aspire to.

Hiddink is one of the most respected managers in the world today, and hails from a long tradition of successful Dutch coaches, such as Johan Cruyff, Rinus Michels (one of the inventors of 'Total Football') and Frank Rijkaard. Apart from being the one-time manager of Real Madrid, and taking the Netherlands to the semi-finals at the 1998 World Cup, Hiddink is perhaps best known for South Korea's fourth-place showing at the 2002 tournament, and leading Australia to the second round in 2006, their first appearance in the competition for 32 years.

Everywhere he had managed, Hiddink had charmed the locals – in South Korea he had become the first foreigner to receive the country's highest civil award, and was also made an honorary citizen. In Australia, while the government had neglected to officially recognise his services to the nation's football, he had nevertheless made a great impression, winning the affection of the entire country.

Although Russia had clearly landed an experienced and capable manager, the Dutch expert's appointment was not greeted with universal approval. Valeri Gazzayev said that he was 'categorically against the appointment of a foreigner'. Nevertheless, once Hiddink had arrived, he made it clear that he had nothing against the man himself, and even went out of his way to stress that he would do anything he could to help the new national team coach. 'I'm against the appointment, as such. I simply think we should give the job to a Russian. Being a top-quality trainer isn't enough. The manager of the Russian team should also understand our culture, traditions, and so on. But I recognise that Hiddink is a well-qualified coach, and I respect him as a man,' expounded Gazzayev in an interview with *Sovetski-Sport*.

Andrei Kanchelskis, the former Manchester United winger, was sceptical about Hiddink's chances of lifting the Russian national side when I spoke to him a few weeks after the appointment. 'I think it will be tough for him. Russian footballers,' he said, 'are quite difficult to work with. If the best of our trainers, Syomin, Romantsev, etc., couldn't do anything, then I really think he will have his work cut out.'

The vast majority of the Russian football world echoed Kanchelskis' feelings that the job should have gone to a native, the general sentiment being that any success the team might achieve under Hiddink's guidance would somehow be tainted, not entirely 'Russian'.

Alexei Smertin was an enthusiastic exception, however, suggesting that 'Hiddink will bring a winning mentality to our team'. While the former Chelsea midfielder may have welcomed Hiddink, feelings were not exactly reciprocal, the new manager first stripping him of the captaincy, and then dropping him entirely from the squad. Hiddink had promised some shake-ups, and this was just one of them.

Russia and the Russians have always had an ambiguous attitude to foreigners, ranging from deep distrust to undisguised admiration. During the Soviet Union's darkest days of repression, contact with a foreigner was a sure-fire way of falling under the suspicion of the KGB or its forerunners, perhaps of even earning an all-expenses-paid trip to the Gulag.

This loathing of foreigners in certain sections of society is typified by the rabid nationalist groups who gather near Red Square every weekend. Alongside their racial supremacy theories and attempts to persuade the Russian Orthodox church to canonise Stalin, it is a commonly held belief among these rag-tag organisations that all of Russia's ills have been visited upon it by outsiders; that, for example, the alarming demographic crisis in Russia is a result of some grand conspiracy by the West, rather than a consequence of a catastrophic collapse of the national health service combined with an ageing population.

At the other extreme, Russia has never had qualms about learning from the rest of the world, Europe especially. Peter the Great is the most obvious example of a Europhile in Russian history: the first tsar to leave the country in peacetime, travelling incognito throughout Europe, collecting ideas and impressions from his journeys in an attempt to drag Russia out from its self-imposed isolation.

Russia had had no contact with the West for over a century before Peter the Great crossed its borders. Upon the young tsar's return, he quickly made his new-found intolerance for the 'old Russia' known, the most obvious examples of his desire for change being an ultimately unsuccessful battle against deep-seated corruption and a ban on long, Russian-style beards. His attempted reforms led some members of the clergy to brand him the Antichrist.

In the early to mid-1990s, being a foreigner in Russia was a great deal different. Back then, foreigners were the unknown. Only a few years had passed since the break-up of the USSR, the world's largest closed state, and foreigners were seen as something special, something fascinating, people useful and prestigious to know. It was easy to get into exclusive clubs just by mumbling a few words of English or heavily accented Russian. As a Russian friend of mine once told me, 'Back in the early days of post-perestroika, foreigners were gods. They were from the West, and the West was a place where everyone wanted to go, but few had been.'

However, as Russia's economy took off under Putin, foreigners became commonplace, in the big cities at least. Hiddink's appointment reflected these altering attitudes to foreigners in Russia. A decade before his arrival, the idea of inviting a Westerner, especially one from liberal Holland, the home of hashish cafés and legal prostitution, to become the manager of the national side would have been unthinkable. By 2006 though, inviting top foreign specialists to work in Moscow had become fashionable and, more importantly, realistic. Foreigners, despite the inevitable culture clashes, were no longer so exotic. In fact, given the salaries on offer, Russia is now in a position to dictate terms to the said specialists, something that Hiddink, in attempting to lift the Russian national side from the doldrums, would quickly find out.

Upon their arrival in Russia, both Hiddink and his wife raved about Russian culture, about wanting to explore the country for themselves. The new national team manager promised to learn Russian, saying that he was already having lessons, but that he would be working with an interpreter until he had reached a satisfactory level.

'We have a hard job ahead of us, but Russia has potential,' said Hiddink at an impromptu meeting with the press on Red Square, stopping to gaze at the sixteenth-century St Basil's Cathedral (a building so beautiful that Ivan the Terrible reportedly had the architect responsible blinded to ensure he would never construct anything to rival it).

'The Dutch weren't at all surprised when Hiddink accepted the Russian job, because he always likes to take chances, to work with sides that can only get better,' a Dutch journalist from that country's *ELF Football* magazine told me, as we sat in the terraces at Petrovsky Park watching one of Hiddink's rare open-to-the-press training sessions.

If Hiddink was to perform his trademark magic on the Russian national side, it was clear that he would have to show something special, to demonstrate the ability to motivate teams that had served him so well in Australia and South Korea. The week he took charge, Russia were languishing in 34th place in the FIFA ratings.

'Hiddink's ability lies in making players believe in themselves. In giving them confidence,' football commentator Vasili Utkin told me a few weeks after Hiddink had begun work. 'Under Hiddink,' he continued, 'Russia will top their qualifying group for the 2008 European Championships.' Seeing that they had been drawn with England and Croatia, I looked doubtful. 'You'll see,' he said, smiling. We agreed to differ.

'I was in Seville last year for a match between Chelsea and Real Betis, and I ran into Roman [Abramovich] there. We discussed the appointment of Hiddink, and Roman seemed convinced that if anyone could do it, then Hiddink was the man to help the Russian team,' Utkin concluded, unashamedly name-dropping.

If, as Hiddink himself admitted, there was still much he had to learn about Russia, then there was a lot the Russians had left to find out about their new manager.

On his first day at work in July 2006, Hiddink arrived at the plush offices of the Russian Football Federation in red trousers and open-toed sandals. Russians are sticklers for dress codes, and the country's papers were soon full of discussions as to whether or not this was the correct way to present oneself at one's new place of employment. They had, it seems, expected Hiddink to arrive, all sombre and professional, in a suit and tie.

Evgeni Aldonin, midfielder with CSKA Moscow and the man that Hiddink would initially make his captain, had this to say on the matter of 'the red trousers', as it became known in the Russian media: 'For Europeans, clothes are not so important. They just wear what happens to be comfortable for them.'

Although hardly of earth-shattering importance in itself, the incident was the first sign of the culture clash that many had feared would disrupt Hiddink's attempt to build a Russian team capable of qualifying for the 2008 European Championships. Russia remains a very formal country, the nation's mores and customs shaped by more than seventy years of communism.

In the West, for example, it is fairly common for the leaders of nations to be called by the diminutive versions of their full names – Tony not Anthony, Bill in place of William, and so on. In Russia, this would be unthinkable – Vladimir Putin is always Vladimir Putin, and when he is not he is addressed by his first name and patronymic (derived from his father's name) – Vladimir Vladimirovich. He is never officially referred to as simply Volodya or Vova, just two of the shorter versions of his first name.

Possessing almost no Russian, Hiddink immediately, although perhaps unwittingly, set about mutating officials' first names to suit himself, disregarding the stifling system of patronymics. After the initial shock, Hiddink's disregard for traditional Russian forms of address did much to break down barriers and open doors for the Dutchman, not to mention introduce an element of humour into the Russian national football set-up.

Within the team, the players, used to addressing the managers as, for instance, Oleg Ivanovich (Romantsev) or Valeri Georgievich (Gazzayev) simply addressed Hiddink as 'Guus'. The lack of over-formality went hand-in hand with the new coach's relaxed approach.

'Russian trainers think it's necessary to shout at us, to harangue us when something doesn't go right, but personally I much prefer the Dutch approach,' said Andrey Arshavin, Russia's 2006 Player of the Year, suggesting that perhaps the traditional Iron Fist techniques may be losing something of their appeal in twenty-first-century Russia.

During an open training session I attended at the national team's base, Bor, just outside Moscow, in the autumn of 2006, Hiddink kicked a ball back to a group of players and dozens of photographers clicked away, capturing the moment for posterity. The new Russian manager stopped and, through a translator, said, 'See, what you are doing is wrong. I'm not the important one. It's these guys who are going to have to go out and battle for Russia.'

His words had little effect. The Russian media remained obsessed with his every move and opinion. *Sovetski-Sport* wangled out the information that the Dutch trainer had already picked up some swearwords, although Hiddink refused to reveal which. Another journalist, having been informed that Hiddink had been reading up on Russian history, gave the new national coach an impromptu test, quizzing him on such significant dates as the founding of Moscow. The Dutchman came through with flying colours.

The Russians were particularly pleased that he had taken the time to learn some oaths. Russians, as they are prone to do about almost anything – women, tanks, home cooking, etc. – vehemently claim that their swearing is superior to any in the world. I'm not sure how they have managed to judge this, there being, as far as I am aware, no serious academic works on topic, yet I have a sneaking suspicion that they are right. Russian swearing is so flexible and precise and, in Russia (where it is still strictly forbidden on TV and radio), shocking, that it leaves me a touch ashamed for the comparative uninventiveness of my native language's artillery of profanities.

Later, at one of his first press conferences, days before his debut match, Hiddink handed over to Russian Football Federation president Vitali Mutko with the words, '*Spasibo, Mister Prezident,*' uttering his first Russian in public, and earning praise from the journalists present for his pronunciation.

Hiddink's first game, a 1–0 victory in a friendly against Latvia on 16 August 2006, came and went. The Russian media refrained from drawing conclusions. Hiddink, however, had this to say on the quality of the players he had to work with, the footballers entrusted with the task of restoring Russia's footballing pride. 'They are good, technical players,' he began, 'but I'd like to see a bit more speed, a bit more decisiveness.'

The first real examination of Hiddink's new Russia came in September 2006, when Croatia came to Moscow for a European Championship qualifying match. Tickets sold at a frenzied rate, outstripping demand for even the upcoming Madonna concert, the pop diva's first visit to the Russian capital coinciding with the fixture.

The heavens chose that week to open up, and the pitch at the normally immaculate Cherkizovo stadium was heavily waterlogged, meaning that neither Russia nor Croatia would be able to play their normal short-passing game.

In the first 45 minutes the Croatians had the better chances but, displaying the lack of ruthlessness that had led to their elimination by Hiddink's Australia during the 2006 World Cup group stages, they failed to take any of them. In the second half, the Russians went close twice, but the waterlogged pitch made it hard for either team to find their rhythm. With fifteen minutes to go, and the score still 0–0, it would not have been unreasonable to expect Hiddink to throw on a couple of extra forwards, but the Dutchman chose to be more cautious. Perhaps he figured that the qualification tournament was long, and that it would be better to earn a point rather than suffer the ignominy of a home defeat in his first official match. The game ended goalless.

Opinions were mixed. Oleg Romantsev said that Russia had played 'primitively'. Others were kinder. Both sides blamed the condition of the pitch for the poor quality of the game. Still, maybe it was best that Hiddink, and Russia, hadn't begun with an overwhelming victory. Since I had arrived in Russia, I had noticed a tendency for Russian managers to do well in their first games, to be hailed as the saviours of the national side, and then being fired or resigning when a few results went wrong. With the 0–0 draw at least there would be no hyperbole, no false expectations that would subsequently prove impossible to live up to.

Despite the disappointing draw with Croatia, Hiddink had already managed to win over the majority of Russians. It was clear to all that he was a man of intelligence and good humour. 'The training sessions are great fun,' said Akinfeev, the CSKA goalkeeper. 'It makes a change to train in such a relaxed atmosphere.'

Indeed, during the training sessions I attended, Hiddink, wisecracking away, had the team doubled up with laughter. More importantly, the Dutchman showed that he was aware of where he was, fully conscious that being the first foreign coach to manage Russia was a remarkable historical privilege, and that he wasn't going to push too quickly, that he was willing to respect the 'Russian way'.

'Every country has its philosophy, its tactics, its style, its culture. I don't think you should go against the culture of a nation. Italians, for instance, like to sit back. England are different, Holland are different. Russian players like to go forward, they like to look to attack. It's a more dominating and more attractive way of playing, with some risks. The Russian nature is to go forward,' he commented at a press conference.

In an attempt to mould the side into a unified group, Hiddink had adopted the practice of allowing players to talk about club football only on the first day of international duty, thereafter forbidding further discussion on the theme. In this way, he explained, he hoped to separate club politics from international football, bolstering the players' sense of togetherness, increasing their willingness to fight for one another.

In interviews and at press conferences, Hiddink was deliberately guarded, usually making only positive statements. On the themes of fixed matches he was diplomacy itself, saying only that 'if there is a problem, then it needs to be sorted out'. But perhaps this was understandable: he was in a strange (and extremely volatile) country after all, and getting involved in local squabbles was clearly not something specified in his lucrative contract.

'We like to concentrate on the positive side of things,' Joop Alberda, the technical manager of the Russian side, told me when I called him after a Spartak Moscow Champions League game in November 2006.

Alberda, a member of the Dutch Olympic Committee, had been the trainer of the Dutch volleyball side at the 1996 Olympic Games in Atlanta, taking the team to Gold. 'When Guus called me and asked me if I would like to come to Russia and assist with the day-to-day running of things, I thought for about half a second before agreeing,' said Alberda. 'It's a fascinating country, and equally as interesting is the opportunity to observe the changes which are going on here, and have been since 1991. It makes life hard sometimes, of course, but that's probably a small part of the appeal. It's a challenge.'

Having had plenty of experience of Eastern Europe during his volleyball days, Alberda was no stranger to the bureaucratic nature of Russian officials, and indeed to Russia itself. 'They have a different way of doing things,' he commented, 'a lot more formal approach to sport. But, you know, in terms of the organisation of sport, of its systematic planning, the West has learned everything it knows from Russia.'

Russia's next qualifying match was a home game against Israel, in early October 2006. Although Israeli football was not as weak as it had previously been, the side just having missed out on a play-off place for the 2006 World Cup, Russia were still expected to win.

The match was scheduled to take place at Dynamo Moscow's home ground – Petrovsky Park. The stadium's ticket offices are embedded in a wall near the Metro, and those fans hoping to purchase a ticket for the game were forced to squat down in order to be able to see the ticket seller, who, bizarrely, was situated below street level. Once sighted, requests for tickets had to be conveyed through the tiny window. It was a ludicrous scene. As ever, there was no explanation as to exactly why fans were being forced to engage in yoga-like exercises to procure a ticket. Someone had simply had the idea that it would be a good idea to lower the ticket-sellers' booths, and no one, as usual, had thought about the fans. In Russia, whenever the public comes into contact with officials, even of the minor variety, a certain self-abasement is necessary in order to facilitate the process of receiving whatever it is – a document, an explanation, a ticket – that you require, and the ticket sales for the game against Israel were no exception.

However, compared with the Under-21 game between Russia and Portugal that took place the day before the Israel match, the Dynamo debacle was a paradigm of efficiency.

As is common all over the world for Under-21 games, attendance was expected to be low. In order to ensure a full house, it was announced that entrance to the game would be free, and many tickets were handed out at local schools. The game took place at the Eduard Streltsov stadium, which has a capacity of nearly 14,000. By the time I arrived, there was a huge queue outside the entrance. The ticket booths, a fan informed me, had run out of tickets. Although the match was free, in keeping with the Russians' reverence for documents, tickets were still required to gain entry. Luckily for me, a policeman sold me one for fifty roubles (about a pound). Guus Hiddink attended the Under-21 game, and Russia ran out 4–1 winners, the long-suffering fans outside finally being admitted in time for the home side's second goal.

Hiddink's press conferences were studies in tedium. Not yet having mastered Russian, and with not many Russians fluent in English, questions were posed in the language of Tolstoy and translated into English for the Dutchman, who then replied, the answer then translated back into Russian for the journalists present. For the bilingual, it was torture. In situations such as this, Russians tend to express themselves very formally, and so instead of, say, a quick, 'What's the pitch like?' we got a lengthy, 'Tell me please, Mr Hiddink, what condition is the training pitch in today?' Multiplied by twenty.

Against Israel, Russia started well, scoring after only five minutes. But then, as so often happens, they lost momentum and wasted chance after chance until finally, inevitably, Israel broke away and equalised. The game ended 1–1. Russia had now played two official matches under Guus Hiddink, both at home, and had yet to win a game. I was sitting in the press box, and the Russian journalists around me shook their heads. 'Same old same,' muttered one. *'Pizdets!'* said another, conveying his displeasure with one of the country's fine and numerous oaths, in this case a uniquely Russian hybrid of 'cunt' and – in as far as usage goes – 'fuck'. I wondered if *'pizdets'* was one of those swearwords that Hiddink had boasted about picking up.

We trailed off to the press conference. Hiddink marched into the room, sat down and said, 'Of course we are disappointed.' Looking at the faces around me, I couldn't help feeling that he had somewhat understated things.

'It was very quiet in the dressing room after the match,' said goalkeeper Igor Akinfeev. The president of the Football Federation was unable to contain his anger, however, reportedly telling Hiddink, 'You're not the magician that Abramovich claimed you were.'

After the draw against Israel, Hiddink seemed to temporarily lose something of his spark, something of his customary energy and good humour. 'I couldn't sleep after the Israel game. I lay awake all night until six a.m. We deserved victory. Now, of course, qualification has been made harder. But I'm determined to fight until the end,' he told the Russian press, face drawn, refusing all further interviews.

Hiddink recovered from his depression in time for the match against Estonia, a former Soviet republic, a mere four days later, on 11 October 2006. If ever a match was vital, this was it. Another draw or, unthinkably, a defeat, and the Russians' hopes of qualification would be almost dead. With just three games gone, Hiddink would be a lame duck, and an expensive one at that.

The Russians had relocated to St Petersburg, to Zenit's Petrovsky stadium, for the game, part of a policy to spread the national side's fixtures around the country. There were, however, as far as I was aware, as yet no plans to host anyone in Vladivostok, Russia's Far Eastern port, and a mere seven hours ahead of Moscow.

During the Soviet era, the authorities had initially discouraged football in Estonia, for fear that it would stir up nationalism and become a focus for the independence movement. When they finally made an appearance in the USSR Championship, Estonian teams played mainly in the Second Division. Since gaining independence along with the other Baltic States – Latvia and Lithuania – in 1990/91, the Estonian national side hasn't exactly made the world sit up and pay attention, highlights being victories over such notable footballing giants as the Faeroe Islands and Belarus.

What would happen if Russia were to lose to Estonia? If all hope of Russia qualifying for Euro 2008 was to disappear with over twenty months remaining until the festival of football kicked off? The man responsible, Vitali Mutko, didn't even want to consider that, saying that he would 'take no action'.

Unnervingly, Hiddink had the support of the Football Feder-ation, a sure sign if ever there was one that things were going badly. The first criticisms had already surfaced in the press, questioning the new manager's substitutions in the Israel game, expressing disappointment at Russia's blunted attack. To be fair, Hiddink had warned them. 'I'm no magician,' he had said in his first week in the job, 'but we'll give it our best shot.'

Russia was demanding more than 'best shots' however. Having been starved of success for so long, the nation was desperate for victory, and was relying on Hiddink to come up with the goods. During the 1998 World Cup in France, Hiddink had taken Holland to fourth place, speaking both before and after the competition of the concept of 'beautiful football', saying that it was more important for Holland to stick to this philosophy than win the tournament. In Russia, he could be sure, no one would care in the slightest exactly how the side won their matches. Beautiful or ugly, the actual football would come a poor second to results.

With just ten minutes of the match remaining in St Petersburg, Hiddink's face was a picture of gloom. The Estonians had closed ranks, and were denying Russiaany clear chances. Then Hiddink made a substitution, bringing on Dmitri Sychev. One of Russia's top forwards, it was, oddly, his first appearance in a Hiddink side. He wasted no time, immediately threading the ball through for another substitute, Pavel Pogrebnyak, to hammer the ball home. And then, in injury time, Sychev himself scored to make it 2–0. It was not quite the mauling most people had expected, but it was a victory, Hiddink's first in an official fixture. More importantly, it was three points, and with matches against Croatia and England still to come, they would most likely prove priceless.

Hiddink is famed for his effective substitutions, having used them to dramatic effect during his time in South Korea and Australia, turning matches by bringing on forwards, and now he had done the same for the Russians. True, the level of the match wasn't as high, and the opponents were not of the same quality as the Italians, Croatians and Japanese undone by Hiddink at the last two World Cups, but it was a glimmer, a hint of a promise. The Russian fans went home happy, and Hiddink flew back to Holland for a week, where he was facing tax-evasion charges.

Whatever the future held, Hiddink, despite his best attempts to remain neutral, had already ruffled some feathers, publicly criticising the head of Russian football after the victory in St Petersburg.

'It's usual international practice for the president of the country's football to come into the dressing room an hour and a half before the match, and wish the players good luck,' began Hiddink in an interview in the Russian press, clearly not wanting to make a great deal out of the issue, 'yet Mr Mutko is so enthusiastic that before the game with Estonia he repeatedly came in and out. In the end, I had to ask him to leave, to let the players concentrate on the match.'

According to a report in *Russian Newsweek*, Mutko, after being kicked out of the dressing room, waited until Hiddink's attention was diverted and sneaked back in, where he collared a couple of Russian defenders and proceeded to urge them to 'cover each other on the field', before Hiddink had him thrown him out again.

Mutko reportedly responded to this affront by saying, 'Hiddink drinks too much coffee. He orders twenty cups a day to his hotel room.'

'Someone take me to a normal café or restaurant,' Hiddink was reported, by *Newsweek* again, to have pleaded to friends in Moscow, 'and not Pushkin (Moscow's most elite restaurant, and a favourite with politicians, celebrities and other members of Russia's tiny upper class) again. I've already been there five times with Mutko.'

There was more to come. The former Spartak Moscow and USSR goalkeeper Vladimir Maslachenko stated publicly before the game with Macedonia that Hiddink was unable to choose the side that he wanted because 'certain people had interests in making sure that their players were chosen for the national team'. It was assumed that he was talking about highly connected agents and club owners. 'The whole system is to blame,' he went on. 'Players belong to certain groups, people well connected with the Russian football authorities. Hiddink is a hostage of the situation, but he can't speak out because he has signed an extremely profitable contract.'

Hiddink, as if in answer to these claims, which he had not commented on, surprised the Russian football world by leaving out a number of 'influential' players for the game against FYR Macedonia, bringing in a handful of uncapped youngsters. It was an indication of the dearth of potential new blood in Russian football that three of the new caps were not even regulars for their club sides, their places filled by foreign journeymen. 'As things stand,' said Hiddink, 'I have sixty players to choose from – and thirty-five of those are reserves.'

In Macedonia, everything finally came right for Hiddink and Russia. Facing a side that had just held England to a 0–0 draw in Manchester, Russia scored two goals in the first half and then comfortably defended their lead in the second. But, more importantly from a Russian point of view, Hiddink seemed to have finally got through to the players, the speed and energy that had been previously lacking in the side apparent to all. The team had positively glowed with the very same self-belief that Vasili Utkin had predicted Hiddink would instil. Suddenly, I was glad we hadn't gone so far as to lay a cash wager on Russia taking first place in the group.

By the end of 2006, Russia lay second in Group E, one point ahead of England, who had played an equal number of games. Perhaps, the Russian media speculated, Hiddink was (whatever Vitali Mutko might think, and despite all of the Dutchman's claims to the contrary) a magician after all, a football sorcerer, casting his spell over the Russian national team?

'Russian players are used to trainers being unapproachable, to being tyrants,' Nikolai Roganov at *Total Football* told me.

'Hiddink is very easy to speak with, even through a translator. You sense the man's communicability straight away. He has created a warm atmosphere in the team, and the players have responded to that, and are ready to give their all for Hiddink, to battle for him. It's strange, Hiddink came to us from far-off Holland, but he has found it easier to get through to our players than any Russian trainer.'

'Guus Hiddink is, odd as it may seem,' Igor Rabiner at *Sport-Express* told me, 'teaching the Russian Football Federation to respect the profession of team manager.

'In the past, the Russian Football Federation officials just looked upon the coaches as employees. They didn't respect them at all. One wrong word and you were out the door. If any Russian trainer had dared kick Mutko out of the dressing room, he would have been fired immediately. But Mutko and the football federation took it from Hiddink. What we are all hoping for now is that when Hiddink leaves, they will continue to show the same respect to the new, Russian trainer of the national team.

'It's very strange indeed,' he laughed. 'A foreigner, respected by Russians, is teaching the Russians to respect Russians.'

'In Russia you can only believe,' Fyodor Tyutchev had written in the nineteenth century. In the twenty-first century, less than six months after arriving in the country, Gus Hiddink had begun to teach the Russian national team, and its football federation, to do just that.

CHAPTER SIX

The fixers – Russian style

'Money, like vodka, makes a man strange.'

Anton Chekov, *Gooseberries*

While Guus Hiddink's attempts to reorganise and restructure the nation's favourite sport were proving largely successful, there was a darker side to the game that he would be unable to reach, a place where foreign trainers had no business, where straight-talking, tactics and man-management could have little effect.

Ever since oil money started to flood into the game at the start of the twenty-first century, Russia's national sport has been engulfed in scandal after scandal, with claims of fixed matches, crooked referees and high-level conspiracies becoming commonplace. At times, the charges border on hysteria, with accusations and allegations of corruption occurring almost every weekend. Despite (like many a Russian fan) half-wanting to turn a blind eye to events, I eventually decided to investigate for myself, to look into reports that the problem was already so deeply rooted as to be an intrinsic part of the game – just another factor, like home advantage and recent form, to be taken into account when predicting the results of forthcoming encounters.

I visited the offices of *Novaya Gazeta*, one of Russia's few truly independent newspapers, at the beginning of November 2006. The first snows had already begun to fall, and there was a sharp chill to the air. Outside the offices lay a framed photograph of Anna Politkovskaya, the *Novaya Gazeta* reporter and fierce critic of the Chechen War, murdered a little over a month prior to my visit. Her death had sparked international outrage, and there were many who saw the hand of the Kremlin behind the shooting. However, in the murky world of Russian politics, things are not always so simple. There is provocation, and counter-provocation, and there were as many who believed that anti-Putin forces, seeking to discredit the Russian leader, were implicated in her murder.

While involved in exposing such matters as high-level fraud, and torture in Chechnya, *Novaya Gazeta* had also made it its business to investigate the sleaze allegedly poisoning Russian football. Following a spate of high-profile incidents, I arranged to meet Ruslan Dubov, the newspaper's sport editor, to discuss the ugly side of the beautiful game.

Ruslan was younger than I had expected him to be, and smoked constantly, taking long drags on cheap 'Winston' cigarettes. Life as an investigative journalist in Russia was stressful, and the nicotine must have proved invaluable in helping him to keep his nerve.

He began by telling me that he considered Russian football to be fundamentally corrupt, that almost every team was, or had been at some time, in some way, tainted.

'The money involved just increases the higher up you get,' he said. 'I'll give you an example. There was a lower-division match, not long ago, that was fixed in advance. The referee was promised money to ensure that the game finished in favour of the home side. He did his job, and afterwards went into the club president's office to get his cash. "Well, we don't actually have any," he was told, "but look, take those sacks of sugar over there, if you want." The referee shrugged, and loaded them into his car. Obviously, in the Premier League, no one is hauling off sacks of sugar.

'The deeper into the forest you go, the fatter the partisans,' Ruslan concluded, illustrating his point with a seldom-used Russian proverb, stubbing out another fag as he did so.

The 1990s saw the start of a crime wave that has plagued Russia from the chaos of the Yeltsin years right through to the economic success story of President Putin's second term. Assassinations and contract killings have become commonplace and football, unsurprisingly, has not remained unscathed.

In September 2006 the first deputy chairman of the Central Bank of the Russian Federation, Andrei Kozlov, was gunned down near Spartak Moscow's sports centre, where employees of the bank had been playing football. He died the following night. Although there was no clear link with football, the scene of his death, within sight of one of the sport's temples, was darkly symbolic, and stirred memories of another killing, one that had a much stronger connection to Spartak.

In the summer of 1997 Larisa Nechayeva, Spartak Moscow's former general director, was shot dead at her country house. The case has still to be solved, yet conspiracy theories abound in the press and the Internet as to the reasons behind her murder, implicating a number of figures, ranging from past members of the Spartak board of directors to the local Moscow authorities.

One theory has it that Nechayeva had been attempting a clean-up of Spartak's finances, and that someone ordered her to be permanently silenced. Another is that the Moscow authorities arranged a hit on her when she attempted to build Spartak their own stadium, thus depriving the city, and its leaders, of the money the club pay to rent the Luzhniki Olympic Arena. There are also those who believe her killing was ordered by a rival Moscow side, enraged by her success in attracting sponsors such as Adidas and Akai to Spartak. None of these theories have ever been proven, however.

Indeed, Nechayeva's murder will probably remain unsolved. The police have little inclination to investigate and, given the number of journalists murdered in Russia since the collapse of the USSR, there are fewer and fewer reporters willing to get involved in such matters. After all, it is a lot simpler, not to say safer, to believe the opinion of the state prosecutor that her death resulted from a 'simple robbery gone wrong'. What is clear, though, is that Nechayeva was a woman with many enemies.

One of the matches that had persuaded me to look into the increasingly frequent allegations of fixed games took place in July 2006, when Spartak Moscow became embroiled in a bitter game in Tomsk, the heart of Siberia. During the match, the referee, Pavel Kulalyev, in charge of only his third fixture in the Russian Premier League, dismissed a Spartak player and disallowed one of their goals. From being 2–0 up, Spartak had to settle for a draw, and for one point in place of three. After the final whistle, the accusations began to fly. Spartak captain Egor Titov said that the referee had 'murdered Spartak'. A Spartak representative went even further went even further, saying that 'there were serious forces in action against us'. Most people assumed that Shavlo was referring to the club's deadly enemies, CSKA. This looked to be a scandal that would run and run.

'They killed us. I mean, I can accept mistakes from a ref, but the first half was fine. No problems. Then the second half comes along, and he is the ref from hell. With all his decisions going against us,' Sergei Shavlo, Spartak's general director, told me as we discussed the matter in his office. 'Russia should keep up with Europe in terms of the battle against corruption. If they can remove the leading clubs from the top division, then we should do the same.' Kulalyev subsequently said in the Russian media that his con- science was 'clean'. The Russian football authorities later banned him from referring top level matches, however.

I met the president of the Russian Football Federation after an Under-21 match in Moscow towards the end of 2006. As well as being the top man in Russian football, Vitali Mutko was also a member of the Federation Council, Russia's upper house of parliament. I had been trying to contact him for months, and had been given the run-around by his two press attachés so much that, in the end, I simply resorted to shouting my usual spiel at him through a fence as he was waiting to get into his Mercedes.

Russian football is in a state of flux, and its president has an extremely high public profile. He was, it occurred to me, the first politician I had ever met. We shook hands. The temperature was hovering around zero, yet Mutko's skin had a tanned, glowing sheen. Mutko speaks with real zeal about cleaning up Russian football, but he is, when all is said and done, a politician, and possesses all the skills that profession demands.

'Give my assistant a call,' he said, after we had spoken for a few minutes, exchanging meaningless pleasantries. 'We'll have tea and biscuits.' I would never get to taste those biscuits, unfortunately, Mutko's minders failing to arrange a meeting with their boss for me.

Mutko had reacted to Shavlo's allegations by promising that a special committee would be set up to investigate, claiming that if any foul play was uncovered he would not be afraid to use the 'Italian option'. This was just weeks after Juventus, Lazio and Fiorentina had been exiled to Serie B. Rumours of fixed matches had long ago become routine, but now it seemed the authorities were set on doing something.

Vitali Mutko went further, promising to remove the people responsible for dirtying Russian football from the game. 'There are,' he had said in interview widely reported in the Russian press, 'many ways to do this. In Russia, it costs $75,000 to buy a game. We all know that. I remember once, when I was the owner of Zenit St Petersburg,' he recalled, 'we were playing Spartak, and leading 1–0. Muscovites were coming up to me, friends of mine associated with Spartak, and thanking me. I didn't know what for. Then, when we lost, I understood. The game had been sold without my knowledge. And I had just sat there like a fool.'

Mutko also told the story of the scandal surrounding the match between Spartak Moscow and Lokomotiv that would decide second place, and a Champions League spot, at the end of the 2005 season.

According to the Russian Football Federation president, the

referee for the match, Valentin Ivanov (the Russian man in black who set a new record for red cards at the 2006 World Cup, handing out four during Portugal and Holland's second-round match) was threatened before the game. As one of the most respected referees in Russia, someone wanted him out of the way for the match. Calls were made to Ivanov, hinting at retribution if he were to take charge of the encounter. The authorities provided security for him, allaying the his concerns, and Spartak won the game and the Champions League berth.

'Those commissions set up by Mutko and the like,' said Ruslan Dubov, puffing away on his third cigarette in fifteen minutes, 'are just run by, excuse the expression, old farts. They sit in their offices, and expect to have allegations proven to them. They are so bogged down in the system that they don't actually do any investigating. As you know, the Russian football authorities declared that they would battle against corruption not so long ago, made a great fuss, and launched a special commission. I met that commission. One guy. That's all. No one does anything. No one can do anything.'

As the season dragged on, Spartak fans, enraged by a series of decisions that had gone against them, unfurled a huge banner at a game in the ancient Russian town of Yaroslavl, home of Shinnik FC.

'Russian League title and Cup for sale. Expensive. Mutko. 637 0834', read the banner.

(In the unique world of Russian advertising psychology, 'expensive' is often used to imply that the item for sale is of real quality.)

'There is an epidemic of fixed matches in Russian football,' went on Ruslan, his ashtray by now overflowing with cigarette butts. 'It goes like this – when the result of a game has been decided beforehand, the players are gathered in the dressing room and told the result. They then call relatives, friends, etc., who bet on the outcome.'

There are a great deal of foreign players in Russia now and, if I could believe that it was possible to "work" with Russian players, I found it difficult, perhaps naively, to accept that foreign stars, seasoned internationals, could be persuaded to throw matches so easily.

'They can persuade anyone to do anything,' shrugged Ruslan, a man clearly used to the omnipotent power of Russia's criminal structures.

Why, I wondered, if all this were true, had no player ever spoken out against the match-fixing?

'And lose their livelihood? I mean, even if a player does speak out, it's just his word against the rest. Veterans of the game keep quiet as well because they are simply used to doing so. Turn off the Dictaphone and open a bottle of vodka, and they tell you a different story.

'There are lots of ways that clubs can punish players who disobey orders,' Ruslan went on. 'Attacks on players take place, and are hushed up. Of course, if anyone is brought to trial, it's always some fans who did it, but it's clear to everyone exactly where these fans get their orders from.

'I'll give you an example. There was a game not long ago featuring [name of club withheld]. The governor of the region, and the owner of the club, had presented the players with expensive foreign cars as a token of his appreciation for their recent efforts. The last weekend of the season came, and someone decided to earn some cash. The team were instructed to throw the game but, somehow, they won that day. Immediately after the final whistle had blown, a series of massive explosions took place in the car park. Five of the very same cars that had been presented to the players were blown up.'

Swift retribution indeed.

I asked if any of the Russian sports papers had written about the incident.

'What are you on about? Of course not.

'You know, in the USSR,' continued Ruslan, after he had gotten over the naivety of my question, 'we had a system of planned economics – Five-Year Plans and so on. Now, we have a system of planned football. Russian football is a swamp. There are teams, especially in the First Division, who have no desire to win anything. The majority of their games are fixed, they sit in the middle of the table, get by, fulfil their social functions, and that's all.

'You know,' Ruslan told me, 'a lot of this information, we get from the police. They just get so frustrated with the situation, with all the never-ending commissions and investigations, that they start to leak things to us.'

As the allegations of match-fixing have increased, more and more pressure has been brought to bear on Russian referees. In 2005, the Russian football authorities began to fly in foreign referees to take charge of big games, but even this was not without controversy. After the CSKA–Spartak derby in September 2006, the CSKA manager labelled the French referee Loran Duamel a 'clown' for his performance.

However, public criticism and terrace taunts such as '*Sudyu na milo!*' are not the only things that home-grown referees, who are paid around £1,500 a match in the Premier League, have to contend with. In the past few years, assaults on the men in black have begun to increase. For some reason, baseball bats seem to be their aggressors' favoured weapons of choice. Although, fortunately, no referee has yet died, serious injuries have been inflicted, the Premier League referee Alexander Kolobaev suffering broken ribs, a broken nose and serious concussion during an attack in Moscow.

Dostoevsky wrote, 'If there is no God, then everything is permitted.'

Certain elements in Russian football seem to think the same applies to referees.

One of the most vocal critics of 'fixed matches' in Russia has been Vasili Utkin. Besides being the most famous football commentator in Russia today, Utkin also writes for *Sovetski-Sport* and has published a number of controversial and accusatory articles in the paper on corruption in the Russian game.

I met Utkin in the sumptuous Gorky restaurant in central Moscow. It is not the kind of place I usually frequent, yet he appeared comfortable enough there, with long-legged waitresses gliding from table to table. I ordered a glass of homebrew beer, and the waitress seemed personally delighted by my choice.

'The way it usually works is that the two teams come to an agreement,' began Utkin, expounding on the problem of match-fixing, Russian style. 'For example, they simply decide to share the points: that is, both sides win at home. That way, for teams who may be faced with a struggle for survival, they are at least guaranteed a certain number of points. Their rivals maybe draw, and pick up one point, whereas they are guaranteed three out of six.'

A few weeks after this interview, a friend of mine, a player in a Sunday League team, told me that his side had arranged to split the points in their fixture with another Moscow amateur side, winning 3–0 at home and losing 3–0 away. At first I had assumed he was joking, parodying the recent spate of accusations that had swept through Russian football, but he was deadly serious. After all, it was logical. To get out of the group, consisting of four teams, his bunch of engineers and office workers needed around ten points. Three at home would only leave them needing seven out of four matches to achieve their aim of qualification for the next round of the Moscow-wide tournament.

This mentality undoubtedly comes from Soviet times and the system of prearranged quotas when, in factories and farms all over the country, targets were, while in reality fallen short of, simply declared fulfilled, or even exceeded. The most important thing was to appear to be successful, to achieve set goals; the methods and, accordingly, the true reality of the situation, were mostly irrelevant. In many cases, factories or farms, lacking the required amount of the specified product, simply borrowed what they needed from neighbouring production centres, returning the loan when the commission in charge of checking quotas had departed.

There is very little difference, I would suggest, between the practice of borrowing a ton of coal and splitting points. The principle is one and the same. The USSR may be dead, but its customs live on.

While the Soviet economy may have been falsified, its football, according to Utkin, was somewhat cleaner. 'In the Soviet era,' he said, pausing to gaze at a group of model-type Russian girls giggling on the first floor of the restaurant, 'the stakes in the game weren't so big, and there wasn't really the material incentive to fix matches. Then, it was more of a political thing. Making sure that the Moscow teams did well, that the Ukrainians were kept happy with a cup or two, and so on. Anyway, that's not really the main point. It's difficult to compare the two. Soviet footballers weren't paid anything like as much, and even if they did get some money there was nothing to spend it on. They played for honour, for their team, for the political or social structure it represented. Basically, comparing Soviet football and Russian football is like comparing a Dostoevsky novel and a modern-day bestseller. The first was created with love, out of the sheer pleasure of the act itself, the second is a commercial thing, with financial concerns behind it.

'The bookmakers are a good indication in Russia of when a match has been fixed. For example, recently Luch Energiya played at home to Krilya Sovetov. The odds offered for a home victory were extremely low, suspiciously so in fact, and meant that for every hundred roubles bet (the equivalent to two pounds) a punter stood to win less than five.'

Luch Energiya were debutants in the Russian Premier League in 2006, and their main strength lay in the fact that they were based in Vladivostok, seven time zones away from Moscow. The away game was a tough one, but the odds offered in no way represented the relative strength of the two sides. Luch eventually ran out 3–2 winners, a fact that Utkin found, to put it mildly, entirely unsurprising. I declined to ask if he had had a bet himself on the outcome.

Match-fixing, in all its forms, is the football fan's worst nightmare. The suspicion that his team have won or lost, not because they played better or worse, but because the result of the game was agreed on beforehand is, in some ways, more insidious than outright bribery. It is enormously difficult to buy all 22 players, and there is always the element of chance. However, if the two sides simply agree on the result, then football is reduced to farce, to ballet, or professional wrestling, the teams merely going through the motions, following preplanned steps.

As an aside, before I left him, I asked Utkin if he could supply me with a contact number for Oleg Romantsev. While I was no longer optimistic about my chances of speaking to the one-time Spartak manager, I was still curious to see what he would make of all this, what he would have to say about the scandals blighting the Russian game. Utkin, a man with many connections within the world of football, could only shrug. 'I'm afraid not,' he said, not even bothering to scroll through the address file in his swanky mobile phone.

Towards the end of 2006, the English online betting company Betfair reported that bets taken for the Luch Energiya and Tom Tomsk match in Vladivostok had amounted to $800,000, approximately one hundred times higher than the usual stakes for such a game. Not a betting person, I nevertheless kicked myself for missing the chance to win a tidy sum. The first fixture between the two sides had ended with a Tomsk victory and, according to what I had learned about the Russian game, it seemed a sure thing that Luch would win the return match (and they did).

Betfair subsequently launched an investigation into the incident, leading *Novaya Gazeta* to comment that the English seemed to be the only ones seriously interested in battling against corruption in the Russian game.

As Russian football's popularity has risen, events surrounding the game have grown increasingly violent. This violence permeates all levels of the game, from the Premier League to the lowest divisions.

Lipetsk is a small town in the southeast of European Russia. Even before the incident that took place in the autumn of 2006, it had something of a reputation for lawlessness and random violence. As my wife, Tanya, an ex-KVN (a Russian entertainment show) member, put it, 'Lipetsk is wild. Whenever we performed there, the local guys were always beating someone up over something or other. Usually vodka.'

In late 2006, Metallurg Lipetsk were a side in the Second Division of Russian football. In the lower divisions, far removed from the sky-high wages and stardom of the Premier League, teams exist on tight budgets, at the whim of egocentric presidents and investors. Bearing in mind that '*gaz*' and '*neft*' are Russian for 'gas' and 'oil', a brief glance at the names of some of the teams scattered around the third echelon of Russian football is enough to get a good idea of the nature of the sides: Gazovik, Souz-Gazprom, Neftekhmik, Kavkaz-transgaz 2005. Nowhere else in Russian sport is the power and omnipotent nature of the gas and oil industries more apparent.

However, having an oil or gas company as a sponsor is no guarantee of success. Teams are formed and then disbanded or, having failed to live up to their egocentric owners' expectations, financially abandoned.

In 2005, after a dismal campaign in which they won only seven of their forty-two matches, Metallurg were relegated from the First Division. The club's sponsors drastically cut their investment in the side, and a new manager, former Metallurg player Stanislav Bernikov, was appointed.

Metallurg, as is often the case following relegation, was split into two camps – the veterans who had been unable to find themselves new, better-paying clubs, and the newcomers from the youth side, moving up in class to the first team.

The season began well enough but, following a series of poor results, it became clear that it was going to take a drastic turnaround in fortune for the club to make an immediate return to the First Division that year. In September 2006, Metallurg suffered two home defeats, putting the proverbial nail in their chances of promotion.

Stanislav Bernikov did not take the result well. He was a man who had given his whole life to football in the region, so the rumours that his players, safe from relegation, with no hope of promotion, had sold the matches for 300,000 roubles ($10,000) apiece, whipped him into a great fury.

According to eyewitness reports, at the next training session Bernikov led the players on a cross-country run. However, halfway through he suddenly stopped for a 'serious conversation'. At the same time, a car pulled up in a nearby clearing. Bernikov began to interrogate the players: 'How much did you get? Huh? How much? Ten thousand, more?'

Five men got out of the car and, according to reports in the Russian media, upon a signal from Bernikov began to beat up Evgeni Shamrin, Denis Zhurnovsky and Alexei Morochko, the goalkeeper, forward and captain. One of the attackers was, allegedly, Bernikov's son. During the attack, a pneumatic pistol was fired at Morochko, who, he says, stopped the bullet from hitting his face by raising his hand. The other footballers stood and watched, while some of the veterans, it is said, helped in the attack. Of all the members of the team, only six players confirmed the incident. The rest said that they saw nothing. Shamrin, Zhurnovsky and Morochko were later hospitalised.

Following the incident, Bernikov denied everything, saying that he too had seen nothing. The club's president suspended him until an investigation had been carried out, and Vitali Mutko and the Russian Football Federation promptly set up yet another commission.

The team's fans subsequently published an open letter on their website in support of the hospitalised footballers. It began, 'We, the supporters of FC Metallurg Lipetsk, lovers of football and simply people indifferent to the current situation, call upon everyone who cares about the country we live in, the country your parents live in, and in the country that your children will live in, to help try and punish those guilty of the crimes against members of our team, citizens of our country.'

While it may seem that Bernikov was simply fighting against corruption with his own extreme methods, there were rumours in Lipetsk that things were not so simple. There were whispers before the attacks that Bernikov had been involved in selling the games himself. Were the assaults payback for something? A dispute over money? Had orders been, perhaps, ignored?

The Bernikovs reportedly have contacts in high places in Lipetsk, and it seemed highly unlikely that any action would be taken against them. There were disputed reports that Stanislav Bernikov was about to be reinstated as manager. The players involved, Shamrin, Zhukovsky and Morochko, have refused all further interviews on the topic.

Maxim, the webmaster of a Lipetsk website devoted to Metallurg, informed me in early October 2006 that the team was playing out its last games of the season under a trainer without a licence, and that Bernikov was under investigation. Somehow however, in Russia, where the well connected very rarely face censure, it seemed naive to expect that, even if he was guilty of the charges being levelled against him, the ex-Metallurg manager and his alleged hired thugs would ever be brought to justice.

I attended a Metallurg home game a little more than a month after the incident. Lipetsk is a prosperous town, by the standards of the Russian provinces at least, and the stadium, although shabby, is one of the best in the lower divisions. The new trainer, Sergei Mashnin, sat on the touchline, shouting instructions to his players. In the sparsely attended stadium, there was a group of fans holding a banner that stated, 'Shamrin, Morochko, Zhuk. We are with you!' After the game, which Metallurg lost 1–0, I went up to them.

'Ah, it's the same everywhere in Russia,' said one of them, a young man in his twenties. 'Money, that's what counts. Bernikov will never be punished because he knows all those guys in power. They all play for the same veterans team.' He waved his hands in disgust.

'This is Russia,' said another. 'Nothing will ever change.'

Despite the fans' pessimism, the Russian Football Disciplinary Committee eventually found Stanislav Bernikov guilty of the charges levelled against him, namely 'organising an attack on members of Metallurg Lipetsk', and he was banned from football for life.

'I was astonished,' a member of the Metallurg fan club told me, on the team's unofficial website forum. 'I never thought that he would be punished. Never imagined that, with all his contacts, he would face any disciplinary measures.'

However, cynics suggested that because of all the media attention the incident had attracted (the story had even been reported in foreign newspapers) Bernikov had simply been punished to prove to the world that justice worked in Russia, that the football authorities were determined to clean up the game.

In May 2007, Bernikov and his son appeared in court in Lipetsk charged with 'hooliganism' and 'intention to cause bodily harm' in relation to this incident. The charges were reduced to 'assault' however, and they were both fined some £800.

In 2008, nearly eighteen months after the incident, Bernikov shows no sign of making a comeback. Metallurg, it seemed, had confounded expectations, bucking the trend for Russia's 'connected' to look after their own.

The club narrowly missed out on promotion to the First Division at the end of the 2007 season. The side's top scorer, with seventeen goals, was Denis Zhurnovsky, the only one of the players allegedly assaulted by Bernikov and co to remain at the club.

In November 2006, the Russian football authorities looked into allegations that the results of certain games had been arranged beforehand, choosing three games from the First Division to investigate, ignoring the fifteen or so Premier League matches that had been widely suspected of being fixed.

A committee of ageing Soviet players and officials were shown three prerecorded matches at the offices of the Russian Football Federation. They uncovered no hint of foul play or wrongdoing. As Viktor Ponedelnik, a member of the committee, commented to *Sovetski-Sport*, 'They should really have had lawyers here. We just aren't qualified.'

'That was ridiculous, just typical of Mutko and the Russian Football Federation,' said Nikolai Roganov, the editor of *Total*

Football, when I touched on the subject. 'To sit a committee of ex-players down to watch three games, and decide if they were fixed or not – to basically judge the integrity of the whole Russian game on the basis of three prerecorded matches, that was just absurd.'

Is it reasonable to expect Russian football, despite Bernikov's disqualification and the Russian Football Federation's numerous commissions, to be cleaned up any time soon?

Realistically, the answer has to be no.

Despite the rampant corruption and accompanying violence, there is a great apathy at the core of Russian society. For example, the Russian army is plagued with the world's most brutal hazing – *dedovshchina* in Russian – the widespread practice in which older conscripts beat up their younger colleagues and generally make their lives a nightmare. Physical and psychological torture is common, as are deaths, mutilations and suicides. Hazing stretches back to the Soviet era, and the Russian Soldiers' Mothers Committee has estimated that around a thousand soldiers die every year as a result of non-combat situations. The committee attributes a large proportion of these deaths to the results of hazing.

With the advent of modern mobile phones, and the willingness of drunken soldiers to record themselves beating recruits, this once taboo subject has exploded, with footage readily available on the Internet, and broadcast on exposé TV programmes. In 2005, the young draftee Andrei Sychev was assaulted by his superiors in a New Year's Eve attack. As a result, both his legs and genitals were amputated. The case became the most celebrated incident of hazing in Russia yet, taking up the front pages of all the major newspapers for days. However, there were no protests, no mass marches to the gates of, say, the Defence Ministry, demanding investigations. This is just one example of blatant injustice. There are others, equally as horrendous, and met with an equally deafening silence.

Given this tradition of silent suffering, it would be naive to imagine that anyone is going to have the commitment to root out corruption in the national sport. After all, football, as we are constantly reminded when the national team loses, is just a game.

For all of the Russian Football Federation's claims to be investigating widespread corruption, results have been minimal, to say the least. Football is money and, in Russia, wealth is backed up by violence, or the threat of such.

CHAPTER SEVEN
Zenit – life's a gas with Gazprom

'At last the damp autumn day, muggy and dirty, peeped into the room through the dingy window pane with such a hostile, sour grimace that Mr Golyadkin could not possibly doubt that he was not in the land of Nod, but in the city of Petersburg.'

Fyodor Dostoevsky, *The Double*

It is a curious feature of football in Russia that teams are, generally, far better supported in the regions. This may very well be because Muscovites, having six Premier League sides to choose from, are spoiled for choice, yet I suspect that live football attracts higher crowds elsewhere due to the simple fact that there are far less distractions the further away from Moscow, with its bright lights and Western-influenced nightlife, one goes. Football has less competition in the provinces.

Despite this, the country's football (like so many other features of Russian life) revolves decidedly around the capital or, more precisely, around the money concentrated there. Once in a while, however, regional sides can upset the order of things, claiming their own, long-to-be-cherished moments of glory. In November 2007, Zenit St Petersburg became the first non-Moscow club to lift the Russian title for eleven years, the club's Dutch coach Dick Advocaat becoming in the process the first foreign trainer to lead a team to the Russian championship.

The city where Dostoevsky's antiheroes brooded on the nature of human existence, and where Gogol's characters went out of their minds, chasing their detached and newly animated body parts along canals and bridges, St Petersburg spreads itself languidly about the River Neva. Its streets are wide, and, due to a law forbidding the construction of buildings exceeding five storeys in the centre, the sky appears somehow larger, more impressive than in other places.

St Petersburg was founded by Peter the Great in 1703. A singular-minded man, he had thousands of slaves transported to a swamp in the north of Russia to build the city he intended to act as Russia's 'Window to Europe'. Thousands of these unfortunates, no one knows exactly how many, perished during its construction. 'The whole city is a graveyard,' someone had said to me the first time I visited, and everywhere I went I imagined the crumbling bones of three-century-dead slaves beneath my feet.

St Petersburg, or Leningrad as it was known from 1924 until 1991, was also the birthplace of Russia's perestroika-era rock, the city where some of the country's finest groups, like Kino (led by the ethnic Korean, Viktor Tsoi) and Akvarium were formed.

Parallel to my discovery of Russian football was my exploration of the world of Soviet rock. There was, I discovered upon my arrival in the country, all this music that I had never heard of, whole musical careers born, flourished and having died without me having had the faintest idea. I became almost obsessive in my love for Kino. Their lyrics were simple, yet possessed of something I couldn't pinpoint; something born out of a time I hadn't experienced, some emotion that wasn't quite clear to me ... It was nostalgia for a time I had never known.

Until their 2007 title victory, Zenit had always been one of Russia's traditional underperformers, winning their only league title in 1984. St Petersburg is dark for eighteen hours a day in winter, and in summer experiences 'White Nights', when, even in the early hours of the morning, it is possible to read a newspaper by the light of the sun. Due to this, mood swings are common, and the residents of Russia's pre-revolution capital are famed throughout the country for their languid, unpredictable characters.

The city also has an undeniable influence over the style of football played by Zenit. Aside from the team's often irrational tactics and erratic defence, it is a decade-long tradition that the side usually starts well in spring, and then fades as daylight dwindles towards the end of the season, all the energy sapped from the players by the almost constant gloom.

Zenit were formed in 1925 as the representative club of a Leningrad metal factory. Up until 1939 the side were known as Stalinets, in honour of the moustached Soviet dictator. However, having lost that year's cup final to Spartak, Uncle Joe, in a fit of pique, decided that the team were no longer worthy of his name, and the side was renamed 'Zenit', taking its new name from an arms industry sports society.

Before being elected president of the Russian Football Federation in 2004, Vitali Mutko was the owner of Zenit St Petersburg from 1997 to 2003. Shortly after bringing in the first foreign manager to ever work in Russia, Vlastimil Petrzhela of the Czech Republic, in 2002, Zenit were soundly beaten by Dynamo Moscow, losing 7–1.

Mutko later told the Russian *Football-Hockey* newspaper, 'There were thousands of our fans at the stadium. The players were afraid to leave the dressing room. There were supporters waiting outside, in a foul mood. I went out and had a chat with them. "What are you shouting about. We lost, so we lost! This is our team, the only one we have," I said. One of them thrust a bottle of vodka under my nose. I had a drink with them, and the situation calmed down. We won the next game, 5–1.'

That match was a turning point, of a sort, for Petrzhela and Zenit. From then on, the team would always be in or around the top four. However, they constantly suffered from a lack of ruthlessness in front of their opponents' goal, and a pathological unreliability in front of their own, forever dropping vital points in crunch matches. Petrzhela had his own theory, though, as to Zenit's inability to achieve any tangible success. 'Zenit will never be allowed to become champions,' he said, 'because everything in Russian football is geared towards the Moscow teams. Referees included.'

There had long been rumours that money supplied by Muscovite businessmen was being used to influence the results of vital games. In 2004, a group of St Petersburg politicians even appealed to the then-prime minister, Mikhail Fradkov, to ensure that the men in black were fair to Zenit.

When Roman Abramovich sold his shares in Sibneft to Gazprom in 2005, the gas giant backed out on Sibneft's previous sponsorship deal with CSKA, and acquired a controlling stake in Zenit St Petersburg instead. 'It is public knowledge in Russia,' a Moscow businessman told me, 'that an executive position at Gazprom has been set aside for President Putin for when he eventually retires from political life. Putin is a native of St Petersburg, and this is undoubtedly the reason why Gazprom have taken control of Zenit, rather than, say, any of the Moscow clubs. While, admittedly, the president is not actually that great a football fan, it's obvious that he would still enjoy seeing his home-town side rise to the top in Russia.'

It is hard to exaggerate both Gazprom's wealth and influence. With access to the largest gas reserves in Europe, and a monopoly on prices and supplies throughout much of the continent, Gazprom is currently one of the world's most powerful companies – a midwinter switch of a button by its top executives would be sufficient to leave huge swathes of Europe freezing. The gas giant has often been called 'a state within a state', and in late 2007 a public opinion poll reported that more than 50 per cent of Russians, given a choice, would prefer to work for the company.

Gazprom's profits annually exceed $10 billion, and in December 2007 President Putin publicly backed the company's chairman, Dmitri Medvedev, to succeed him as Russian leader. Taking into account these unlimited resources and unrivalled influence, Gazprom's decision to invest in the world's favourite sport may well have consequences for not only Russia's footballing hierarchy, but also Europe's.

When Peter the Great founded St Petersburg in the early eighteenth century, he invited Dutch craftsmen to come to Russia to assist him in the construction of the city. Three hundred years on, in July 2006, Gazprom and Zenit likewise looked to the Netherlands for inspiration, sacking Petrzhela mid-season and appointing the Dutch trainer Dick Advocaat, fresh from managing South Korea at the 2006 World Cup. At one time a candidate for both the England and Russia posts, Advocaat's reign began with three 0–0 draws, as the 'Little General' set about bringing some order to Zenit's leaky defence.

This accomplished, Advocaat turned his attention to the side's attacking powers, Zenit slowly rising from ninth place to fourth, to within three points of the league leaders as the season drew to a close.

In mid-October 2006 Zenit went to Moscow for a game against Spartak. One of the largest contingents of Zenit fans ever seen at an away fixture travelled to the capital. Following their winning run, and the new confidence Advocaat had brought to the team, there was real hope among the fans that the 2006 season might be Zenit's, that they would be able to grapple the championship away from Moscow. The Zenit fans revealed a huge banner featuring a red-eyed Advocaat smoking a joint. 'The Dutch Plan', it proclaimed, a pun on the identical-sounding Russian word that means both 'plan' and 'marijuana'.

However, Zenit's play was anything but chilled-out, the St Petersburg side launching a series of raids on the Spartak goal. Zenit's pressure failed to pay off though, and with just minutes to go the match remained goalless. Advocaat's charges had looked the better team, but had been unable to put away any of their numerous openings.

And then, in a move that suggested he had already partly succumbed to St Petersburg's famed irrationality, Zenit's new manager took off a defensive midfielder and brought on Alexander Kerzhakov, a striker. Zenit, playing away from home, now had three forwards on the field. In the pouring rain, urged on by their fans, Zenit surged towards the Spartak goal. And then, a change in mood, a flash in the heavens, and the Muscovites broke, sweeping down the field where Vladimir Bistrov, transferred from Zenit to Spartak during Petrzhela's reign, put the ball in the net. It was the last kick of the game, and Zenit's title hopes were dead, for that season at least.

'Football isn't always fair,' said Advocaat. 'Sometimes you just don't deserve to lose. But when I took over we were in the middle of the table. My task was to build a new team, and to lift the club and its supporters. I think I have achieved both,' he added, clearly already looking to the future.

With a few games to go in the 2006 campaign, Zenit again travelled to Moscow, this time for a match against CSKA. Both teams needed the points desperately, CSKA to stay ahead of Spartak at the top of the table, Zenit to continue their bid for a UEFA Cup place. However, like many matches that season featuring CSKA, the fixture was full of controversy. First the referee incorrectly disallowed a Zenit goal for offside, then failed to send off CSKA's Vagner Love for a blatant punch, then disallowed another goal by Andrei Arshavin, the Zenit striker, and finally, to top it all, gave an extremely dubious penalty to the reigning champions. The Brazilian Carvalho stepped up to the spot and stroked the ball into the net. That was the only goal of the encounter, and CSKA moved closer to their third championship in four years. Immediately after the game, Zenit demanded a rematch, but the Russian football authorities turned down their appeal. The referee and the linesmen involved were, however, banned until the end of the season.

'We'll do them next year,' said a local St Petersburg sports journalist. 'They should have realised who they were playing against, just who they were up to their old tricks with,' he added, referring to the financial muscle that Gazprom had brought to Zenit.

Big signings were on the cards for the club, and the general mood was reflected by another banner that the Zenit fans had unfurled before the game. 'Zenit's Golden Future,' it read, 'Without a Hint of Green', getting in a dig at CSKA's alleged greasing of palms for good measure.

A few weeks after the 2006 season had finished, Zenit taking fourth place, the club began to invest heavily in the transfer market. First the hulking Russian international Pavel Pogrebnyak was convinced to leave the Siberian side Tom Tomsk in a $10.5 million deal. The transfers then followed thick and fast, as Advocaat began to shape his side for the following season. Alejandro Dominguez, an attacking Argentinian midfielder, was poached from the Russian Republic of Tatarstan side Rubin Kazan for $10 million, and then Anatoly Timoschuk, in the fiftieth-largest transfer in football's history, signed for $20 million from Ukraine's Shakhtar Donetsk. Added to the $10 million that Zenit had already spent on the Turkish striker Fatih Tekke, Gazprom were keeping their promise to invest heavily in the club.

There were those, however, who questioned Zenit's transfer policy, suggesting that the club were paying inflated prices for talented, yet not exceptional players. The Timoschuk deal, they pointed out, came a month or so after Ronaldo had signed for AC Milan for almost half the sum Zenit had paid out for the Ukrainian international.

'You try to get Ronaldo to move to Russia,' said a Zenit spokesman, shrugging, going on to suggest that the club were being forced to pay huge transfer fees to bring players to Russia, or, in Fatih Tekke's case, to force their clubs to sell them. Indeed, Zenit had outbid a rank of clubs, including Arsenal and Wigan, to secure the Turkish international's signature. As for Timoschuk, Dick Advocaat saw the player as 100 per cent vital to Zenit's title chances, and what the Dutch manager wanted, it seemed, he got.

'This city is mad about football,' Advocaat later told me. 'It has a population of six million, and we are the only team. There are plans to build a new sixty-thousand capacity stadium. The support here is already incredible,' he enthused, 'but if we win the Championship, the city will go, I assure you, completely crazy.'

I visited St Petersburg in late November 2006, almost a year prior to the day that Zenit would eventually lift the title, arriving on the 5.30 a.m. train from Moscow and then wandering the city's dark and windy streets until 11.30 a.m., when I presented myself at Zenit's Udelni Park training camp.

Before my meeting with Advocaat, I watched a training session, the players taking turns to practise free kicks, the two goalkeepers getting covered in mud as they dived from post to post. Amongst the new Zenit signings was Fernando Ricksen, the Dutch international and former Glasgow Rangers defender. Originally loaned out to Zenit, following an altercation with the Scottish side's new manager Paul Le Guen, Ricksen had recently made the move permanent, signing a three-year contract.

'I thought for a long time before agreeing to come to Russia,' said Dick Advocaat, as we sat in his office a couple of hours after noon, what light there had been already starting to fade. 'I had already had some offers from other Russian teams, but for me, like a lot of people, the word "Russia" remained a mental wall, and I had always refused. But then Zenit made me a very good offer. They flew me over here in a private plane, showed me the plans for a new stadium, for a new training centre, told me about the money that would be available for signings, and it all looked very promising. It sounded like a good challenge, so I accepted.

'The financial support of Gazprom is apparent in all aspects of daily life at the club,' Advocaat went on. 'It's not a problem to sign players; the main problem is convincing them to come. Russia has a bad reputation, and that can put both players, and their families, off. The weather might also have something to do with it, especially in St Petersburg,' joked Advocaat, gesturing at the dark rain clouds lurking outside the window.

Zenit had recently been linked with the Brazilian international Ze Roberto, yet at the last moment the player, who had already arranged a Russian visa, backed out of the deal.

'That was, again, connected with the reputation that Russia has. But that will change. There is a lot of money in the game here now, and that, along with the new stadiums being built, will eventually attract stars.'

Both Guus Hiddink and Advocaat had turned the fortunes of their new teams around, and I questioned Zenit's new manager as to the secret of success. 'Organisation is everything,' replied Advocaat. 'That was the first time I had seen a Russian side pressing so effectively,' he added, referring to Russia's confident 2–0 victory in Macedonia a little over a week before our talk.

Like Hiddink, Advocaat was not afraid to make unpopular decisions. As the new Russian manager had dropped two former captains from the national team, so Advocaat had relegated Alexander Kerzhakov, Zenit's star and pin-up boy, to the substitute's bench. At the post-training press conference I attended, a thin, angry-looking woman journalist repeatedly berated Advocaat over his decision not to include Kerzhakov, once a target for Tottenham Hotspur, in recent line-ups. 'The past is the past,' snapped Advocaat, his tone somewhat softened by the translator. 'You need to prove your worth, week in, week out.' A short while later Kerzhakov was gone, to Spain and Sevilla.

Advocaat spoke in awed tones of Russia's size, of the logistic difficulties involved in travelling around the largest country on Earth. 'Flying to Vladivostok for an away game, for example. That's eight hours on a plane. The same as from London to Los Angeles. I was ill that day though, and didn't make the journey. I had a problem with my nose, and they wouldn't let me fly. Some people don't believe me,' he added, laughing, 'but I would never let the club down. I love flying.' As the manager of a side forced to make a ninety-minute plane journey to its *nearest* away fixture, that was, we agreed, most fortunate.

Despite having worked in Scotland for three years, managing Glasgow Rangers from 1998 to 2001, Advocaat speaks English without a hint of a Scottish accent. 'How could I pick up a Scottish accent when I can't even understand the Scots?' he joked.

'I enjoyed life in Scotland,' he went on. 'I know the people, the culture, the places. Life was a lot easier for me there.'

I enquired as to Advocaat's impressions of St Petersburg, a city known throughout Russia as the 'Venice of the North'. At the time of our interview, Advocaat had been in Russia for five months, and his answer illustrated the hectic life that football managers lead. 'Well,' he said, 'I've been here for five months. I've seen a cathedral, St Isaacs' – that was really beautiful. But, basically, it's training, back to the hotel, watching DVDs of matches, getting to know the club. Outside of football, I don't really have much time for anything else.'

There has always been a great rivalry between Moscow and St Petersburg. Natives of Russia's northern capital, for the most part, view Muscovites as uncouth and uncultured. St Petersburg, they maintain, is a city of culture, and Moscow just a 'big village', where money rules supreme.

Unlike in Moscow, where there are six, St Petersburg has only one Premier League team, and so, as a result, Zenit are extremely well supported. (An English analogy would be Newcastle United.) Their most famous group of supporters are Nevsky Front, whom Zenit have even set aside a section of the stadium for. In order to gain membership of Nevsky Front one is obliged to pass an interview at the fans' St Petersburg offices.

Nevsky Front were formed in the mid-1970s, when a small group of fans began to travel to away matches in neighbouring Soviet republics. As Pasha, a regular visitor to the group's Internet forum, told me, 'At the time, the other sides were just supporting their teams with their fists. They were just mobs. We decided to create something different, something a lot more cultured. We began using banners, flares, chants and so on. We were heavily influenced by both the more spontaneous Italian style of supporting, as well as by the traditional English way.'

Above Wolverhampton Wanderers take on Spartak Moscow 'Under the banner of Marx, Engels, Lenin and Stalin'
© Getty Images

Right Lavrenty Beria – Secret police chief, sadist and Dynamo Moscow fan
© Getty Images

Below The USSR national side in the 1980s – 'The good old days'
© PA Photos

Above left Andrei Kanchelskis focuses on the ball © PA Photos

Above right The 'Iron Fist' Oleg Romantsev keeps his ears warm
© Tim de Waele/Corbis

Below Russian football hooligans show their displeasure at the national
side's 1-0 defeat to Japan at the 2002 World Cup © Getty Images

Above Terek and Ramzan Kadyrov celebrate the Chechen side's
2004 cup victory © AFP/Getty Images

Below CSKA's Vagner Love heads for goal
© Stephane Reix/For Picture/Corbis

Vladimir Putin
marks CSKA's 2005
UEFA Cup triumph
with a display of
presidential
ball skills
© PA Photos

Life after Chelsea -
Alexei Smertin (right)
celebrates a goal at
Dynamo
Moscow
© Getty Images

Guus Hiddink
takes a stroll
on Red Square
shortly after
becoming
Russian coach
© Getty Images

Spartak Moscow take on Slovan of the Czech Republic in a 2006 Champions League qualifier
© William Bennetts

The author (head bowed) under the watchful eye of the Russian authorities at one of Dynamo Moscow's more poorly-attended games
© Jo Bennetts

Lenin awaits Steve McClaren and Co at the Luzhniki ahead of Russia and England's vital Euro 2008 tie in Moscow
© Marc Bennetts

Above Guus Hiddink's Russia look to the future © Getty Images

Below England train in the Moscow chill before their 2-1 defeat to Russia in October 2007 © Marc Bennetts

Lokomotiv fans
celebrate a goal
against CSKA
Moscow
© Dmitry Dudenkov

Dynamo Moscow's
Petrovsky Park
hibernates
© Dmitry Dudenkov

Lev Yashin
eternally defends
the honour of
Dynamo Moscow
© Dmitry Dudenkov

Left It's only the pros who take the winter off in Russia. (Moscow State University in the background)
© Dmitry Dudenkov

Below A few months on, the Luzhniki reflects on the national team's October 2007 victory over England (The Luzhniki from 'Sparrow Hills')
© Dmitry Dudenkov

Nevsky Front, although now a well-known St Petersburg institution that likes to make clear the distinction between hooliganism and fandom, had little choice, however, in the early 1990s at least, but to combat fire with fire.

'We realised that travelling to away games was a risk, and so we formed units of guys who knew how to fight, tough guys, mainly in their late teens to early twenties, with plenty of energy, and they became our warriors, so to speak, at away matches. Still, we had the hooligans under control at that point. It all got out of hand a bit later, when Zenit made it through to the final of the Russian Cup in 1999. Half the city went to Moscow for the final. There were so many fans who just got on trains, hitched lifts, anything. The young kids though, looking for trouble, sensed that they had power, and things have never been the same since.'

After my interview with Advocaat, I got into a conversation with the club's security officer, the man responsible for ensuring the safety of Zenit's players and officials. Having heard that I was writing a book about Russian football, he asked me if I would be interested in meeting up with some representatives of Zenit's organised hooligan element. After a series of phone calls, I eventually met up with Slava, and we went to the local sports bar to talk. 'That guy, the Zenit security officer, he's FSB (formerly the KGB),' said Slava almost immediately. 'He's not one of us.'

So why had he put me in touch with an organised hooligan group?

'I guess he just thought it would be interesting for you, for your book,' answered my new acquaintance, shrugging. However, the truth is that in Russia there is a clear link between the security services, nationalists and football hooligans, and I was not really so surprised.

Slava was in his mid-twenties, and as pale as the St Petersburg sky. 'By day', as he put it, he was a clerk in a local bank. 'Zenit has never had a black player in the team. Not one, in its whole history,' he told me as we took our seats. I got the feeling he expected me to be in some way impressed.

Of course, for seventy-odd years of the club's existence, the absence of coloured players was hardly surprising, as the USSR Championship was entirely made up of Soviet citizens.

Nevertheless, since 1991, in a country where players from Africa, South America and the Caribbean were becoming a common sight, Zenit had remained, as Slava put it, 100 per cent white.

'The club has always had an unofficial policy of not buying coloured players, partly because the administration has always been in favour of this, and partly because they have always known that the fans would be against it. I mean, since Advocaat has been at the club, Zenit have bought a few Korean players, and some people have stopped going to the stadium. If he buys coloured guys, I don't know what the reaction will be. I really can't say. Nothing good will come of it though.'

A club spokesman denied that Zenit had ever operated such a policy, yet this is of little consequence. What matters is what the fans think of the club. With the arrival of Advocaat, clearly no racist, a confrontation may soon be on the cards.

St Petersburg is a city of startling contrasts – the cultural capital of Russia, the birthplace of some of its finest writers and artists, and the centre for the burgeoning nationalist movement.

In recent years, the city has gained the reputation as one of, if not the most, dangerous for non-whites in Russia. Attacks, sometimes fatal, on coloured residents and tourists take place on a regular basis. Citizens of the USSR's former Middle Asian republics are likewise targets for the city's skinheads and nationalists, the most shocking example being the murder of a nine-year-old Tajik girl by a group of white-power fanatics in 2004. While the city – and, indeed, the Russian – authorities make all the right noises about combating the rise of far right-wing groups, there has never been a serious commitment on their behalf to educate the population, or seriously punish the perpetrators of hate crimes.

The 2007 season saw Zenit shake off some early-season blues to claim the Russian title for the first time since the collapse of the Soviet Union, ending more than a decade of seemingly unbreakable domination by Moscow sides.

The city on the River Neva went out of its mind with joy, just as Advocaat had predicted, celebrations continuing all night long as Zenit fans ran riot in the city's legendary and sumptuous Metro stations, smashing chandeliers and wrecking escalators.

'Without a Hint of Green', Zenit fans' banners had taunted CSKA in 2006, yet there was little doubt that Gazprom's decision to invest in the club at the expense of CSKA had made the difference, lifting Zenit to heights it could have only dreamed of in the bad old days of Russian football. A golden plane took Zenit's players to Moscow for the final game of the 2007 season, flying them back again for the post-match celebrations after a 1–0 victory against Saturn had assured the club of the title.

'Today is a historic day for St Petersburg,' Gazprom chief, Alexei Miller, told journalists at the city's Pulkovo airport as fans gathered to greet the team. 'This is just the beginning,' he went on. 'The time has come to write a new chapter in the history of St Petersburg football. The capital of Russian football has made a move to St Petersburg.'

'We have waited twenty-three years for this,' said the city's mayor, Valentina Matviyenko, as the side did a lap of their home stadium. 'And now we can say, "Zenit are the champions!"'

'We have joined the ranks of clubs like CSKA, Spartak and Lokomotiv, and now Zenit will battle for the title every season,' said Advocaat at a press conference.

No one was entirely certain, however, if Advocaat would be around to witness this 'new chapter in Russian football'. The Dutchman's contract was due to expire, and he had reportedly signed a preliminary agreement with the Australian FA, agreeing in principle to lead them through their 2010 World Cup campaign.

However, after Zenit's title success, Advocaat had already begun to hint that Champions League football and a reported £2.5 million-a-year deal would go some way to persuading him to remain in Russia's pre-Soviet capital for just a little while longer. 'We are already thinking about the future,' he said.

Indeed, less than a fortnight after Zenit St Petersburg and Gazprom had wrestled the Russian league title away from CSKA and the capital, Dick Advocaat put pen to paper with Zenit, extending his contract by a year. The Australians, with a little over two months to go until the their first 2010 World Cup qualifier, were furious, and launched a compensation claim against the Dutch trainer, as well as attempting to have him disqualified by FIFA.

Advocaat spoke of his decision to remain in St Petersburg at the end of the 2007 season, telling a press conference, 'I had wanted to stay at Zenit at the beginning of the season, but the fans weren't too pleased with the way we began. I said then, "If we don't win the title, I'll leave." But now, after becoming champions, everything has changed.'

A couple of weeks after winning the league, Zenit flew to England for a UEFA Cup tie against Everton. The newly crowned Russian champions wrongly had a man sent off after half an hour, and eventually lost 1–0. 'We don't need that UEFA Cup, anyhow,' a Zenit fan told me after the game. 'It's still covered in the CSKA players' spit from 2005. The 2009 Champions League Final is our aim.'

'The Russian Chelsea' the Russian media had called Zenit, and while it was a convenient moniker, it could do nothing to disguise the fact that, despite the wages on offer, Zenit would continue to struggle to attract players.

In November 2007 the captain of the Egyptian national side, Ahmed Hassan, turned down a $3 million a year move to Zenit, saying by way of explanation, 'It would be very hard for me to play in Russia. It's very cold there, and I can't take it. I don't want to take any risks.'

His words, with minor variations involving crime, racism and corruption, were ones that Zenit and Advocaat had become used to hearing. This was not the first time, and certainly not the last, that money had failed to convince a player to pack his bags and make the move to Russia.

But perhaps money wasn't the be-all and end-all. There were other things in football that counted for more, as club president Sergei Fursenko pointed out in an interview after Zenit had claimed the title. 'Money isn't everything in football,' he told the

Russian *Izvestiya* newspaper. 'The philosophy of the game and strategy are. Money is just the means by which they are realised.'

For the head of a club based in one of the world's most literary and atmospheric cities, it was a fitting statement to make and, taking into account Dynamo Moscow's utter failure to capitalise on the millions invested in the club, contained more than an element of truth.

I took the midnight train back to Moscow, sharing a four-berth cabin with a well-spoken grandmother and her small grand-daughter. Lying on the top bunk, I stared out of the window as we pulled out of the train station, the train rocking gently from side to side, giving the buildings shimmering past an oddly askew look.

St Petersburg had once been the Russian capital, the Bolsheviks only moving the government to Moscow after the 1917 revolution. There had been, of late, growing calls for its former status to be returned. Moscow, supporters of the idea maintained, was just too big, its streets gridlocked, its citizens growing fat and lazy. Transferring the capital of the Russian Federation to the 'Venice of the North' would give St Petersburg a boost, while the mass exodus of government officials would free Moscow up to concentrate on what it did best – make money.

In some ways, the process had already begun, and the colossal injection of funds into Zenit was a clear indication of this. In Russia, football teams are dependent on the goodwill of big business and government, and Zenit's upturn in fortunes was a clear signal that President Putin's birthplace was currently enjoying the position of 'most favoured city'. Even if the proposed transfer of power did not take place, St Petersburg was, undoubtedly, on its way up.

Perhaps, I mused, it would be Zenit who would prove Arsène Wenger right, taking the Champions League by storm, forcing the world of football to sit up and pay attention to Russia? Would St Petersburg, centuries on, and in a way he could never have imagined, finally turn out to be the 'Window to Europe' that Peter the Great had intended it to be?

CHAPTER EIGHT

Professor Hooligan expounds

'Countless as the sands of sea are human passions.'

Nikolai Gogol

I had travelled to St Petersburg to investigate the other side to the Muscovite dominance of the country's football, and I had found a lot more than I had bargained for. True, in Zenit I had discovered a team with ambition and the financial backing to match, but I had also scraped the surface of the country's growing hooligan problem.

Football is, of course, more than a sport. It is also violence and mass disorder, crowd disturbances and intolerance. The Russian variety of the world's favourite pastime is no different. Although football hooliganism existed in the USSR, it was not widespread. Today, however, as the game has recovered from the nadir of the early 1990s, 'firms', modelling themselves on English or, less frequently, Italian models, have mushroomed. The biggest 'fixtures' take place between the Moscow sides, fights erupting all over the city after virtually every derby. The phenomenon is not confined to the capital or St Petersburg, however. All across the Russian Federation, every team has its own firm, its own group of hardcore hooligans ready to defend their side's honour with fists, bottles or knives.

I met Vadim, or 'Sirop' (Syrup) to those who know him well, at a bar in the southeast of Moscow at the start of 2007. The founder of Flint's Crew, one of Moscow's most infamous hooligan firms, Vadim was a fanatical Spartak fan, albeit one clad in a nifty Liverpool FC jacket.

I had expected him to be shaven-headed and semi-articulate, yet my expectations were confounded. Long-haired, around forty years old, he was as passionate and opinionated about the very concept of football hooliganism as some people are about fine wines or ballet.

'Strange as it may seem, the first hooligans in Russia,' he told me, 'were hippies. It was around 1973, 74, and anything that guys could get their hands on from the West became immediately popular and fashionable. First they found out about The Beatles and all that stuff, from magazines smuggled into the country, and then, a bit later, about football hooligans. You look at the old photos of the first organised hooligan gangs, and they all have long hair and patched jeans. Actually,' he added, laughing, 'one of those guys, one of the original Soviet football hooligans, became a priest later. I tracked him down not long ago. He was paying off his sins, I suppose.

'You know,' he went on, 'there is a real football hooligan boom in Eastern Europe right now. Even though it's over fifteen years since the collapse of the USSR, there is still that feeling that the youth have something to prove. After living in what was essentially a prison for so long, these young hooligans want to flex their muscles, to show the world, England in particular, that anything you can do in a hundred years, we can do in ten.'

Vadim was a great admirer of the English football hooligan scene, and told me the story of how in 1996, during the disturbances in Trafalgar Square following England's semi-final defeat to Germany at the European Championships, he had been in England and recorded events on a video camera.

'Some of your guys, hools, big guys, came up to me, and said, "What you doing?" I explained that I was recording the action to show our lot back in Russia how to be real hooligans, making a kind of "how to" study guide, and they said OK and took me with them, stuck me up on one of the lions, and I filmed the whole thing from there. I was,' he went on proudly, 'the only person to tape the riots from the hooligans' side. Look at the BBC footage, you'll see me.'

Russia had been in the midst of an economic crisis at the time, and I wondered how Vadim had managed to afford to travel to the UK for the month-long tournament.

'Easy,' he said, shrugging, 'I sold my flat.'

At the time, a flat in Moscow would have gone for some £15,000. In 2008, the minimum price for a one-bedroom flat in the centre of Moscow was around £100,000. I couldn't help feeling his decision had been somewhat flawed, from a financial point of view at least.

However, notwithstanding Vadim's admiration for and dedication to English hooliganism, the truth is that, despite the media hysteria that inevitably accompanies English fans abroad, the English hooligan movement has undoubtedly had its heyday.

Vadim shrugged. 'I've heard the Ecstasy theory, that the guys got into acid house, and all that, and just mellowed, but I don't buy it. I think that it happened because the authorities began to relate to the fans better. I mean, they improved the stadiums and everything, stopped treating the fans like animals. It's all a matter of collective responsibility. If there are a thousand people, and they are herded into stadiums, treated like shit, then fifty start to fight, the other nine hundred and fifty are going to join in. But if they are treated well, allowed to watch the game in civilised conditions, then when those fifty begin to cause trouble, the other nine hundred and fifty will just turn their backs. In Russia, we still have the former situation. In England, you have, now, the latter.'

Vadim's argument was persuasive, and he was certainly the first football hooligan I had heard use the term 'collective responsibility'.

Another hooligan I met in Moscow (a member of another of the city's biggest firms, but who preferred to remain, as he put it, 'incognito'), had this to say on the subject of the decline and fall of English hooliganism. I shall call him, for convenience's sake, 'Gosha'.

'Liverpool came to Moscow in 2003, but they were nothing. Not serious opponents for us. Basically, in recent years, British fans have just shouted a lot and chucked bottles. I was at the 2006 World Cup and saw how they behaved. They'd find a camera, chant, wave their fists and run off. Ridiculous. In Russia, there is nothing of the sort. When two groups of fans meet, they get right down to business, and fight until the opposing fans are either on the floor, or run away. It's the same all over Eastern Europe right now. We respect the English tradition of hooliganism, but we no longer fear them. They are weak, right now, compared to Russia, Poland, Serbia and so on.'

Patriotism can sometimes be an insidious thing and, while having never been involved in football hooliganism (or, indeed, having considered myself a patriot), I felt an absurd need to defend the honour of my fellow countryman. I pointed out that real British football hooligans had problems travelling these days, and that football hooliganism itself was no longer so popular in the United Kingdom, that many of the fans they had fought had been just that – businessmen and family men following their teams around Europe.

'Lots of the guys in my firm are the same,' countered Gosha. They have their own businesses, kids, but, nevertheless . . .'

Nevertheless, indeed.

'The biggest problem for Russian football hooligans,' he went on, 'is not that they might take your passport away, but that you will simply be refused a visa. Russians need visas to go to most European countries and I, for example, know that I am extremely unlikely to be granted a visa in the near future. I've been in prison abroad too often – in Spain, in France, in Turkey, in Norway,' said Gosha, listing the countries he had done time in.

Russian football fans, even now, after all the changes that have taken place in Russian society, have almost no rights. A hangover from Soviet times, they are forbidden to celebrate goals too raucously, soldiers occasionally wading into the crowd to drag out the rowdier elements. At a recent match in Rostov, Lokomotiv fans, tickets in hands, were refused admission to the stadium, because police were standing in their places, having felt it necessary to occupy sections of the terraces in order to deal with any potential trouble. Upon protesting, pointing out that they had travelled around 500 miles to get to the match, and had already paid for their seats, they were set upon by the police and a pitched battle ensued. Questioned by the Russian media about his men's behaviour, the head of the local police was unrepentant, and warned Rostov's future opponents that their fans would 'face the same thing'. 'It'll take a long time for things to change here,' Vadim had said during our meeting.

There was something slightly incongruous in all this, I thought. Vadim was no monosyllabic thug; he was nothing at all like the popular media image of a football hooligan. So why did he need it? Why was he, in essence, a hooligan? He had, as he himself told me, eyes glinting at the memory, led fans into battle, helped organise mass street fights. I had recently re-read Bill Buford's *Among the Thugs*, and I recalled his theory that hooliganism is a substitute for sexual release. However, I didn't particularity want to get into the issue of Vadim's virility, and so instead settled for asking him why he was so proud to be a hooligan, exactly what it was he found in the act of violence.

'Firstly,' he began, as if he had been anticipating the question, 'the British and the Russians are very similar. When we are not technically at war, we need some conflict, as we say in Russia, *voinushka* – 'a little war'. Something to get the blood up. Secondly, a football club is a nation, and the hooligans are its army. You ask any of these respectable fans what they think about hools and they will say that they are awful, and so on. But ask them if they would like to see us disappear, and they say 'no, no'. They know that they need us to defend them from the other teams' hooligans. We are a form of mutual deterrence,' he explained, 'just like nuclear weapons.'

Gosha had his own explanation.

'Yeah, it can be a problem sometimes, being a hooligan, especially one that the police have on record,' he commented. 'I mean, they can come to your house, "invite" you down to the station for a chat. But, well, it's like an illness. I just can't resist following my team to away games, and testing myself against opposition fans.'

Being a hooligan, or just a supporter, in Russia and following your team around the country is a trial of both stamina and determination. As a fan in St Petersburg put it, 'In England, yeah, the longest a fan is going to have to travel to an away game is from the south to the north, from Portsmouth to Newcastle, for example,' he said, showing off his knowledge of English geography. 'That's about four hundred miles, right? In Russia, for Zenit St Petersburg fans at least, that's the shortest journey. Most of the time, travelling to an away fixture means two days on the train. But it can be more. Three, four days. To Vladivostok, it's eight days by train.'

When, in 2005, CSKA lifted the UEFA Cup, fights erupted across the capital as Spartak fans launched a series of assaults on celebrating CSKA supporters. While the rest of Russia had put aside club differences to cheer on CSKA, many Spartak supporters had openly rooted for Sporting Lisbon. When the final whistle blew, the bitter truth sank in. It was CSKA who had put Russia firmly on the European map, not Spartak, and that hurt. Spartak, it was true, had reached the semi-finals of the Champions League, the UEFA Cup and the old Cup Winners' Cup under Oleg Romantsev, but they had never managed to make that final step, had never appeared in a European final, let alone claimed a major

European trophy. Someone, it stood to reason, was going to suffer for that.

As one Spartak hooligan told me, 'That night, we stormed a CSKA bar in the north of Moscow. CSKA fans were in there drinking, celebrating, and we took them completely by surprise. The police turned up pretty quickly though. They had to fire into the air to break up the fights.'

At the beginning of March 2006, the Russian season opener, the Super Cup, between Spartak and CSKA, was marked by some of the most violent encounters yet. The two sets of fans met in a series of arranged meetings throughout the city. The largest gathering took place in the north of the capital, outside the '1905' Metro station, a combined six hundred fans charging at each other from opposite sides of one of Moscow's busiest roads. There were many injuries, some of them serious.

'We never go to the hospitals after these fights,' Gosha told me, 'not unless an injury is particularly bad. I mean, a broken arm or leg, or something. Even then, we usually go home and wait, then go to the nearest medical centre and make up some story about falling over.'

The media reaction to the mass confrontation after the CSKA–Spartak derby was extremely odd to say the least. The broadsheet *Izvestiya*, at one time known for its relatively objective reporting, ran an article detailing the history of battles between the two groups of fans, listing the victors in each encounter. The paper even went as far as to give the nicknames of some of the more infamous hooligans involved, documenting the brawls without the slightest hint of condemnation. 'According to the majority of eyewitnesses, *Izvestiya* concluded, 'CSKA's fans were triumphant, putting an end to the series of defeats they had suffered the previous year.' All in all, it was an edition for the football hooligan's scrapbook.

In the USSR one of the most popular pastimes for young men (and some women) was '*Stenka na Stenku*' or 'Wall on Wall'. This consisted of the youth of two areas – an English analogy would be

New Cross and Peckham in London – meeting at an arranged point and assembling themselves into two lines, or 'walls'. They would then walk towards each other, and the aim was to take out your corresponding number in the opposing 'wall' by any means necessary. People were routinely maimed, or even killed. Although cases of *Stenka na Stenku* still occur in Russia today, the pastime took a dramatic nosedive in popularity in the late 1980s.

My mother-in-law, 66-year-old Tamara Nikolayevna, told me that, 'In Soviet-era Belarus, in the years after World War Two, the guys from my village, Dubovka, would go and fight with the guys from the neighbouring village, Savichi. They would carry long poles, and stand in two lines, facing each other, whacking each other with these sticks. People would get crippled; there would be blood everywhere. The women and children from each village would come and cheer on their men. "Come on, give him what for!" we would yell.'

And, I wondered, did the police get involved, make arrests?

'No, no,' she replied, laughing. 'At that time there was only one policeman for every four villages. What could he do?'

Eventually, however, the Soviet authorities cracked down on *Stenka na Stenku*, imposing a ban in the mid-1950s. 'They wanted to draft guys into the army, you see, but half of them were suffering from injuries from *Stenka na Stenku*,' Tamara recalled. 'Still, it continued, of course.'

Stenka na Stenku has its roots in traditional medieval Slavic village games popular on the territories of modern-day Russia, Ukraine and Belarus. The basic idea has not changed much down the centuries. In fact, if a surviving set of rules is anything to go by, the earlier form of *Stenka na Stenku* may have even been more organised than the modern version.

(a) Those combatants who have been knocked down are not to be judged a part of the fight.

(b) Fighting shall be carried out face-to-face, chest-to-chest. There is to be no entering the battle from the sides.

(c) There is to be no swapping sides.

'Football hooliganism just replaced *Stenka na Stenku*,' Vadim told me. 'Up to then, there was no focus to the violence. Football just provided that focal point. The whole scene is just an extension of *Stenka na Stenku*. It's like I said, we always need a little war.'

I had seen some of this ruthlessness at first hand on more than one occasion. Russians tend not to bother with prolonged 'c'mon then, go ahead' build-ups when involved in street fights, but rather get straight down to business. They also regularly supply champions of the semi-legal 'Fighting without Rules' competitions, held in Moscow and other cities of the former USSR.

'Like FIFA,' a St Petersburg hooligan told me, 'we have the concept of "Fair Play" – that is, fighting exclusively with your fists. There is, of course, the opposite, "Unfair Play", the main proponents of which in Russia are Dynamo Moscow. They killed a young fan a few years ago, and since then we have hated them with a passion.'

Nashi are a political youth movement with strong ties to the Kremlin. The youth organisation has its origins in the *Idushie Vmeste* ('Walking Together') movement, which gained notoriety in 2001/02 for organising book-burnings of 'offensive' or 'morally repugnant' works by modern Russian authors, such as Viktor Pelevin and Vladimir Sorokin. Nashi, however, do not go in for book-burning, and are more concerned with organising pro-Kremlin and pro-Putin rallies.

Although Nashi declares itself to be an anti-fascist movement, it is an open secret that the group's leaders hold racist and nationalistic views. It is likewise no secret that Nashi's security is supplied by skinheads, many of whom have ties to hooligan movements with strong connections to racist groups.

In 2006, it was reported that a top Nashi member, Aleksei Mitryushin, was the head of a CSKA fan club, while two more Nashi members were said to be in charge of a Spartak Moscow fan club. Indeed, reports surfaced in the Russian fringe press in the summer of 2005 that some of Nashi's football hooligans had been present at a meeting between the youth organisation's leaders and Vladislav Surkov, an aide in the Putin administration.

In 2005, the then-Nashi leader Vasili Yakemenko announced that he would, and indeed could, were such a thing to ever occur in Russia, have brought in football hooligans to deal with political demonstrations such as those that had led to the Orange Revolution in Ukraine in late 2004.

'I would have contacted my colleagues in the Spartak fan movement and they would have assembled five thousand of their supporters to chase away those who came out onto the streets of Kiev in support of the Western-backed politicians,' he said.

In late 2007, after Nashi had held rallies and marches in support of the pro-Kremlin United Russia party, which took some 65 per cent of the vote at that year's Russian parliamentary elections, Yakemenko was rewarded for his loyalty and efficiency with a position on a ministry committee on youth affairs.

There are those in Russia who believe that racist and nationalist groups are being formed by, and with the assistance of, the Kremlin, in order to provide the powers that be with a viable 'enemy' if the need should arise (for example, to frighten the population with a 'fascist threat' before elections).

'It is a fact, it's not even concealed,' Ruslan Dubov at *Novaya Gazeta* told me, 'that the president's administration finances Nashi, who, in turn, finance hooligan elements. If, say, it is to the government's advantage to have a large-scale disturbance somewhere, money that Nashi and other "fascist" organisations receive from the Kremlin is simply used to pay skinhead gang leaders to make sure that things kick off.'

Vadim was sceptical when I asked him about it. 'I know these guys, the leaders of mobs who are also members of Nashi. But it's blown all out of proportion by the press. The truth is, just because some Spartak fans support Nashi, doesn't mean they all do. Some are into the communists, some Putin, some are apathetic. We try, basically, to keep politics out of the scene. Try not to get used.'

Football hooliganism's big day in Russia came during the 2002 World Cup, when downtown Moscow was engulfed in an orgy of violence that broke out following the national side's 1–0 defeat to Japan.

There was a political subtext to the 9 June match, one that the usual rabble-rousing nationalists had had no hesitation in bringing to the public's attention. The uncomfortable fact was, and is, that Japan and Russia have never signed a peace treaty to formally end World War II because of a dispute over four islands, known to Russia as the Kuril Islands and to Japan as the Northern Territories. The USSR occupied the islands towards the end of the war and Russia still, to this day, controls them. Although both countries have been making conciliatory gestures over the last decade or so, the issue remains unresolved, mainly as a result of the outbursts of patriotism that erupt whenever the matter is brought up.

The authorities had decided to erect a huge screen in the centre of the city, in Manezh Square, a short walk from Red Square, and by the time I arrived a huge crowd had already assembled. I even saw a few Japanese. I had heard that their embassy had advised its citizens to stay at home, fearful of the repercussions in the event of their nation taking its first-ever European scalp. Perhaps, I figured, despite their creditable 2–2 draw with Belgium in their opening encounter, they just didn't rate their team's chances.

Russia had won their opening game against Tunisia 2–0, and another victory against the hosts would have seen them progress to the play-off stages for the first time since the break-up of the USSR. Oleg Romantsev was in no mood to throw caution to the wind, however, and had stuck to a defensive formation, relying on ageing Spartak players.

Japan were obviously primed for the match; roared on by the crowd of 66,000, their opening passes and runs at the Russian defence immediately silenced a significant section of the crowd gathered in Manezh Square. The Russians were a lumbering force, unable to deal with the agile Japanese midfielders, and making very little progress towards the opposing goal.

And then, inevitably, Japan scored. A diagonal ball was played into the penalty area. Yanagisawa diverted it into Inamoto's path and the midfielder took one touch before hammering the ball into the net past Ruslan Nigmatulin.

In Moscow, Manezh Square reacted badly to the goal. The crowd began booing and, before long, bottles were being hurled at the screen. Vladimir Beschastnykh had the chance to save the situation a few minutes later by levelling the score, but he put his shot wide of an open goal from a few metres out. Russia were doomed. We all sensed it. The bottles started to fly in greater numbers. Some of them were still half full, sending vodka or beer raining down on the heads of those in front of them. Girls started to scream.

I made a move, pushing my way through the crowd. There was ugliness in the air, the unmistakable scent of violence. I was reminded of the Poll Tax riot in London in 1991 that I had been caught up in. There was the same sense of unloosed rage. Except here there was no clear enemy, and the source of discontent was not hiding behind the Downing Street gates, but was being played out on a football field halfway round the world.

I headed off towards the Metro, but the crowds around the entrance were too large, and I was forced to turn back and set off in the direction of the main street, Tverskaya, where there was another station. And then the final whistle blew.

Mobs of drunken fans began pouring up the street, kicking at windows and shaking the expensive cars parked nearby. A girl staggered past me, bleeding from a head wound, the blood soaking through her 'Rossiya' T-shirt.

The police moved in, but they were outnumbered by the waves of allied skins and drunks. I saw a cop taking a kicking, a few well-placed blows to his head rendering him unconscious, and later I would wonder if he had been one of the afternoon's reported fatalities.

A nearby car was set alight, and then another was overturned. I felt suddenly worried for the Japanese we had seen, and hoped they had had the good sense to get out of Manezh Square after their countrymen had scored. A teenager walked past, brandishing one of the poles that had been used to hold the Russian tricolour aloft during the game. I caught his eye for a moment, and he smiled, flashing me a toothy grin before hurling it through the window of a nearby boutique. I watched him, expecting him to go in and grab some stuff, but he seemed to have no interest in looting.

I wondered for a second how many of the fans knew that Russia still had a chance at the World Cup, that defeat to Japan had not meant the end of the team's participation in the tournament? Russia only had to draw with Belgium in their final game to go through. That wasn't such a colossal task, surely? (In the event, it turned out it was, Russia going down 3–2 to Belgium on 14 June.)

The next day, the news reports began. There was some confusion as to the exact number of fatalities. Was it two, or one? And what about the attempted suicide that *Sovetski-Sport* was reporting? Was this true? An Associated Press photographer had seen a mutilated corpse lying on the street during the chaos, and police later confirmed a man had been knifed to death. A drunken fan had driven his car into a crowd, running down three pedestrians. The Interior Ministry was, however, denying reports that a policeman had been killed.

What was known was that there had been at least one death, that more than seventy people had been hospitalised, nineteen of them in a serious condition, and that one hundred and thirteen people had been arrested. Crowds had also gathered near the former KGB headquarters, now home to the renamed FSB, and begun setting light to cars there.

And then the conspiracy theories began. The Thursday before the game, parliament had given an initial reading to a so-called 'anti-skinhead' bill to crackdown on extremism, whose legal definition under the new law would include 'hooliganism'. It was suggested that those close to power, in order to ensure the bill would pass, had orchestrated the violence. Critics of the bill maintained that it wasn't aimed so much at the growing skinhead element, as at demonstrators, protestors and political gatherings. Indeed, the extremely low amount of police on duty coupled with large groups of football fans with easy access to alcohol was either a blinding oversight on someone's behalf, or a stirred and shaken Molotov cocktail. It was, the conspiracy theorists muttered, just another example of the authoritarian turn that President Putin's reign was taking.

'You know,' said Vadim, 'there were no real football hooligans at the riot after the Japan game. They were just drunken teenagers, and FSB officers. Putin needed something to crack down on, to prove his "hard man" credentials. There were no hools there, because the police had warned us not to go. They'd called up all the known "faces" and said that anyone caught there would do three years, no questions. The whole thing was orchestrated by the FSB. They were the ones who started breaking windows, burning cars, etc. Then the teenagers and other drunks joined it. That kind of thing, it doesn't take much to get it going.'

Football hooliganism and racism are invariably linked, and in Russia even more so. Since the split-up of the USSR, with every passing year racist attacks have become more and more frequent. In 2007 the Russian media reported that teenage race-hate gangs may have been responsible for over fifty murders in Moscow alone that year.

'We'd never really seen black people before in the USSR, apart from as diplomats or students,' Vadim told me. 'For people living in the provinces, there were, really, no coloured people at all. For the older generation of football fans, in particular, it is a really staggering thing to see coloured guys from Tunisia, from Mali, or wherever, playing for sides like CSKA, Spartak and Dynamo. These clubs are Russian institutions and, I don't know, it's difficult for you to grasp probably, but it really was, and continues to be, a culture shock.'

I was in the Russian supporters' end for a Euro 2004 qualifying match against Ireland. 'Look,' said the guy next to me, pointing at one of the Irish players, 'they must have got citizenship for that one. A naturalised Brazilian or Cameroonian probably.'

I wanted to tell them that the 'Brazilian' was Phil Babb, that he had been born in England, that his mother was Irish, and that there were quite a few black Irishmen. But I couldn't be bothered. It was too loud, and I didn't feel like shouting my explanation over the noise of the crowd. I understood where he had got the idea from though. There are a minuscule amount of black Russian citizens. The vast majority of them are the result of encounters between African students and native Russians.

In 2000 the former Spartak defender Jerry Christian Tschuisse almost became Russia's first coloured international. He would have undoubtedly been a valuable asset to the Russian national team, plugging a hole in their leaky back four. The process of naturalisation usually takes about seven months, and the requirements are fairly strict. For Tschuisse, however, the whole procedure was sped up, some say with the personal intervention of President Putin himself. A month after applying, Tschuisse had his citizenship in his hands. However, it turned out to be a case of 'thanks, but no thanks' as Tschuisse had a rethink, accepting an ill-timed offer to join up with the Cameroon squad. And thus Russia was denied its first black international.

There are quite a lot of black footballers in Russia these days. They mainly come from South American, African or Caribbean countries. Since the oil boom, they can expect a salary considerably larger than they would receive playing in their own leagues. The downside is the racism prevalent in Russian society and, accordingly, football. The situation was so bad by 2005, with regular attacks on coloured footballers, especially in Moscow, that some teams were forced to hire bodyguards to protect players from their own fans.

Andrei Bikey, the former Lokomotiv defender now playing for Reading in England, had bad memories of his stay in Russia. 'Russia has a different mentality,' the Cameroon international told the English media. 'For a person with black skin it is very hard to live there. There is racism. In England it is better: it is possible to walk along a street without being hassled. The Lokomotiv fans are fine but when we played against other teams, racism is everywhere, especially when playing against Spartak. Nevertheless, the police will not protect us. Once, I was followed by three guys, but I managed to escape. In order to protect myself, it would even have been necessary to get a weapon,' he stated.

'There is no racism,' asserted Vadim, 'we just want young Russian players to get a chance in teams. That's why we have to set these African players straight, that's why our guys beat them up. For every black footballer who comes to Russia, a young Russian player loses out. Club presidents just think, "Well, it's cheaper to hire a black guy from Africa, so I'll do that." That's why the national team performs so badly. There is no one to choose from. It's not their skin colour that bothers me, but the fact, as I've said, that they take Russian lads' places in the teams.'

So, following this line of logic, were he and his mates likely to attack any of the Slavic players from, say, Serbia or the Czech Republic currently keeping 'Russian lads' on the major clubs' benches?

Vadim shook his head, 'No, no, you see, it's all a mass-media thing. Fascism, racism, they are fashionable words, but it's not as simple as that.'

He hadn't quite answered my question, and I doubted he could. I thought back to my childhood, to the 1980s, to the days of Cyrille Regis, Laurie Cunningham and Viv Anderson, to the first coloured footballers ever to play professional football in England. I recalled the monkey noises that had greeted them at stadiums all over the country, and the debates and the disbelief when Anderson became the first black player to pull on an England shirt. If the process of adaptation had been a slow and tortuous one in England, then in Russia it would be far, far more painful.

In England, the first black footballers had sprung from English society: they were representatives of the first generation of Afro-Caribbean males to come of age in Britain, and it was inevitable that some of them would end up playing for their local professional teams. Had they not, there would have really been something seriously wrong with British society.

The coloured footballers turning out for Spartak, CSKA and so on every weekend are, for those Russians who have never been abroad (the vast majority), truly and utterly alien. Many of them will have never spoken to a coloured person; all of them will have grown up with racist jokes and stereotypes as the norm. Many of my acquaintances in Russia – educated, intelligent people – are capable of the type of casual racism that I doubt I will ever grow hardened against. It will take a long time for the Russians to grow used to seeing black faces, and not only on the football field. Until they do, the prospects for dark-skinned footballers remain bleak.

In 2002 the Russian football authorities, under pressure from UEFA, launched a half-hearted campaign to 'Stamp Out Racism', including an annual match between the Russian national side and the foreign 'legionaries'. However, with hardly any chance to practise before the game, the hastily gathered team of foreigners invariably suffered heavy defeats, doing little to dissuade the skins and nationalists of the validity of their racial superiority theories or to diminish the increasingly noticeable 'Russia for the Russians' slogans. The friendlies were discontinued in 2005.

In the middle of the autumn of 2006, Spartak fans, faces masked, unfurled a swastika at an away match against Shinnik in Yaroslavl, one of Russia's oldest cities. 'The swastika, it was just picked up by the mass media,' Ruslan Dubov at the *Novaya Gazeta* newspaper told me, 'but the whole skinhead thing has been growing for a while now, and is continuing to do so.'

A week after the swastika incident, marches took place across Russia, ostensibly for National Unity Day, but hijacked by crowds of extremists and skinheads. The Russian Football Federation made an appeal for football fans to stay away, but it was hard to judge exactly which of the shaven-headed marchers was a football fan, hard to judge the effectiveness of the appeal.

Chidi Odiah, CSKA's Nigerian defender, like most Nigerians in Russia, speaks excellent Russian. After CSKA's visit to Putin's out-of-Moscow residence following the team's UEFA Cup victory, he was interviewed by a Russian TV reporter.

'What were your impressions of the president?' asked the reporter.

'I just remember thinking I've never even seen the leader of my own country, and here I am with the President of Russia.'

'And do you remember his name?'

Odiah stared at the journalist for a moment.

'What?'

'Do you remember his name?'

'Look, you don't understand me, I knew his name beforehand.'

The TV reporter was stunned. That a black footballer who had been living in Moscow for a few years should know the name of the President of the Russian Federation! Truly, times were changing.

'I get a lot of journalists asking me for interviews,' said Vadim. 'From England, Germany, Switzerland. I spoke to some guy from an English newspaper not so long ago, but they totally mixed up everything I said. They wrote that Russian hooligans love to chant, "You're gonna get your fucking heads kicked in", as a tribute to the English hooligan scene.'

I had also read that interview and been, to put it mildly, surprised. English is not a second language for most people in Russia, let alone football hooligans.

'They get a lot of things wrong. Still, they pay well,' said Vadim, laughing.

(In case you are wondering, Vadim declined to take my cash. I was, he said, 'a good guy'.)

Both Vadim and, to an extent, Gosha, were a puzzle. There had been much talk of a poorly educated, inarticulate and aggressive underclass fermenting in Russian society, open to manipulation by the ruling powers. The football hooligans, or so the theory went, were ripe for deployment as 'shock troops' in order to counter any future social unrest.

However, the hooligans (and this was the term they used to refer to themselves) that I had met clearly did not fit this model. Aggressive, without a doubt, but poorly educated and inarticulate they were not. At least, they had not appeared that way to me. In a crowd, however, in the midst of their firms, I imagined both Vadim and Gosha would be entirely different prospects.

For me, the most poignant moment of the riot that followed Russia's defeat by Japan came the day after the match. The Russian NTV television station was continuing reports from the scene of the clear-up operation, and I watched as a journalist interviewed a driver standing next to the charred remains of his Saab. Indignant, dragging his gaze away from the carcass of his beloved vehicle, he stared straight into the camera, his face twisted in equal measures of anger and sorrow. 'They are just pigs, these so called "fans",' he began. 'I know that these things happen in England, but to think that it could happen here, that's just so painful'.

CHAPTER NINE

Chechen champions

'Over the rocks the Terek streams, raising a muddy wave.'
Mikhail Lermontov, *Cossack Lullaby*

My journey into Russia's hooligan scene had proven to me without doubt that football in Russia was intimately bound up with politics. An indication of this is the frequency with which President Putin's name crops up in this book (seventy, if you are interested). In comparison, I can't help but wonder how many mentions Gordon Brown would get in an equivalent tome dedicated to the English game.

In Russia, football is open to hijack by political forces looking to use the game for their own ends. As the country's most popular sport, it is the ideal place to make political points, reaching out to, and attracting the attention of, those segments of the population usually apathetic towards such matters.

Despite the loss of large swathes of territory that the break-up of the USSR entailed, Russia is still an extremely ethnically diverse country, more so than most people imagine. As a result, ethnic conflicts constantly simmer, boil over and erupt in sporadic outbursts of violence.

One of these ethnic groups, the Chechens, has been battling against Russia since the seventeenth century, revolting against the armies of Catherine the Great and Alexander I. Although colonial rule was eventually established following the capture of the Chechen leader Imam Shamil in 1859, Chechnya was never entirely pacified.

In 1944, after falsely accusing them of collaboration with Nazi forces, Stalin ordered the entire Chechen population exiled to Central Asia, to the harsh lands of the Kazakhstan steppe. Many died on the journey and in the first few months, as the Chechens struggled to come to grips with the harshness of their new surroundings. The survivors were eventually allowed back to Chechnya in the late 1950s, after Stalin's death.

The accusations of collaboration with the Nazis were particularly cruel, even by Stalin's standards. Thirty-six Chechens were awarded the title of Hero of the Soviet Union for bravery shown as Red Army soldiers during WWII, and indeed, as many historians would later point out, the Nazis had failed to even make it as far as Chechnya during the war.

Not unsurprisingly, there existed widespread resentment of the Russian authorities amongst the Chechens upon their return to their homeland, and as perestroika took hold in the USSR, calls for independence from Moscow grew louder and louder. These demands were finally answered in late 1991, when the charismatic ex-Soviet Air Force General Dzhokhar Dudayev, who had spent the first thirteen years of his life in exile in Kazakhstan, seized control of the republic, declaring it independent.

In 1994 President Yeltsin ordered an invasion of Chechnya in order to, ostensibly, restore Russian control over the region. However, witnesses later said that Yeltsin was drunk that night, and had demanded a 'small victorious war' that would improve his ratings before the not-too-distant elections. The ensuing conflict was vicious and brutal, with atrocities and heavy losses on both sides.

It was in 1998, during my second year in Russia, that I realised the extent to which the average Russian loathes Chechens. 'You have to understand, Marc,' a doctor acquaintance told me, 'that all Chechens are killers. It would be best to exterminate them all.'

'All of them?' I asked, as we drove through the centre of the city.

'All of them,' replied the doctor, carefully stopping for a red light.

Around the same time as this conversation was taking place, Vladimir Zhirinovsky, the leader of the extreme right, confusingly named Liberal Democrat Party, suggested that the best way to solve 'the Chechen problem' would be to drop an atomic bomb on the whole region. His suggestion was met with enthusiasm by a large section of the Russian public, the only subsequent snag being that it would be impossible to prevent the radiation drifting across the borders of the Chechen Republic.

Terek Grozny FC, named after the river that flows through the Chechen capital and onto the slopes of Mount Kazbek, were formed in 1946. However, in the mid-1990s the team was forced to disband due to the escalating violence in the Chechen Republic. Despite the continuation of hostilities, the side re-formed in 2000 and a mere four years after rising from the ashes, Terek lifted the Russian Cup.

Khaider Alkhanov's promise had come true. In late 1999, Alkhanov, the then Minister of Sport of the Chechen Republic, by way of persuading the Russian football authorities to grant Terek a licence to re-form, had declared with what sounded like insane optimism that, 'Within a year, maybe two, Terek will be playing in the UEFA Cup.'

The train from Grozny pulled into Paveletsky train station in south Moscow early in the morning of 29 May 2004. The fact that a train from Grozny was arriving in Moscow was an event in itself, but what was even more remarkable was that it was carrying supporters from that war-ravaged city to watch their team play in the Russian Cup final. The journey had taken more than 24 hours. The fans were, at least, used to travelling.

As it's not really a good idea to hold football matches in one of the world's most brutal war zones, Terek are forced to play their 'home' games in Pyatigorsk, in the Russian North Caucasus. To get to the stadium, supporters have to negotiate their way through military checkpoints in Chechnya, and then travel through three North Caucasus republics – Ingushetia, North Ossetia and Kabardino-Balkaria, none of these places exactly holiday resorts either. North Ossetia, for example, is where the Beslan tragedy took place in September 2004. It makes, you have to agree, the average London fan's complaints about an away game 'up north' pale in comparison.

A reported 8,000 Terek fans had made their way to the capital, where they were met by OMON troops, Russia's special forces, specially trained to deal with terrorism and hostage crises.

The fans, at any rate, had paid no attention to Chechen rebels' taunts that the team was a mere propaganda exercise by the Kremlin, intended to show that life was returning to normal in Grozny. In fact, Terek (or 'Terek Kremlin', as the insurgents prefer to call the team) were, and are, tremendously well supported in Chechnya, the very fact of the club's existence considered something of a miracle in itself. The fans, having watched their team get to the final, spectacularly knocking out Premier League sides on the way, were hoping now for an even greater miracle – to take the Cup back to Grozny.

Terek's opponents were Krilya Sovetov, from Samara, and the hot favourites. Terek were, after all, a First Division outfit, albeit with a so far almost perfect record in that league, and Krilya were a Premier League team who could boast Andrei Karyaka, the division's top scorer.

'Ah! We're not worried about Karyaka,' said Arslan, a former resident of Grozny, now living in Moscow, and who would be attending the match with me, 'we've got Fedkov!'

Andrei Fedkov, Russian Premier League top scorer in the 2000/01 Championship, with a handful of caps to his name, was playing his first season for Terek. A perpetual provincial-team journeyman, his career had never really taken off. But now, at the age of 32, he had the chance to lift his first trophy. Fedkov was typical of many of the ethnic Russian players who had been drafted into the Chechen side. Most of them were over thirty, and had been discarded by teams from the elite of Russian football. This was their opportunity to prove that they still had something to offer.

But perhaps it was just as well that the team wasn't entirely made up of Chechens. Vait Talgaev, Terek's Kazakh manager, had once complained that one of the problems with coaching a team of Chechens was that the respect they had for their elders could be an disadvantage on the football field. He cited examples of young ethnic Chechen players, finding themselves with a scoring chance, failing to shoot because an older player was also in a favourable position, electing to pass the ball in acknowledgement of the senior player's status.

'I always tell them, "If you can see the goal – shoot! Don't worry about if an older player is nearby. Just shoot!" It's hard to imagine, for example, Wayne Rooney having the same problem upon spotting, say, Michael Owen lurking in the penalty area.

By the time of the cup final however, following a number of successful transfer bids for experienced Russian players, there was not a single Chechen left in the Terek side, something which only gave fuel to the critics' claims that the club was a mere political project, Chechen merely in name.

In early 2007, nearly three years on from the cup final, I put these criticisms to Bulat Alanov, a successful Chechen business-men and Moscow resident, who had fled Grozny in the late 1990s. An acquaintance of an acquaintance, Bulat had taken a big shine to Terek, and his office was plastered with their pennants and posters. He even had a Terek tie that, he told me, he had had specially made.

'How many Londoners are there in Arsenal?' he asked me. 'Very few,' he went on, not giving me time to reply. 'Does this make Arsenal any less English? Any less of a London side? This,' he continued, as his secretary brought in a teapot full of sweet green tea, 'is modern football, it is the same everywhere.'

There was no arguing with his point, but then, I put it to Bulat, Arsenal are not held up by the British Government, as Terek are, as proof that the political situation in southern England is stabilising, returning to normality after a long period of brutal warfare. Arsenal may be full of foreign stars, but they do, at least, still play in north London, and have strong ties to the area. Terek were, at the time of our last conversation at least, based hundreds of miles away from the region they supposedly represent.

'You know how many young men have died in the war in Chechnya?' asked Bulat, fixating on my first point. 'Thousands,' he continued as I tried to come up with a figure. 'Maybe amongst them was the Chechen Pele, or the Chechen Maradona. Who knows? We will never find out.'

It was a convincing argument, yet the simple fact is that Chechens have never really been great footballers. They excel at wrestling and judo, but football has never really been their forte. I declined to mention this though, sensing that Bulat would not react well.

Before the cup final, in the cafés around the stadium, those Chechens who had made their way independently to the match were sitting around waiting for kick-off. It is, in fact, extraordinarily hard to distinguish Chechens from some of their North Caucasian neighbours. However, the women employed in the cafés, fore-warned of the arrival of large numbers of Terek supporters, were exceptionally jumpy, eyeing the clusters of dark-skinned supporters with undisguised apprehension. In Moscow, in Russia, the word 'Chechen' is almost synonymous with 'terrorist' and from the looks on their faces you could see they were expecting a bomb to go off at any moment.

The women's concerns were more than understandable, how-ever. It was less than a month since a blast had claimed the life of Akhmad Kadyrov, the Kremlin-backed president of Chechnya, during May 2004 Victory Day celebrations at the Dynamo stadium in Grozny. The bomb, planted by Chechen rebel forces, had torn through the VIP stand, killing President Kadyrov and six others, despite heavy security in the stadium and in the streets around it. Given that Akhmad Kadyrov had also been Terek's president, and that Ramzan Kadyrov, Akhmad's son and the club's new president (and then the Chechen deputy prime minister), was scheduled to attend the match, it was not unreasonable to expect another attack.

I wondered, however, if the women would have felt any less nervous had they known that Shamil Basayev, the notorious rebel leader who had claimed responsibility for the Victory Day massacre, was an avid football fan, and had even been the head of the Chechen Football Association in 1998? It seemed unlikely, somehow, that he would attack a football match, but the Moscow authorities were taking no chances, the streets around the stadium full of gun-toting soldiers and tough-looking cops.

We made our way into Cherkizovo Stadium with just under an hour to go until kick-off. To be honest, I wasn't really sure who I was rooting for. A Terek victory would be like a fairy tale come true, and it would be fun to watch Russians' reactions to the news that a team from Chechnya had won the Cup. A defeat for Krilya would also have been a pity though: the team played attractive, attacking football, and they, like Terek, had never won anything. The game was the first time for seventeen years that the final would be taking place without the appearance of a Moscow team. In the end, I decided I would just attend the match as a neutral, supporting only, as the Russians are fond of saying, 'beautiful football'.

Once inside, we made our way to our seats. Perhaps due to the fact that no Moscow teams were playing, Cherkizovo was about half full. It is, after all, over a thousand miles from Chechnya, and a good five hundred from Samara.

I looked in the direction of the VIP box. I was pleased to see that it was quite a safe distance away, just in case any bombs started flying, but there was no sign yet of Ramzan and his ubiquitous bodyguards. We were in the end reserved for the Chechen supporters. Not far from us there was a huge banner featuring the smiling face of Ramzan's dad. On the other side of the stadium was another banner. This one read: 'Death to Chechen Terrorism'.

A minute's silence was announced for Akhmad Kadyrov. He was the fourth Chechen president to be killed since the break-up of the Soviet Union. That's an average of about one every three years, which kind of made me wonder why anyone would want the job in the first place.

In Russia, as in many other countries, such silences are not always observed. After the death of Pope John Paul II in 2005, at one of CSKA's UEFA Cup matches in Moscow, a large proportion of the crowd burst into chants of 'Orthodoxy! Orthodoxy!' when requested to pay tribute to the leader of the world's Catholics, as if the two branches of Christianity were nothing more than rival teams with a long history of grudge matches.

Krilya, as befitted their higher status, had most of the ball in the first 45 minutes, but couldn't find the breakthrough they were after. Terek looked content to sit back and hope to snatch a goal on the break. To be honest, it was pretty tedious stuff. Both teams were, understandably, nervous and this was reflecting on the game. It was only the occasion itself that was making the match into something worthwhile. Half-time came and went, and we were deep into the second half when Krilya suddenly burst into life, hitting the woodwork twice. The Terek fans around me looked anxious. Could it really be that Terek were going to blow it? To get all this way and then lose, that would be too much to take. Better to have lost in the semifinal!

Krilya continued to dominate. Ten minutes left. Karyaka got into a good position, but again wasted his chance. And then another open goal went begging. Maybe luck was on Terek's side after all?

Injury time. The prospect of extra time, and then a penalty shoot-out. Denis Kedluev picked the ball up inside Terek's half, looked up and, seeing Fedkov unmarked, played a through ball to him. Fedkov was one-on-one with the keeper. Terek's very own goal machine glanced at the keeper rushing out to meet him and, with the most delicate and casual of touches, lobbed the ball over him, into the net.

There was a split second of silence while that image burned into everyone's head. The ball in the back of Krilya's net. Fedkov leaping with joy, the keeper sprawled on the ground – 1–0 to Terek! With less than a minute remaining! The stadium, the Chechen half at least, erupted.

Krilya restarted the game, but it was clear that they were finished. The team from Samara tried to surge forward, but it was too late – before they had managed to launch another attack, the referee blew his whistle for full time.

On the pitch, it was pandemonium. Ramzan Kadyrov was there, and so was Khaider Alkhandov, the man who had promised glory when Terek hadn't even existed. The Terek players unfolded a huge banner of the late Akhmad Kadyrov, taking it on a lap of the stadium. They then grabbed Ramzan and began throwing him up and down in the air in celebration, a bit like the birthday bumps without the kicking. Ramzan's security forces, numbering several thousand, have been accused of torture and abduction in the Chechen republic. He denies the allegations. I didn't know what truth there was in these claims, but I just hoped the Terek players wouldn't drop him. One should always be careful around people who own private armies.

As Cup winners, Terek had earned the right to take part in the UEFA Cup. I wondered who their opponents would be. Millwall had also qualified for the competition by finishing as runners-up in the FA Cup, and a tie between representatives of the nation that has been at war with Russia in its various guises for the last 500 years or so, and the nutters from the Den seemed like quite an enticing prospect. But why stop at Millwall? Anything was possible.

Real Madrid! Manchester United! Barcelona!

Any of these teams, if they failed to get through the group stages of the Champions League, could have found themselves up against Fedkov and co.

'I dedicate my goal to the Chechen people,' said Fedkov,

immediately after the match. Which, if you stop and think about it, was quite a remarkable thing for a Russian footballer to say.

Of course, there would now be the question of where the UEFA Cup ties would take place. There had been talk of constructing a new stadium in Grozny, but even if it was ready for the opening round it seemed highly unlikely that UEFA would allow any team to travel there. Glasgow Rangers had in 2001 successfully appealed against travelling to Makhachkala, the capital of Dagestan, a republic ostensibly at peace, when they had been drawn against Anzhi, the local team.

Although UEFA initially insisted that the game go ahead in Makhachkala, Rangers refused to travel, their chairman saying in a statement, 'Having fully considered the decision from UEFA this morning advising that the match against FC Anzhi should proceed in Makhachkala, Rangers have responded that a team cannot at this time be sent to Makhachkala for safety reasons.'

Dagestan was just too close to Chechnya, it seemed, and the fact that car bombs had gone off near the stadium in the days before the match was due to be played had understandably unnerved the Scottish club. The Anzhi vice president couldn't see what the problem was, however, saying that extra security would be drafted in for the match, and that: 'We think that Rangers will like it here in Dagestan and they will be satisfied with everything.'

UEFA eventually agreed with Rangers, however, switching the match to Warsaw, and deciding that the tie be played over one leg instead of two. (For which, incidentally, Glasgow Rangers gained the reputation of snivelling cowards throughout the entire Caucasus region.)

'Now I understand why Scots wear skirts!' a Dagestani friend commented at the time, notwithstanding the fact that there were about as many Scots in that multinational Rangers team as there were Dagestanis. Rangers won the game 1–0.

A new stadium was being built in Grozny because, or so the story went, President Putin had recently flown over the city in a helicopter and been shocked by what he had seen. He had then ordered that reconstruction projects be undertaken immediately.

It's not clear what he was expecting to see in a city that had been subjected to the heaviest bombing since World War II, but, anyway, he'd ordered a stadium. And in Russia, the president usually gets what he wants. It was to be named in honour of Akhmad Kadyrov.

The season finished in November 2004, with Terek in first place, earning promotion to the Premier League. They had become the first team ever in the history of that league to gather over a hundred points, and, until the final few matches when, already ensured of promotion, they had fielded weakened teams, had had an almost perfect record.

The top scorer at the end of the season? Andrei Fedkov, with an incredible 38 goals in 42 matches. And the UEFA Cup? Well, Millwall didn't come, but Terek beat Lech Poznan of Poland before going out to Basel, the Swiss champions, over a close two-legged tie. The 'home' games were all played in Moscow, in Cherkizovo once more. There were again trains from Grozny, except this time it was the start of a regular service between Moscow and the Chechen capital, the first for years.

The rebels' 'Kremlin Terek' snipes seemed to take on greater significance when Terek were invited, in honour of their victory, to the Kremlin to meet the president. During the meeting, President Putin congratulated the team on helping to bring stability to the region, and presented the side with a sabre that had once belonged to Akhmad Kadyrov.

After the Cup victory, plans to hold Terek's end-of-year celebration ceremony in Grozny were abandoned due to predictable security risks, and the event took place in another Chechen city, Gudermes, in December 2004. There was something about that celebration that soured the whole Terek story for me. Before that I had, if not exactly supported the team, then been sympathetically inclined towards them; it was too much like one of those childhood football films or books I had been so keen on; something like a cross between *Escape to Victory* and *Roy of the Rovers*, with Fedkov in the role of Roy Race leading his band of Premier League cast-offs to cup glory in a hostile land. The rebels' taunts seemed distasteful somehow. Terek were, after all, just a football team, and claims that the side was merely a Kremlin propaganda device spoiled a good story.

But then, reading about the award ceremony in Gudermes, in the 'Ramzan' sports complex, the team being showered with awards and prizes, including thick envelopes stuffed with cash personally presented to them by Ramzan Kadyrov himself, and the announcement that Andrei Fedkov was to have a street named after him in Chechnya, I started to go off the idea of Terek as peace-bringers from the Chechen war zone. The romance began to fade, and what was left was just a bunch of ex-Russian internationals (for the Russian players, the event in Gudermes was the first time they had ever set foot on Chechen territory) and the odd token Chechen, receiving vast amounts of cash from the republic's budget.

But still, despite all this, I couldn't entirely condemn the players. After all, they were just pawns in the larger political picture, and they all had families – wives, children, parents – it would have been ludicrous to expect them to turn down the chance of one final payday.

Things, as they so often do in Russia, had turned out to be a lot more complicated than they had appeared at first.

The rumours and whispers began even before Terek's Kremlin visit. Krilya Sovetov had received $7 million to throw the game, went the allegations. The authorities had needed to show that life in Chechnya was returning to normality, and had been willing to do so at any cost.

In a way, even though there may have been no truth in the claims, it made sense. The fuss made over Putin receiving the victorious Terek team in the Kremlin had been quite unprecedented. Chechnya was an important project for the Kremlin, and sport, football, was just a part of it. Propaganda plays out at all levels, and what better than the nation's favourite pastime to get the message across that the war had been won in Chechnya, and that, as President Putin would regularly proclaim with great pomp for the next few years, only the 'mopping up' remained.

'Terek were on the news all the time [before and after the cup victory], if you remember,' a *Novaya Gazeta* journalist told me. 'Chechnya and football. It sounds a lot better than Chechnya and war, I'm sure you'll agree.'

So why did the team not build on their success?

'They had fulfilled their duty, and they simply weren't needed. That was why they went down again the very next season. With no one to buy results for them, with an ageing squad, it was obvious they would have trouble staying up.'

'Perhaps,' Vasili Utkin told me, a few weeks after becoming the voice featured on the Russian version of the FIFA soccer computer game, 'the Kremlin took advantage of the situation. It's possible that when the team had reached the semifinal, a decision was made to make the most of the situation. But, really, you should speak to Ramzan Kadyrov about that.'

Utkin contacted the Chechen leader for me, but Kadyrov was reluctant to be interviewed by an English writer about the beautiful game.

Terek's first season in the Premier League was an unmitigated disaster. Fixed games or no fixed games, the club invested little in new players, relying heavily and unrealistically on the ageing Fedkov to continue scoring at the same phenomenal rate in the top flight. The one acquisition they did make, however, was of real quality.

In 2005, the goalkeeper Ruslan Nigmatulin, Russian Sportsman of the Year in 2001, signed a contract with the Chechen team. Nigmatulin's career was at something of an impasse at that point. After having left Russia in 2002 for Italy, he was unable to pin down a place in the starting line-up at Verona and eventually returned to Russia, to Lokomotiv, but found himself on the bench again, covering the new national team keeper, Sergei Ovchinnikov.

When the offer from newly promoted Terek came, Nigmatulin, hailing from the Russian Republic of Tatarstan, accepted, saying that he hoped he could help his 'Muslim brothers'. After Terek were relegated at the end of the 2005 season, Nigmatulin quit football. He was just 31 at the time, an unusually young age for a goalkeeper to retire, especially one who, just four years earlier, had been touted as one of Russian football's brightest prospects.

I met up with the ex-Spartak, CSKA and Lokomotiv goalkeeper in a café in the centre of Moscow. He was absorbed in his laptop when I came in, and smoking a cigarette. I expressed surprise that he was a smoker. Was this a recent thing, perhaps a pleasure he had decided to allow himself after leaving the world of professional sport?

'No,' he said. 'A lot of players smoke, it's no big thing.'

That cleared up, I asked him why he had taken the decision to quit. I got the impression he had been asked this a lot recently. 'I decided to leave football because I didn't want to play in the First Division again. Basically, I felt that it would just be downhill from that point. I'd achieved a lot, played at the World Cup, for example, and came to the conclusion that it would be better to stop while I was still ahead.'

We talked of Terek, and it was immediately plain that the subject was a sore one for Nigmatulin, and that he would have preferred to talk about the acting career he was attempting to build. 'I've been for some casting. I see myself in the role of a lover,' he confessed. I turned the conversation once more to Terek. Nigmatulin, to give him credit, answered my questions in detail.

'Terek just weren't ready for the Premier League,' he said, taking a drag on his menthol cigarette. 'Everything was poorly organised. I mean, the training sessions, the delays in the payment of salaries, the entire infrastructure.'

I knew that the club had been financed from the republic's budget, but I wondered if Ramzan Kadyrov had also invested in the team. By the time the interview took place, Terek's headman had become the prime minister of the Chechen Republic, second only in authority to the president. He was, however, reportedly de facto running things, and looking to assume eventual control of the war-stricken region.

'As far as I understand, yes. He supported the team. Came to the matches, training sessions.'

How then to explain the delays in the payment of salaries? Money was set aside for the team, and Kadyrov, a well-off man, had made a personal investment.

'Perhaps it was some kind of punishment? We played pretty badly. Maybe they deliberately withheld our wages?'

It was becoming more apparent that Nigmatulin was extremely uncomfortable discussing Terek. 'Look,' he said, 'really this is a very unpleasant topic for me. For an English book, I'm prepared to talk, but, really, I try not to answer questions on this theme.'

I pushed on. How involved was Kadyrov with the team? Had he yelled at them, say, when they lost?

'Of course.'

Being screamed at by a man with thousands of former Chechen rebels at his command sounded like a pretty terrifying prospect, and I didn't imagine that it was the kind of thing that Nigmatulin as a young up-and-coming footballer had ever imagined he would have to face. He didn't complain about it, though. At least, not to me.

Midway through the season, Terek, frustrated by a perceived prejudice on the part of Russian referees, had drawn up and sent a letter to President Putin. The letter complained that they were being discriminated against, that penalties were being unfairly awarded against them, and appealed for the president to intervene. As can be imagined, this only made matters worse. Despite having a vested interest in Terek ('Every day that Terek play in the Premier League is another day that the Kremlin can point to stability in the area,' *Russian Newsweek* had written), President Putin, understandably, declined to interfere, and Terek's players were mocked and taunted as snitches at stadiums around the country.

'I only found out about that from the newspapers,' said Nigmatulin. 'I have no idea whose idea that was, but it was, well, to bother the leader of the country with such a thing . . . football is only a game after all. It was ridiculous.'

Before the 2005 campaign began, there were worries that a team representing the Chechen republic would have problems in their travels around the country, that it would be a red flag to the growing nationalist and right-wing movement.

'I had the feeling that we weren't exactly loved. There was a war going on in Chechnya,' Nigmatulin replied, 'and people shouted at me that I was betraying Russia by playing for a Chechen team.' He shrugged. 'But look, I'm a professional footballer. I play for the team that I play for. I don't concern myself with political matters. That said, there are a lot of Chechens in Moscow, and they came to all the matches to support us when we played Spartak, or CSKA, or whoever.'

Had he ever been to Chechnya itself, ever paid a visit to the land that Terek represented, the republic on whose behalf the team had claimed the 2004 Cup?

'No, never,' replied Nigmatulin. 'Fortunately.'

2007 saw Terek earn a second chance at top-level football, claiming the runners-up promotion sport in the First Division. Despite the fact that life in Chechnya was calmer than it had been since the outbreak of fighting in the early 1990s, sporadic violence continued, and there seemed little chance that the 2004 Cup winners would realise their dream of playing home matches in Grozny for some time to come.

Ramzan Kadyrov became Chechen president in 2007, the former boxer bringing an Iron Fist to bear on the Caucasus republic, pledging loyalty to Moscow and United Russia, the pro-Kremlin party that would subsequently sweep aside all rivals at that winter's parliamentary elections. In Chechnya, where Kadyrov had promised an overwhelming victory for United Russia, the party took some 99 per cent of the vote.

Terek applied to begin the 2008 season in Grozny, and incredibly, despite militant activity in the region, the Russian Football Federation granted the side permission to host Premier League football. Russian football fans began to nervously plan their away trips to the Chechen capital.

'Ramzan Kadyrov has promised to find the kind of sponsors that will ensure that Terek will want for nothing,' the republic's Minister of Sport told *Sport-Express*. It remained to be seen, however, if Terek's second season in the Premier League would bring them more success than their first.

'Say what you like about Terek,' Bulat Alanov had told me, just before I left his office, 'but I'll tell you this, the fighting stopped on cup final day in 2004. The rebels, even if they hated the side, put down their guns and went looking for the nearest TV. See, only football has that power, and it works its magic everywhere, even in Chechnya.'

Even though the Terek story was far removed from the football I had grown up with, where rebel leaders and war zones were not exactly everyday fare, Bulat's observation about the Chechen separatists putting aside their weapons to watch the cup final proved that, in some respects, Russia was not so different after all. Russia, even its combat zones, was under the spell of football, hopelessly lost in the beautiful game, all other concerns secondary when compared with the miracle that is match day.

CHAPTER TEN

New rope for new times

'The capitalists will sell us the rope with which we will hang them.'
Vladimir Ilyich Lenin

Russia is desperate to attract foreign stars to its Premier league, and money is no object. As a result, every month the papers are filled with rumours that eventually turn out to have little grounding in reality. 'Ronaldo is coming to Dynamo!' 'Luis Figo has signed a contract with FC Moskva!' scream the headlines for a couple of days before the truth is finally revealed.

Despite the salaries that the leading Russian sides can offer, as Dick Advocaat at Zenit pointed out to me, top players are still reluctant to sign contracts with Russian clubs. Russia suffers from an appalling image problem that, until altered, will undoubtedly remain the stumbling block to real, lasting success. When, or if, this mental block is removed, Russia will have a real chance of becoming the new centre of European football power. That is, if oil prices don't plummet first.

At the beginning of March 2006, the Scottish international Garry O'Connor signed for Lokomotiv Moscow from Hibernian for a fee of £1.6 million, and a reported £70,000 a month, becoming the first British player to conclude a professional contract with a Russian club in the process. Roman Abramovich, it was true, had attempted to send Joe Cole to CSKA on loan in 2003, but the Chelsea and England midfielder had refused the move. O'Connor had no such qualms, and arrived in Russia towards the start of the 2006 season.

Even by the standards of the English Premier League, O'Connor's wages seemed unnecessarily generous for a player who had made just six international appearances. Hibs manager Tony Mowbray said that, while not wanting to lose a player of O'Connor's calibre, he had not stood in his way. 'The personal terms proposed are exceptional and will simply be life-changing for Garry and his family,' he told the club's website.

O'Connor, it was true, was not a real star, no Figo or Ronaldo, yet as an import from the birthplace of football, his arrival was taken as an indication in Russia that things were at least moving in the right direction. If, the logic went, a Scot could be tempted to leave the 'civilised' world of Britain and British football, then surely it would not be long before bona fide stars were playing week in, week out all over the Russian Federation.

Russians have always had a deep respect for British, and in particular English, football, even during the Cold War. Although they have rarely gone so far as to practise the British long-ball game, its influence is apparent to anyone who attends a match, or opens a newspaper in Russia. Fans parade around in Union Jacks, and English football is hotly discussed on the pages of all the sports magazines. Indeed, for communicating with the police and other officials in Russia, English football is the lingua franca. Personally, I can recall countless occasions when I have been able to defuse potentially nasty situations by getting into a conversation about Chelsea's chances in Europe with a bribe-hungry Russian cop.

Immediately after having signed for Lokomotiv, the Scottish international made all the right moves, getting his name on the scoreboard in only his second game, a 2–2 draw with Spartak Moscow in the quarter-finals of the Russian Cup, and even promising to learn Russian, although for starters he gave interviews in a thick Scottish burr that had the local journalists scrambling for translations from their equally bemused interpreters.

The former Hibs striker's third game in Lokomotiv's ranks was an away match against Luch Energiya, from Vladivostok, in the Russian Far East, a gruelling sixteen-hour plane flight to the match and back, passing through numerous time zones. However, to be a success, mammoth plane journeys were not the only thing O'Connor would have to cope with.

Lokomotiv Moscow's history can be traced back to 1923, when the best footballers of the Moscow railway service were brought together in the side Klub Im. Oktyabrskoi Revolutsii, or 'Club of the October Revolution'. In 1935 Lokomotiv was formed, most of the players coming from this team. In Soviet times they were spectacularly unsuccessful, spending much of the 1980s in the Second Division. It was only after the fall of the USSR that Lokomotiv's fortunes began to look up. Their sponsors, the Russian Railway Ministry, built them a glistening 30,000-capacity stadium, and in 2004 they became the first side apart from Spartak to claim the Russian title twice.

Traditionally cursed with extremely low (even by Russian standards) crowds, Loko began to attract more fans with their attacking football and youthful set-up, and by 2006 were the best-supported Moscow side apart from Spartak. In 2005 the club brought in their first-ever foreign manager, Slavoljub Muslin, a Serb who had previously managed sides in Belgium, France and Ukraine. As a fellow Slav, the reasoning went, he would find it easier to adapt to life in Russia than the Italian, Brazilian and Portuguese trainers who had failed so miserably at Spartak, Dynamo and CSKA.

Although O'Connor was widely reported to be the first British footballer ever to play for a Russian side, this was not in fact entirely accurate. He was, as the more pedantic of my friends in

Moscow pointed out to me, actually the first to play *professional* football in Russia. In the 1960s, Jim Riordan became the only Briton to play for a Soviet football team, turning out for Spartak Moscow. Having joined the Communist Party at university, he was sent to Moscow, where he reportedly made the acquaintance of double agent Guy Burgess. Noticed by Spartak scouts at a kickabout, he was drafted into the Spartak team as a central defender. He played for the side from 1962 to 1965 and received the nickname 'Chopper', presumably for his no-nonsense defending and trademark British tackling. It was Riordan who introduced Alexei Smertin to the late novelist John Fowles during the player's stint at Portsmouth.

O'Connor was a regular in the Lokomotiv starting line-up until early August 2006, when he lost his place in the team to Dramane Traore from Mali. The Scot's performances up to this had been solid enough, but his goal rate was miserly, with just five goals in twenty matches. Considering that he had been bought to solve Lokomotiv's traditional goal-scoring problem, the fact that he was lying behind the midfielder Dmitri Loskov in the overall goal tally was indication enough that he had, so far, failed to meet expectations. Slavoljub Muslin had little choice. O'Connor was out, his appearances restricted to the odd cup match, and coming on as a substitute.

The same month that O'Connor was relegated to the bench, I attended a Lokomotiv training session at the team's Cherkizovo stadium, and afterwards was introduced to the Scotsman. He was open enough, and promised to find time for an interview in the following days, giving me his telephone number. I called, as arranged, but O'Connor's wife informed me that Garry would be unable to keep his promise, as his agent had ordered him not to speak to the press. It turned out that the Lokomotiv striker had recently given an interview to a Russian journalist, who had then written, inaccurately according to the Scottish international, that O'Connor preferred life in Moscow to that in Edinburgh. The reason? In Moscow there was not so much attention from the fans.

The article went on to say that O'Connor had labelled the Hibs fans 'parasites'. O'Connor also denied this, however.

Despite O'Connor's reluctance to speak, I arranged an interview with Dmitri Sychev, Lokomotiv's young striker, and set out the next day for the team's out-of-town Moscow camp. I hadn't, it suddenly occurred to me, riding the bus through the Moscow rush hour, made it clear to O'Connor that I was an English writer, not a Russian journalist. If the occasion presented itself, I could rectify matters. It was to my fellow countrymen that I was looking to convey my passion for Russian football, after all, and a British face in amongst all the unfamiliar names would only serve to make my tale easier to digest.

I arrived in Solnochni Gorod (Sunny City), and set about trying to catch a car to Lokomotiv's training camp. The system in Russia works like this: due to the lack of official taxis and the need of most of the population to earn a bit of extra cash, the quickest way to get from A to B is to stick out your hand. It's quite simple; you stand by the side of the road with your arm outstretched, much like the Lenin statues that dot the former Soviet Union, and wait for a passing vehicle to stop. You then negotiate your price with the driver, and off you go.

You can meet some interesting people that way. Once, in Moscow, I met the brother of the Azerbaijani linesman who ruled in favour of Geoff Hurst and England for that crucial third goal in the 1966 World Cup Final against West Germany.

'It wasn't a goal though, was it?' I asked, perhaps unwisely. 'I mean, the ball never crossed the line.'

'Of course it was, modern technology has proven it!' came the indignant reply.

I eventually settled on a price with a passing driver, and we set off. I had agreed to meet Dmitri Sychev at the training camp at eleven, and at two minutes to the hour we were still searching for the right turn-off. After coming across a soldier who supplied us with exact directions, we proceeded to hurtle down a muddy path at breakneck speed. I prayed that we wouldn't hit a pothole; the race for the title was proving to be the hottest for years, and shuffling off this mortal coil before the season has reached its conclusion has always seemed like a terrible way to die to me.

Fortunately, we made it to the training camp intact. It was summer, yet the weather in Moscow was distinctly unseasonable, dark rain clouds lurking above the training pitch where the Lokomotiv players were limbering up, a harsh wind racing up and down the length of the fence that separated us from the outside world.

'Come at eleven a.m.,' the press attaché had stressed, 'and don't be late!'

So there I found myself, a few minutes after the designated time, watching O'Connor and co jogging around the pitch. I had assumed that 11 a.m. was the appointed hour for my interview with Dmitri Sychev, yet Alexander Udaltsov, the side's press attaché, had obviously presumed that witnessing one training session hadn't been enough, and that it would be necessary for me to attend a second.

Lokomotiv had been having real troubles scoring of late, and Slavoljub Muslin had clearly decided to practise the fundamentals. Time after time, a winger or midfielder would run down the side of the pitch, cross the ball, and there one of the forwards or attacking midfielders would hammer the ball towards the net. The only hitch was that they just couldn't do it. With no defenders to obstruct them, a mere quarter of shots ended up on target. I started to feel a touch embarrassed, as if experiencing something that I shouldn't be privy to, an unwilling witness to some dark family secret. Accordingly, I made my excuses, and went to examine Lokomotiv's trophy cabinet.

The training centre is also where the players spend the two days before games, and everywhere there were signs requesting guests to be quiet between two and four o'clock in the afternoon, the footballers' nap time, or 'quiet hours'. The concept of the 'quiet hour' comes from the Russian kindergarten system, where children are forced, tired or not, to sleep after lunch. Wandering around the training centre, I couldn't quite shake the image of rows and rows of footballers in cots, thumbs in mouths, snoozing before the next vital fixture.

The Lokomotiv players tramped in after their training session. Garry O'Connor was there, but we didn't speak. I was already feeling uncomfortable, as if I had somehow intruded, paparazzi-like, on his privacy. He glanced in my direction, but didn't acknowledge my presence. Alexander came up to me and asked if I had arranged anything with O'Connor. I explained the situation. He thought for a moment, and then went over to the Scottish international.

'They're just trying tae stitch me up, like!' yelled O'Connor.

Alexander seemed to speak English well enough, but I doubted very much if the phrasal verb 'to stitch someone up' was part of his vocabulary. Especially when spoken in a gruff, no- compromise Edinburgh accent.

O'Connor continued, 'An' I don't know why they wanna talk to me anyway, I'm not even in the team!' And that was that.

O'Connor had given a few interviews before clamming up, and basically, the sum of these was that he thought Moscow was a great city, that he wasn't studying Russian yet, that he missed his friends more than he missed Edinburgh itself, and that he thought Lokomotiv were a top team. He hadn't known much about Russia, the country, or its football teams before deciding to sign a contract with Lokomotiv, but he had found out some vital facts on the Internet before putting pen to paper.

After quitting professional football in 2005, the ex-Terek and Spartak keeper Ruslan Nigmatulin tried his hand as a football agent. Although he is now out of the business, he was involved in O'Connor's transfer.

'Garry is a good player,' he told me, 'but soft.'

Soft?

'Yeah, soft. He needs hardening up. It's hard for him, he misses Scotland, but he's not the only foreigner here, and he's being more than adequately compensated for his exile.'

How had his move to Moscow come about?

'I'm no longer an agent, you understand, but I was involved in the transfer business for a while. Originally, Lokomotiv were interested in Derek O'Riordan, O'Connor's team-mate at Hibs, but he wasn't too keen on moving to Russia. So I sent Lokomotiv some videos of Garry in action. They liked what they saw, flew over, and a deal was struck.'

Could it be that the language barrier was the root of all of O'Connor's woes?

'Well, there are a lot of players at Lokomotiv who speak English,' answered Ruslan. 'More or less, anyway. But, yeah, it's undoubtedly a problem, especially if he can't be bothered to make the effort to speak a bit of Russian.'

It was true. O'Connor had shown no inclination to learn the local language. It was now seven months since he had begun playing in Moscow, yet he, as Alexander the press attaché confessed, spoke 'no Russian at all'. The young Scot was, it seemed, dutifully following in the footsteps of other British footballers abroad, making no attempt to assimilate into the local culture, and pining for Britain, with its 'proper food and TV'.

'I'm away two days before every game,' O'Connor had commented in the English media, 'and flying around the country, so it's hard for my wife. You can get British TV if you buy a Sky card from over here, and get someone in to fix it, but we haven't managed to do so,' he added, illustrating the hardships of life in the Russian capital.

I was reminded of Ian Rush, the legendary Liverpool striker, who, back home after a spell with Juventus, allegedly commented on his time in Italy that 'it was like a foreign country'. Rush subsequently denied in a 2005 *Observer* interview that he had ever uttered the phrase, but even accepting this, the quote perfectly sums up the attitude of the majority of Britons abroad – footballers or otherwise.

Anyway, it is actually possible to live in Moscow without knowing more than a few words of Russian. I myself have met many long-term American and British expats who are experts at mime and gesture, and repeating things slowly and loudly in English when they aren't understood.

In this respect, they have a lot in common with Russians themselves. The USSR was made up of fifteen republics, each with their own language, but it was quite uncommon for a Russian living in any of them to speak, say, Uzbek or Estonian, relying on the fact that most people were at least semi-fluent in Russian, the language of the masters.

There is a story about the USSR national side that illustrates well the problems the language barrier can cause. According to Alexander Chivadze, the former USSR captain, the team were once gathered in the dressing room before a match against Argentina, when the trainer sat down next to Tengiz Sulakvelidze, Chivadze's team-mate and fellow Georgian, and began giving him detailed instructions on how to mark Maradona, and how to try to neutralise the threat that he was sure to pose. After about ten minutes, he got up and shook the defender's hand.

Sulakvelidze, who didn't speak Russian that well, remained silent, but as they were running out onto the pitch he turned to Chivadze and asked, 'Hey, what was he going on about, then?' Surprisingly, despite the defender's failure to fully grasp the instructions given to him, the USSR managed to hold Maradona and co to a 1–1 draw.

'Most Britons,' Olga, manager at a local recruitment company and a Lokomotiv fan, told me, 'have an extremely hard time adapting to life in Moscow. However, they don't make it easy for themselves. Very few of them have a serious go at learning the language, and they tend to frequent places that cater exclusively to expatriates. O'Connor has fallen into the same trap, and has failed to make the most of his stay here. Still, it probably doesn't help in a way that the club has provided everything for him. He hasn't been forced to try to integrate. It must be even harder for his wife, cooped up in her luxury flat in a strange country.'

O'Connor may not be Britain's sole ambassador to Russia for long. There is speculation that other leading Russian clubs are looking to the UK for players to boost their squads. Improbable as it may seem, Russia is fast becoming a viable and attractive option for British footballers looking to spread their wings and please their bank managers at the same time.

Despite all this, the nagging suspicion at the back of many

Russian football fans' minds is that the money currently being invested in the country's football will merely lead to Russia becoming a rest home for ageing footballers, a chance to earn one big, fat, final pay cheque.

'The risk is,' one Russian journalist told me at half-time during a Lokomotiv game, 'that Russia will just end up like one of those oil-rich Middle Eastern states that ageing South American stars always seem to end up playing in. The kind where players go at the end of their careers to ensure their financial futures. The worst-case scenario would be if Russia turns into something like this. A kind of Qatar with snow. Play a couple of seasons in Russia, and guarantee your future. Our league is undoubtedly a lot stronger, but this danger certainly exists.'

Before Garry O'Connor (and unlikely as it sounds), the most skilful British footballer of his generation, Paul 'Gazza' Gascoigne, had almost become the first British footballer to play in Russia. Approached by a number of teams, including Torpedo-Metallurg (now FC Moscow), the deals, for reasons not entirely clear, fell through one after another. Perhaps, however, with hindsight, it was for the best that the ex-England star hadn't moved to the land of vodka and month-long binges.

As he tells it in his autobiography, *My Story*, England's finest footballer of the last twenty years hadn't been so lucky coming into Russia the first time he decided to visit.

Having met a Russian girl somewhere on holiday, he decided, on a whim, to go and visit her in Moscow. As he admits, he was pretty tanked up by the time they got into Sheremeytovo international airport, but even so, he was surprised to be pulled out of the passport control queue by 'two huge guys'.

As Gazza tells it, he had been a bit 'noisy and stupid' on the plane on the way over, and he assumed he would be getting into trouble over his behaviour. This was not the case, however.

'I didn't have a visa for Russia,' admitted Gascoigne. 'I hadn't realised you had to have one.'

After O'Connor's outburst, it was a real relief to talk to Dmitri Sychev. Although I had decided not to dwell on the matter, I couldn't help thinking, as I sat talking to Russia's best player at the 2002 World Cup, and one of the youngest ever to score for the country, that the more players achieved, the easier to approach they became. Possibly it is something to do with having nothing to prove. I wouldn't know, I'm not a professional footballer, but in Russia, at least, that was what I found.

Dmitri Sychev was born in Omsk, in the heart of Siberia, and started his career in the Russian Second Division, at Spartak Tambov. However, it was at another Spartak that he was to make his mark, both on the field and off it.

Invited by Oleg Romantsev for a trial at the beginning of 2002, Sychev performed extremely well in the pre-season games, scoring in virtually every match he was picked for. Not surprisingly, he was offered a contract by the club. It was this contract that was to form the basis of one of the scandals that would tear Spartak apart, and force Sychev into exile in France.

Sychev continued his good form when the season began for real, regularly finding the net. Despite his youth – he was just eighteen at the time – Spartak began to increasingly rely on the Siberian wunderkind to get them out of trouble, so much so that Oleg Romantsev, a man who normally avoided praising individual players, was to remark that 'Spartak are surviving on Sychev'.

Romantsev, who was simultaneously managing the national team, then took the logical step of selecting Sychev for that year's World Cup in Japan and South Korea. From the third echelon of Russian football to the World Cup in a little less than six months! Such a thing was unheard of, leading Sychev to exclaim, 'If anyone had told me that I'd be going to the World Cup six months ago, I'd have advised him to seek psychiatric help!'

Once at the World Cup however, Romantsev showed faith in the old guard, in veterans like Vladimir Beschastnykh and Viktor Onopko. When the chips were down though, as at Spartak, Romantsev set loose Sychev. In the first match against Tunisia, with the score 0–0, Sychev came on to set up one goal and earn the penalty that led to the second. After a rioting crowd in the centre of Moscow had watched Russia lose 1–0 to Japan, Russia only had to draw against Belgium in their last game to qualify.

Sychev again came off the bench. This time he scored, and fuelled a late, late storm on the Belgium goal, but it was too late. Russia lost 3–2, and were out.

After the final whistle had blown, the camera panned across the faces of the Russian players. Maybe it just seemed that way, or perhaps the older players were hardened by years of underachievement, accustomed to the inevitability of defeat, but they didn't appear to care that much. Except for Sychev, that is. Sychev and the young St Petersburg forward Alexander Kerzhakov. Sychev was sobbing, tears streaming from his eyes as, sniffling back emotion himself, Kerzhakov led him off the field. 'Not all is lost if boys still cry!' was the memorable *Sport-Express* headline the next morning.

Sychev became the new golden boy of Russian football after the World Cup, the antidote to the cynicism poisoning Russian football, a welcome gust of enthusiasm in place of the ageing stars with their fat wage packets and seeming indifference to the state of the national game.

As the Russian writer and satirist, Viktor Shenderovich, commented, 'I was so happy to see the boy Sychev cry at that evil World Cup. I was so pleased to see tears from at least one person! Those tears were wonderful, because the boy went out to save his motherland.'

'I don't think I would cry now,' said Sychev, commenting on the tears that turned him into an icon. 'I've grown up a bit. I'm not so emotional.'

The process was inevitable. The grind of league football, the training, the away games, were all bound to take something away from the eighteen-year-old boy who had poured his misery out in front of the nation, to make him into a harder adult. A bitter truth indeed.

After the 2002 World Cup, Sychev asked for a pay raise from Spartak Moscow. There is some confusion as to the sums concerned. Those close to Sychev claim that he was earning $800

a month – far, far less than the rest of the team, who were all receiving five or six thousand, still a miserly sum compared with today's wages. When Andrei Chervichenko, who had only recently taken over the club, refused his request, Russia's new golden boy decided to take drastic measures. On the morning of 16 August 2002, the day of a Spartak home game against Alania Vladikavkaz, Sychev handed in his notice.

Under Russian law, any employee is entitled to quit his job after giving two weeks' notice. However, this was the first time that a footballer had ever done so. Chervichenko immediately slapped a $6 million buy-out price on Sychev, and came to an agreement with the presidents of the other fifteen Premier League teams that the player would not play for them, or be allowed to use their training facilities. Sychev, in response, turned to the civil courts. For this act of open rebellion he was banned by the Russian Football Federation for six months.

Oleg Romantsev, still the Spartak manager at the time, took Sychev's actions literally to heart and was admitted to hospital for an operation related to high blood pressure shortly afterwards.

Soon after Sychev had dropped his bombshell, the rumours began to circulate. One of them had it that a notorious criminal gang had muscled in on the Spartak player, and that was the real reason behind his refusal to play for the club. They, or so the whispers went, wanted a cut of any cash that would be the result of a transfer deal. Supposedly, they were already taking his wages, and had sold the Porsche he had received from the national team's sponsors as the Man-of-the-Match in Russia's 2–0 World Cup victory against Tunisia.

'You should have seen the meeting of the Russian Football Federation's Disciplinary Committee when they were discussing Sychev's contract,' a journalist at *Novaya Gazeta* told me. 'Sychev was driven to the Football Federation's building by guys in black cars with tinted windows. There was a whole convoy of them that stretched down the street. Andrei Chervichenko also turned up with his own heavy mob. In order to ensure that he remained in Moscow, Sychev had had a minder, a convicted killer, assigned to him by the gang that had muscled in on him, to accompany him everywhere he went.'

Novaya Gazeta also claimed, after submitting the contract that Sychev wished to break to expert analysis, that the signature on it was a fake. This is a common enough phenomenon in Russia. Having inherited the Soviet Union's reverence for documents, the country is drowning in a sea of paperwork, and often in a firm there will be at least one person who can forge the boss's signature simply to save time and not get bogged down in bureaucratic red tape. In Sychev's case, however, it was a lot more sinister. If the allegations were true, Sychev was, in effect, seeking to tear up a contract that he had not even signed. In August 2003, the country's brightest young player disappeared for a few days, and it remains a mystery to this day as to where, and with whom, he was.

Eventually, after sitting out his six-month ban, Sychev left Russia, effectively forced into exile, and signed for the French side Marseille, helping them through the 2003 Champions League qualifying stages. According to Vladimir Beschastnykh, Sychev's one-time team-mate, the young star sobbed as he packed his things, leaving the Spartak training camp for the last time.

Andrei Chervichenko had his own version of events. 'Sychev was just a young kid,' he told me. 'He was no superstar; he'd come on as a substitute at the World Cup, and scored a goal. He was on five thousand dollars before the World Cup, and we offered him double that when he came back. "No," Sychev told us, "I want forty thousand.' We refused, and so he tried to walk out on the club. The whole situation was insane. I mean, imagine if, say, Ronaldinho went to the president of Barcelona and said that he wanted an eight-fold wage rise. Of course they would refuse. Just like we did. As for the stories about gangs taking his wages, about wanting a cut of any transfer fee, well, that wasn't my business. Anyway, we solved that problem for him by selling him to Marseille.'

Chervichenko offered to show me the said contract, but, aware of the murky nature of legal documents in Russia, I declined. As far as I have been able to ascertain, Sychev has never commented on these claims.

Dmitri Sychev's father, commenting on the situation, said, 'Spartak's nickname is "Meat", and, you know, sometimes I get the impression that the owners of the side take it literally, and just look upon the players as mere product.'

'They were good to me in France,' said Sychev, recalling his time on the French south coast.

How did he feel now, I wondered, about Spartak? Sychev shrugged, but behind the casualness I could sense something more.

'Yeah, Spartak . . .' he began, turning his face away for a moment. 'There was some unpleasantness, but . . .' his words died away.

Sychev hadn't spoken about the events of 2002 to any Russian journalists since returning to Moscow, to Lokomotiv, and he was hardly likely to open up to a foreigner.

'All of them have contracts,' the same journalist at *Novaya Gazeta* told me, 'and they need to live here, in Russia. That's why no one will speak about what goes on. All of the teams and managers are connected. If a guy speaks out in one team, he will just be forced out of the sport.'

The truth about the 'Sychev affair' will probably never be known, but what is certain is that it had a profound effect on the young forward. During our interview, I made a comment about a major Russian businessman with a large investment in the country's football, and, not expressing myself 100 per cent clearly, implied, unintentionally, that the said figure was ill-disposed to Sychev. The striker looked startled, his eyes narrowing for a second before I cleared things up. Despite everything that he has been through, Sychev remains a likeable young man, as open as he can realistically be, and lacking the airs of many Muscovite players.

Around the time I met Sychev, there was another scandal involving a Russian sports star, the ice-hockey player Evgeni Malkin, who fled to America, escaping from his club Metallurg Magnitogorsk, in the summer of 2006. Malkin had recently put his signature to a new contract with the team, but there were rumours that he, too, was under the control of a criminal gang, and had been coerced into doing so.

'All of them, all of the clubs,' a businessman associate told me, 'are controlled by gangs. They take the young stars' wages and leave them with peanuts. Malkin and Sychev were just brave enough to take them on.'

While Sychev is undoubtedly a player of quality, even his most ardent supporters would have to admit that he has failed to live up to his early promise. Touted as Russia's answer to Michael Owen after the 2002 World Cup, Sychev has never quite managed to rediscover the sparkling form that brought him to the attention of the Russian public in the first place.

This is a constant feature of Russian football – the inability of home-grown stars to fulfil their early potential. Although things are undoubtedly looking up, it is hardly surprising that they so often fail to make the leap from promising youngster to stardom given the current relatively low standard of players in the league. Unlike young players in say, the Italian or English leagues, a forward will rarely come up against defenders of international calibre, perhaps only during European cup games, or matches for the national side. In these circumstances, it is extremely difficult for them to hone their skills. True, Sychev went to play in France, but the French league is no longer a great step up from the Russian Premier League.

It is no coincidence that the only Russian players to have made the jump to that elusive 'star level' are players such as Kanchelskis, Alenichev, Mostovoi, Smertin, etc., those who have left Russia and gone to play abroad in one of Europe's top leagues, like England, Spain, or Italy.

Andrei Chervichenko, however, considered that leaving Spartak Moscow was the root of all Sychev's problems. 'If he had stayed at Spartak,' he told me, 'Sychev would be a world star by now. But these days, he's just a good footballer, and one of many.'

'Low-quality foreign players just hinder the national game,' Sychev told me. 'Players like Garry, of course, they help Russian football, but it's very hard to attract them. You know, Moscow, at least, is becoming more and more like a European city every day. But Russia still has this image as a wild place, dangerously exotic, full of bears and shootouts on every corner, and I guess that's the reason why top players are still reluctant to come.'

Russians are obsessed with the negative image they assume their country has abroad. While, undoubtedly, the country does have the reputation of being an unpredictable place, and dangerous to boot, the Russians themselves are certain that life in the Russian Federation is far too brutal and stressful for the vast majority of pampered Westerners. Russians are convinced that all foreigners believe Moscow to be a city where snarling bears roam eternally snow-covered streets. Indeed, it is even possible to buy T-shirts on the Arbat, Moscow's main tourist stretch, that state, 'I have been to Moscow, there are no bears'.

Lokomotiv were one of Russia's two representatives in the 2006 UEFA Cup. Before the tournament started, hopes were high that Loko could repeat the success of CSKA in 2005.

'If we play as we have been, then we've got no chance of lifting the trophy,' said Sychev, 'but if we play as well as we are able, then why not?'

It was, however, a case of the former. In the first round of the UEFA Cup, Lokomotiv were drawn against the semi-professional Belgium side Zulte Waregem. Faced with a team made up of shoe salesmen and insurance agents, Lokomotiv were expected to walk the tie. At first, everything went more or less to plan. With seconds remaining in the first leg, their home game, the Muscovites were 2–0 up. Not the massacre that some had expected, but a comfortable enough scoreline. And then, a mix-up in the Lokomotiv defence, and . . . 2–1.

Still, the side were confident of overall victory. When asked about the second leg, Slavoljub Muslin replied that he had no concerns, and that he wasn't at all worried about the game. Accordingly, the manager rested Sychev and other leading players, and gave a start to some of the side's substitutes, including Garry O'Connor. The increasingly unhappy expat failed to take any of his chances though, despite twice being one-on-one with the goalkeeper in the first fifteen minutes, and was eventually substituted in the second half. The result? The Belgians won 2–0. Lokomotiv's European adventure was over before it had even begun.

'The trainer gave some of the subs a game,' said Sergei Gurenko, the side's powerful Belarusian defender, after the defeat. 'I just don't understand how those guys failed to show what they could do. I mean, I'm not going to name names, but if you don't like sitting on the bench, well, give your all when you do get on the pitch. We had three one-on-one situations, and we didn't take any of them.' It was more than clear just whom he was talking about. I suddenly felt glad for O'Connor's sake that he didn't read Russian.

In October 2006, back in Britain, O'Connor announced that he would more than likely leave Russia come the end of the season. 'I like Moscow,' he said, 'but my family can't adapt to life here. My wife doesn't speak Russian. It's difficult for her to adapt to life in such a large city.'

And then, following Scotland's 1–0 victory over France, O'Connor, in a move perhaps indicative of his state of mind at the time, failed to join up with the rest of the squad for the next match against Ukraine in Kiev, preferring to fly home to Moscow, leaving his agent to inform Walter Smith, the Scottish manager, of his decision.

Back in Moscow, O'Connor explained that he had flown to Moscow to be with his wife, again quoting her problems with adaptation. Speaking to the local press, O'Connor denied that he was thinking of leaving Lokomotiv. As Alexander Udaltsov, the club spokesman, put it, 'We never hear that Garry is upset when he is in Moscow: it's only when he leaves that we hear all these stories.'

Happy or not, O'Connor had failed to secure a first-team place, and paying a player astronomical amounts of cash to warm the substitutes' bench, even taking into account the vast wealth floating around the Russian game, hardly made economic sense. True, he had put in some good performances, including scoring a bizarre goal against Luch Energiya in August 2006 with his chest, puffing out at the ball rather than heading it, but he had not provided the goals that Lokomotiv had hoped he would.

O'Connor's failure to take his chances in the UEFA Cup were to have grave consequences for Slavoljub Muslin. The two eternal Russian questions, posed by the nineteenth-century Russian intellectuals Nikolai Chernyshevsky and Alexander Gertsen, respectively – 'What is to be done?' and 'Who is guilty?' – were in Muslin's case, combined – 'What is to be done with he who is guilty?' The Lokomotiv president Valeri Filatov decided that the answer was the sack, and with just seven games of the season to go, Muslin was dismissed. It was a harsh decision but, nevertheless, the Serb with a French passport was out, replaced by Oleg Dolmatov, a Russian journeyman manager, famed for 'drinking vodka and never using a sweeper', as a Russian fan, Stas, memorably described him to me.

Muslin was clearly shocked when he spoke the day after his dismissal. 'They didn't forgive me Zulte Waregem,' he said.

'Muslin didn't suit Lokomotiv,' countered Filatov. 'He was too mild, too soft.'

'O'Connor had a hard time at Lokomotiv,' Nikolai Roganov at *Total Football* told me. 'The club changed trainers, and no one played particularly well for Lokomotiv that season. Basically, a year is not really enough to adapt to either Russia or the Russian game. Maybe he didn't score so many, but he always gave his all. He was always in the thick of things, and that is something that we could do with more of in Russian football. If he leaves for good, it will be a great pity.'

The first Briton ever to play professional football in the Russian Federation flew back to Scotland as the 2006 Russian season

NEW ROPE FOR NEW TIMES

wound down, having picked up an injury in Siberia during Lokomotiv's 3–1 victory against Perm in mid-November.

Once home, O'Connor reiterated his reluctance to return to Russia, mentioning again his family's lack of Sky TV in Moscow. The player eventually signed for Birmingham City in the summer of 2007, a little over a month after coming off the bench to claim the Russian Cup for Lokomotiv, finally winning the adoration of the club's fans with almost his last competitive kick of a ball in Moscow.

Back in England, he immediately gave an interview to the *Daily Mail*, speaking of the horrors he had experienced in the Russian capital, hinting at CSKA's mafia connections and, bizarrely, his difficulties in catching taxis.

'Even getting a taxi was a nightmare. Nobody really spoke English and the drivers would charge you a hundred pounds if they could. And, yes, I got ripped off a few times,' he said.

Although he has struggled to hold down a starting place in the Birmingham side, O'Connor is, presumably, a lot happier back in the UK.

O'Connor's arrival in Moscow had, even if ever so slightly, increased awareness of Russian football in Britain, particularly in Scotland. However, the striker's (and his wife's) reluctance to continue his career in a city where events like the 'Sychev affair' were, if not exactly commonplace, then nothing out of the ordinary, was a sharp kick in the teeth for the country's national sport.

There was a paradox at the heart of the matter. The very same things that made both Russia and its football so unique – the chaos, the anarchy and the unpredictability – were, conversely, the elements that were hindering the country's endeavours to lift its Premier League football to the next level. However, I couldn't help feel that if these features of the Russian game were eliminated, then the nation's football would lose something, becoming blander in the process. True, it may very well attract a few more big-name players, but something of the spark would be gone for ever. If

Russian football was ready to trade off spontaneity for stability, then the stars would eventually come. But at what cost?

In many respects this is the larger dilemma that Russia as a whole is struggling with today – the issue of making the successful transformation to a democratic, free-market economy without losing the country's long-celebrated uniqueness, without bidding farewell to, dare I say it, its 'soul'.

Garry O'Connor, for all his apparent ignorance of Russia and its culture, had played a larger part in that on-going struggle than he would perhaps ever realise.

CHAPTER ELEVEN

The sixteenth-richest human in the world

'Silence is for you and not for me,
because I, my friends, have been to England, you see.'

Daniil Kharms, *Untitled* (1933)

While Russia's top clubs continue to face problems in persuading world-class players to sign contracts, the issue itself would be a moot point were it not for the oligarchs and their spending power. Russian football's upturn in fortunes can be directly traced to Roman Abramovich's purchase of Chelsea in 2003. From then on, as the remaining oligarchs attempted to play 'keeping up with the Abramovichs', football became fashionable in Russia, and the cash began to flow.

While I have no desire to come across as overly pedantic, I feel I have to point out that it's Abram<u>o</u>vich, not Abram<u>o</u>vich. It was, I believe, Vladimir Nabokov, the author of *Lolita*, who said that if you can't even pronounce the names of your literary heroes correctly then you have no hope of understanding their works. I wouldn't go so far as to suggest that a case of misplaced stress could confuse the Chelsea supporters singing their saviour's name as to the meaning of the untold wealth invested in their team, but still, it would be nice if they didn't make their idol cringe every time they mangle it.

The mayor of Moscow, Yuri Luzhkov, reacted to Abramovich's purchase of Chelsea in 2003 by accusing the billionaire of 'spitting on his homeland' by having failed to invest in a Russian club. Others were more understanding. The climate in Russia was moving firmly against the oligarchs. According to Kremlin insiders, at the start of his presidency, Putin had gathered all the oligarchs together and told them that they could keep their ill-gotten riches on the condition that they stayed out of politics. Around the time that Abramovich's Chelsea deal was going through, Yukos, the Russian oil company, was being hounded through the courts in a saga that would eventually see its owner, Mikhail Khodorkovsky, once the richest man in Russia, sentenced to nine years' imprisonment. Khodorkovsky claimed that the court case had been instigated by Putin as revenge for his involvement in the 2003 elections, in which he had dared to fund opposition parties. Putin won the subsequent election by a landslide in any case, but it was indicative of the way things were moving – the president was displaying an obsessive need to be in control of every aspect of life in the Russian Federation, from football to the economy, from education to pig farming in the Urals.

In the autumn of 2006, a source at Millhouse Capital, Abramovich's management company, told *Russian Newsweek* that CSKA's president visited the company's Moscow offices 'at least once a week'. The implications of the statement were clear, and related to unproven rumours that Abramovich was continuing to fund CSKA, despite the end of his former Sibneft company's sponsorship deal with the club in 2005.

'Abramovich,' a *Novaya Gazeta* journalist told me, 'is not really such a great football fan. In Russia, all the money he spends on football, is tax deductible, and anyhow, it makes him look good, opening kids' football fields and so have you. In fact, I'm not even convinced that he really wanted to buy Chelsea. He wanted to get out of Russia, he saw the way the mood in the country was going, or rather, the way Putin's mood was going, and decided not to hang around and wait to see if he would be the next of the oligarchs to fall.'

So why the Chelsea deal then?

'Well, I think it's no secret that Chelsea has always, apart from having an extreme right-wing following, been the team of the British Establishment. The favourite of prime ministers and so on, and perhaps it was 'suggested' to him that he might do better in his bid to integrate into British high society by buying Chelsea and making them into world beaters.'

Abramovich is one of those I like to call the *New* New Russians. The original New Russians were those members of Russian society who made their fortunes through dodgy deals in the early 1990s, and set about flaunting their new-found wealth. They were filthy rich long before Russia announced its first official millionaires and billionaires in 2002. They were, as the stereotype went, loud and stupid, uncultured and with criminal ties. The *New* New Russians are a different breed altogether, although many of them may have originally been New Russians themselves. They have mellowed with time, caught the culture bug, and now, in place of flash cars and flamboyance they prefer fine wines and modern art. And, strangely enough, football.

However, as an acquaintance of mine, the owner of one of Russia's most successful companies, complained, 'They don't care at all about the sport, these people. They just want to be seen at the top games. If Abramovich is at a match, be it in Moscow, London or Monaco, they crowd around his box, trying to see who is with him. Gossiping like little girls.'

Once, after CSKA had won the UEFA Cup, one of these new Russian businessmen football fans told me, with the confidence of one used to having the inside word, that the forthcoming Super Cup tie between CSKA and Liverpool had been 'arranged' by Abramovich as a present for CSKA, a way of thanking the club for a job well done. I decided not to waste my time and his by filling him in on the long history of the fixture, traditionally played every year between the winners of that season's UEFA Cup and Champions League. There was something about these businessmen that I didn't like; something distasteful in their assumption that everything was up for sale. Even if, most of the time, it seemed to be.

Ordinary Russians, those distant from the oil money and political power being argued over, are basically in favour of Abramovich's adventures. 'At last,' went the joke, when Chelsea broke the British transfer record to bring Andrei Shevchenko to Stamford Bridge in the summer of 2006, 'Sheva is going to play for a Russian side.'

They may resent the money being tossed around like confetti, but they weren't, and aren't, going to see any of it anyhow. No one has any doubt that Abramovich's fortune could be put to better use in Russia itself, building up, say, the country's health and social welfare system, but it is a vague wish at best, a lazy-day wistfulness.

In the Soviet Union there existed the phenomenon of *nesuni* – the illicit carrying away of fully functioning items by workers from the factories they were employed at. In a sense, the Russian oligarch's alleged siphoning off of the country's assets is just an extension of this, and one that most people can easily identify with. To many Russians, to the majority of those standing on the terraces week in, week out, Abramovich, irrespective of the exact source of his wealth, is 'one of the lads'. A Soviet boy made good. A Slavic Del Boy, if you will – albeit with a touch more business acumen.

Abramovich, as the whole world now knows, is the governor of Chukotka, an inhospitable oil-rich region in the northeast of Russia. Chukotka is home to the Chukchi, the indigenous people who have long been the butt of Russian jokes, perceived as a race of almost subhumans, a touch higher than Neanderthal man. The Chukchi reaction to Chelsea's ever-strengthening squad has yet to be recorded. Chukotka even had a football team itself once, Spartak Chukotka. I had been planning on visiting one of their home games. It would, I reasoned, make an interesting segment, a visit to Abramovich's Ice Kingdom, a chance to compare the Chukchi team with Chelsea, but then someone pointed out that, due to the Arctic climate, Spartak Chukotka used to play their home games in Moscow, 6,500 miles away from their potential fan base. I say 'used to play' because Spartak Chukotka are no more, the previous governor of Chukotka having cut off cash to the team in 2000. Abramovich, upon becoming governor of the remote republic, followed in the footsteps of his predecessor and declined to fund the side. Spartak Chukotka faded into history. One can only wonder what would have happened had Abramovich elected to first revive, and then pump his billions into that humble club, bringing world stars to Moscow, leading Spartak Chukotka to the Champions League. Maybe then the jokes would have finally stopped.

When CSKA were drawn with Chelsea in Group H of the Champions League in 2004, UEFA immediately began an investigation into the financing of the Russian team, trying to prove that they were funded by Abramovich, a breach of the rule that no two clubs can be financed by the same individual. UEFA's inspectors were unable, however, to prove that any such links existed, and CSKA were free to fly into London for the first match between the two sides on 20 October 2004, where Chelsea ran out comfortable winners, headed goals from John Terry and Eidur Gudjohnsen giving the English side a 2–0 victory.

The return game in Mother Russia two weeks later was, as many had predicted it would be, a Moscow social occasion, a meeting of the rich and famous. The VIP box was filled with politicians and other unsavoury types; even the late Boris Yeltsin (although he was far more fond of tennis) made an appearance, leading to the people sitting behind me to crane their necks to see who had arrived.

'Ah, it's only Yeltsin. I thought it was Abramovich,' one of them grunted.

Right at the beginning of the match, Yuri Zhirkov, the little CSKA midfielder, set off on a Brazilian dribble all of his own, but Glen Johnson managed to get a foot in, and CSKA floated in the first of three successive corners before Chelsea got the ball upfield.

In the 24th minute, Arjen Robben flashed past the CSKA defence and stroked the ball into the net; 1–0 to Chelsea.

As the teams came out for the second half I wondered what Abramovich was feeling, up there in the VIP box, if he was experiencing a touch of guilt at bringing his expensive toy to Russia, stealing the points from CSKA that would have secured the Muscovites passage into the next round of the Champions League.

And then it hit me. Abramovich had fallen for England in the same way that I had for Russia. For one special instant, there in the Cherkizovo stadium, I understood Abramovich – we were both self-exiled, both of us strangers in a strange land. A moment of empathy crackled between us. And then, fortunately, as quickly as it had begun, it passed.

The second half kicked off and within two minutes CSKA had a penalty, Johnson bringing down the livewire Zhirkov.

Up stepped Vagner Love, and blasted the ball way over the bar.

The Chelsea fans taunted Love, shouting, 'Who are you mate, Beckham in disguise?' This was not long after the then England captain had sent a vital penalty high over the bar, blaming a 'tuft of grass' for the miss.

Vagner, despite not understanding any English, looked gutted anyhow, and played out the rest of the game in a fog of depression that had more to do with the famous Russian Soul than the Brazilian samba, sea and sun stereotype. Maybe, I thought, he had already been infected by Russia. He had, after all, dyed his dreads in CSKA's colours for the first time for the match.

After Vagner Love's failure to convert the penalty, the second half was, with the exception of a few flashes of skill, tedious to say the least. There were few chances, lots of substitutions, and some of the crowd, despite CSKA only being one down, started to leave before the end of the game.

I stayed until full time and then trailed out with the rest of the crowd. The CSKA fans, even the hard core, didn't seem too upset at their side's failure to take any points from the game. A 1-0 defeat at home to a team that, in the form of Abramovich's wealth, possessed the footballing equivalent of a 'cheat', enabling them to unlimited resources and credit, wasn't really so bad. If only, though, Vagner hadn't blasted that penalty kick over the bar.

We walked to the Metro, past the soldiers begging for cigarettes and spare change. Actually, at one time, this appeal for a cigarette was the thing that you were most likely to hear from a Russian soldier. I have been to matches where the way from the stadium to the Metro was completely lined by military conscripts, supposedly to ensure that there would be no trouble. However, the ten-minute walks were, in reality, nothing more than pitiful choruses of 'Got a cigarette?' 'Got any spare change?' from the spotty, mal-nourished-to-a-man draftees.

I thought about Abramovich, jetting out of the country to London. Although I'm not so naive as to suggest that the world could ever be a fair place, I couldn't help feeling that there was something wrong here. But then that was obvious; only a fool could fail to notice such things.

If the truth be told, Abramovich, and those like him, other oligarchs, as yet lacking such fame, are no longer even really Russians. Unable to live in their native country for fear of reprisal either by the political class, criminals, or some as yet to be defined social threat, they send their children to school abroad, travel the world, returning occasionally to keep an eye on their assets, like slave masters returning to the plantation.

In 2007, according to the *Forbes* business magazine, 14 of the richest 100 people in the world were Russians. Their combined wealth was equal to 26 per cent of the country's GDP. In comparison, 39 of the top 100 richest people on the planet were US citizens, yet their combined wealth was a mere 4.6 per cent of the nation's GDP.

A social explosion may one day occur in Russia, impoverished provincial Russians rising up to claim the property and resources stolen from them at the start of the 1990s. But that day, despite whatever Western-leaning opposition-movement figures in Russia might like to think, is a long time off. For now, the oligarchs are free to continue to humour their whims, to buy into the world of football, with all the political and social influence that ownership of a leading club brings.

CHAPTER TWELVE
Kanchelskis on the Volga

'Look, you have seen a lot, and travelled a lot, so tell me, where do they appreciate a Russian man more; on this, or that side of the Pyrenees?'
Venedikt Erofeev, *Moscow Stations*

Despite the setbacks of the O'Connor and Maniche sagas, in 2006 and for a small part of 2007 the Russian Premier League was able to boast a player who was a genuine household name all over Europe, a man who had once thrilled crowds in Britain and Italy with his speed and talent. And what was more, there were no problems with adaptation, no complaints from this legend of international football. Fluent in the local language, he had, at least, no need for Sky TV.

Samara, a pleasant, medium-sized town in the southeast of the European part of Russia, sits tidily on the Volga River. During the Cold War, it was a closed city, due to the fact that Soyuz launch missiles were once produced here. It is also home to the Lada, the economy car loved by small-vehicle enthusiasts throughout the British Isles.

It is also where Andrei Kanchelskis, the one-time Manchester United and Rangers legend, came to finish his professional career, spending the 2006 season at the club before retiring in February 2007 to become sporting director of the Russian Ural-based First Division side Nosta Novotroitsk.

The local team in Samara is Krilya Sovetov, or 'Soviet Wings', a moniker that grows more and more incongruous with every passing season. The fans here are some of the most fanatical in the country, with the team enjoying the highest average home gates in the whole of Russia. The club, while never having come close to winning the title, are basically a solid mid-table side, occasionally vying for top honours, flirting (as in 2007 when they finished thirteenth) with relegation every few seasons.

After playing his last season in Britain in 2003 for Southampton, Kanchelskis signed a contract with Saudi Arabian club Al-Hilal. Twelve months later he was in Russia, playing for Saturn FC, an ambitious side based just outside Moscow. Before this, however, he had been training with Dynamo Moscow, and had even signed a contract as a player/trainer's assistant, but was dismissed before ever having officially kicked a ball for the Muscovites. The reason? The club accused the former Manchester United winger of turning up drunk for training during a camp in Spain, something Kanchelskis strenuously denies.

I met up with Andrei Kanchelskis after a match with Spartak Moscow in the autumn of 2006. Even at 37, he looked sharp, his raids down the flanks proving that he had lost little of the speed that once thrilled crowds at Old Trafford and Ibrox. He was substituted after an hour, but this was not a regular thing; the week before, for example, he had played the full ninety minutes, and been included in that week's symbolic Premier League team as voted for by Russian journalists. Not, you must agree, the kind of thing you would expect from an ageing drunk.

'I would never allow myself to turn up drunk to training,' said Kanchelskis, categorically. 'I've been playing professional football for sixteen years, and I've never done such a thing. Dynamo couldn't get their story straight. First they said that I didn't turn up for training at all. Then they said that I turned up, but drunk, and now they are saying I trained, but with a heavy hangover.'

So why was his contract torn up? We were speaking in Russian, although when Kanchelskis heard that I hailed from the birthplace of football, he had begun in English, but quickly switched back to his native tongue, claiming that he was out of practice.

'I was signed as a playing member of the training staff. I wanted to share my experience with the team. You know, I've played under some pretty good managers,' he said, the master of understatement. 'At the time, Dynamo were managed by Yaroslav Gzhebik, the Czech trainer. I could see that his training methods weren't effective. What could I do? I mean, look, they hired me as a trainer, so I spoke out. Gzhebik didn't take too kindly to that . . .'

So the whole incident was thought up as an excuse to force him out of the club?

'That's right.'

Vasili Utkin had his own view on the whole episode when I spoke to him about it. 'Who doesn't turn up for work drunk sometimes, Marc?' Russia's very own Brian Moore began, taking a sip of his wine. 'I mean, that wasn't the reason they sacked him. He didn't get on with the manager, and they used it as an excuse,' he claimed, perhaps illuminating more about the Russians' attitude to alcohol than the Kanchelskis issue.

What, I wondered, did Kanchelskis make of today's Manchester United compared with his?

'We'd have beaten them. I don't know by what score, but we'd have won, that's for sure.'

I had heard rumours of disagreements with Alex Ferguson, but Kanchelskis denied any hard feelings. 'Ferguson is his own man,' he said.

Like Oleg Romantsev was his own man? 'You can't compare Romantsev and Ferguson,' said Kanchelskis. 'Romantsev's football was far more primitive.'

Kanchelskis recalled his first days in Manchester. 'I was straight from the Soviet Union, you understand, and although I can't say that I was earning particularly badly back in Ukraine, by Soviet standards at least, in Manchester I encountered things that I'd never seen before. I have to say, however, that United were very good at supporting foreign players. They helped me with banks, bills, everything. I remember they gave me a credit card. Of course, there were no credit cards in the USSR, and I continued using cash for quite a while. Then I got used to them; it turned out they weren't so difficult to use after all.

'I really loved living in Britain. I remember feeling so pleased when I got my British passport. I worked on that for six or seven years. I was so happy that my children could become British citizens.'

I got the impression that, for Kanchelskis, playing abroad was a real adventure, one he had grasped with both hands.

'Yeah, I really enjoyed it,' he confirmed. 'Well, perhaps not my time in Saudi Arabia. That wasn't real football. That's why I didn't stay there long.'

It wouldn't be too much of an exaggeration to say that Kanchelskis is as famous, if not more so, in Britain as he is in Russia.

'In England, especially in Manchester of course, people came up to me all the time for autographs. I don't get that here so much.'

Although Krilya Sovetov have more than respectable attendances, the turnout at their away games in Moscow can be pitifully low, and I wondered what Kanchelskis made of performing in front of a mere handful of spectators.

'It's tough, of course, especially after Old Trafford and Ibrox. I mean, at the Luzhniki, where the capacity is eighty thousand, even twenty thousand seems like nothing. It's a bit disheartening at times. But that's the job. Anyway, in Samara the fans are great.'

Given that Kanchelskis had never actually played in Russia before his ill-fated move to Dynamo, I enquired if there was anything that he had been surprised by, pleasantly or otherwise.

'Not really surprised, because I had been following the game here anyway. Just a bit disappointed by the attitude to football. But that was only to be expected, really. I mean, after Britain and Italy, where the game is the lifeblood of the country, it would have been naive to expect that level of commitment. Having said this, the Russian Premier League is undoubtedly stronger than the Scottish Premier League. In Scotland, apart from Celtic, Rangers and Hearts, there aren't many good teams. In Russia, especially now after all the investment, there are a lot more sides with talented players.'

FIFA, like the rest of the world, had not been expecting the USSR to fall apart as quickly and finally as it did in 1991, and, not finding places for the remaining fourteen republics, handed Russia the only available slot for the forthcoming 1992 World Cup. Players throughout the Soviet Union were free to choose whom to play for. Not surprisingly, the majority of them plumped for Russia, rather than the republics in which they had been born: Belarus, Kazakhstan, and other Soviet republics, now fully fledged countries, with less than glorious footballing heritages.

Andrei Kanchelskis was born in Ukraine of Lithuanian parents, and after the break-up of the USSR he became a member of the Russian international side. Strangely though, it wasn't until 2004 that he played in Russia, having played for the Ukrainian teams Dynamo Kiev and Shakhtar Donetsk before signing for Manchester United in 1991.

Given these tangled roots, I asked what nationality Kanchelskis considered himself to be. Ukrainian? Lithuanian? Russian? Or like so many people in the former USSR with similar problems, Soviet? The question was particularly pertinent. When Kanchelskis left Donetsk for Manchester United in 1991, the USSR was still a world power.

'I feel Russian,' he answered, after a moment's hesitation.

Russian he may feel, but Kanchelskis also has British citizenship, as do his two children. 'I learned a lot from the managers I've played under, and I'd like to go into management when I hang up my boots,' he replied, when I asked him about his future plans.

In England, perhaps?

'Why not? I love England and its football. During the last World Cup I supported three teams – Ukraine, England and Italy.'

2006 was an *annus horribilis* for Kanchelskis' Krilya Sovetov. After taking part in the 2005/06 UEFA Cup, the side were looking forward to a top-four place and qualifying for Europe once more. Then, things began to go wrong. The club's owner German Tkachenko ran into financial problems, and was no longer able to finance the club. Krilya had accumulated debts, and began selling players to stay afloat. There were delays in the payment of wages, and the team's results suffered.

Despite all this, the low point in the year came in September, when Serge Branco, the club's Cameroonian defender, fled Samara, accusing a member of Krilya's training staff, former Russian international Omar Tetradze, of threatening him with a gun.

Tetradze is a moustached Georgian, a man known throughout Russia for his solid performances at the 1994 World Cup and 1996 European Championships. He saw out his playing days in Samara, at Krilya, and then joined the coaching staff in 2006.

'I've worked hard to build up my name, and I'm not going to let some Branco dirty it,' he said in *Sovetski-Sport*, reacting to the player's accusations. As Tetradze tells it, the Cameroonian was late for a meeting before a Premier League fixture. Branco claimed that no one had called him, and he had overslept. However, the club's translator apparently, according to the same report, subsequently showed both Tetradze and the team's manager, Gadzhi Gadzhiev, his mobile phone with a record of the call.

Gadzhiev then told Branco that he would be on the bench for that day's match, and that he would have to pay a fine. The defender then 'went berserk'. Security was called to 'get him out of the dressing room'.

After the game Branco reportedly came to the club canteen and began swearing at Gadzhiev.

'I just lost it. I went after him with a stool. I admit it. We were pulled apart, but there was no pistol! When I read about the gun, I was lost for words,' Tetradze went on.

After the incident, Serge Branco fled Samara and headed for Moscow, for the French embassy. 'Those people threatened my life! I'm afraid to go out on the streets in case they kill me. I am a French citizen,' he said, 'and they are obliged to give me protection.'

He later surfaced in Germany, where, seemingly calmer, he said that he was waiting for a decision from the Krilya Sovetov directors. He was, however, extremely reluctant to return to the team.

Branco, even before the incident, had a reputation for unpredictability and undisciplined behaviour. Not long before the pistol episode, he had been involved in a fight with CSKA's Brazilian international Daniel Carvalho. In the middle of a game, for no discernible reason, Branco, deep in his own half, sat on the ball. Carvalho, incensed, ran up to the Krilya defender and dragged him to his feet. Following the ensuing fracas, both players were dismissed and subsequently suspended for three matches.

Upon leaving Shinnik FC, at the time struggling at the foot of the Premier League, in 2006 to join Krilya, he gave his reasons for doing so as: 'I understood that no great trainers, for example from Real or Inter, would have a chance to see me in action.'

Once, upon being substituted at Shinnik, he threw his shirt on the ground as he was leaving the pitch. 'You know,' he had said, by way of explanation, 'I just can't stand it when people don't respect me. If the manager says he believes in me, and then pulls me off, well . . .' Branco had also been, at one point, a Leeds United player, signing for the club on 1 September 2004. However, a mere fourteen days later he was released, ostensibly due to 'fitness-related problems'.

In Russia, most people found it hard to believe that Omar Tetradze would have threatened a member of the side, or anyone come to that, with a gun. As a local journalist told me, 'Branco had been unhappy in Samara for a long time. There were delays with salary payments and the like. He had had some offers from German teams and, well, after the 'pistol' incident he turned up in Germany. I'll let you draw your own conclusions.'

Had Branco, unhappy with his club, decided to make the most

of a situation, to exploit Russia's wild and lawless image by concocting the story of Tetradze and the pistol? Had he figured that Krilya would release him after that, that he would be free to find a side in Germany or England, places where those 'Real and Inter trainers' would have the opportunity to see him play?

Kanchelskis had this to say about his team-mate. 'If the club decides to have Branco back, then they are only humiliating themselves. After what he did and said, there is no way they should forgive him, no matter how much he might apologise. The sooner we get rid of him, the better. As a player, he wasn't much anyway. Decidedly average.'

However, in 2007, having apparently decided that life in Russia wasn't that dangerous after all, Branco returned to Krilya Sovetov. With Gadzhi Gadzhiev having already left the side, Branco quickly regained his place in the team. He had lost none of his appetite for controversy, storming off the pitch during a Premier League match at Khimki, near Moscow, in response to alleged racist chants by the home side's fans.

'That stuff wouldn't go on in a civilised country,' he said.

Whatever the truth of the gun-threat accusations, the incident only served to underline the fact that Andrei Kanchelskis, one-time hero of Old Trafford and Ibrox, had exchanged European football, and indeed Europe, for something very different indeed.

CHAPTER THIRTEEN

Moving on up with FC Khimki or Frankness from 'he without happiness'

'To free the age from its confinement,
To instigate a brand new world'

Osip Mandelstam – *The Age*

When I first fell for Russian football, I naturally enough at first grew familiar with the country's top clubs and players. But then, as my passion deepened, as I began to lose myself in my adopted homeland's national sport, I started to delve into the lower divisions. Like a record collector who has bought everything by his favourite artist, and who is forced to get his fix through low-quality bootlegs, my obsession took me beyond the Russian Premier League into a world that was obscure even within Russia itself.

The Russian First Division is notoriously tough, akin perhaps to those celebrated Iron Man marathons where athletes have to run a hundred miles and swim the English Channel twice, or something equally ridiculous. Teams play 46 games a season, and can travel anything up to 8 time zones in order to play an away match. This would be the equivalent of, say, Nottingham Forest flying on a regular basis to the heart of Africa for away fixtures.

One example is the game between Baltika, from Kaliningrad, Russia's enclave to the north of Germany, and CKA-Energiya, from Khabarovsk, a short boat ride away from Japan. When the sun is rising in Kaliningrad, the working day has long finished in Khabarovsk.

The Russian Second Division avoids this by splitting the league into more manageable chunks – the Northern Zone, the Eastern Zone etc., a bit like England in the post-war years. Although Luch Energiya from Vladivostok forced their way into the elite in 2005, immediately becoming the least popular away game for visiting teams, players in the Russian Premier League, while still forced to undertake mammoth journeys to away matches, play fewer games, more of them in the Moscow region, and have more chance to recover between fixtures.

On 11 September 2006, five years to the day after terrorists had ploughed planes into the Twin Towers and the Pentagon, I met, for the first time in my life, and possibly the last, a person responsible for the birth of a professional football team. The man was Boris Khalfin, and the team was Khimki, lying in second place in Russia's First Division and strong contenders for promotion to the Premier League the following season.

My contact at the club, Boris only let it slip during our conversation that he had been one of the men behind it, that everything I saw around me was in someway connected to him. Boris was not, as you may have imagined, of advanced age, mumbling away about the glory days of Soviet football. No – he was, I guess, in his early to mid-forties. Khimki was formed in 1997, the same year I came to Russia for the first time.

'There used to be two teams – Novator and Rodina,' began Boris. 'Amateur sides. We thought, "Why not try and get something going here?" I remember printing out match-day programmes at home on an old computer.' He laughs at the memory. 'And now, well . . .' He looked around him, at the training field, at the newly signed ex-Spartak Moscow players wandering around. 'And now,' he continued, 'Just look!'

Khimki is a small town just outside Moscow. It was where I had spent some of my early days in Russia, experimenting with vodka and oblivion. Then, it was a Soviet hangover, a place where skins, glue-sniffers and wild dogs ruled supreme. The team was a joke, in the lowest division of Russian football. But now, Khimki is on the move. The town is a mishmash of construction projects and glistening new shopping centres, of 24-hour cinemas and imported cars. Somehow though, passing the bars and parks where I used to drink with people I hadn't seen for more than half a decade, I found myself pining for the old Khimki.

In England, where the football hierarchy is, and has been for some time, more or less established, it is extremely rare for professional clubs to be formed. In the New Russia, on the other hand, where society as a whole exists in a constant state of flux, it is a common enough phenomenon.

One of the most famous examples is that of Asmaral. In 1990, an Iraqi businessman by the name of Husam Al-Khalidi took over Krasnaya Presnya, a Second Division side, and renamed the team using the first three syllables of his children's names. When they eventually dropped into the third echelon of Russian football, the club was disbanded, the entrepreneur having lost interest.

Khimki, however, were formed entirely from scratch. And they are, as the club's yearbook has it, 'here to stay'.

The week I visited the club, Khimki had four former Spartak players on their books. All of them were over thirty, and there was talk that more ageing stars from the team that had made the 1990s their own would soon be joining. One of the ex-Spartak stars already in the side was Vladimir Beschastnykh, the Russian national side's all-time top scorer. Beschastnykh's other claim to fame was as the scorer of the only two goals in the 1992 USSR Cup Final, a perhaps unique occasion in world football as Spartak and CSKA battled it out for a trophy bearing the name of a country that no longer existed.

Another former Spartak star playing out his final seasons at Khimki was Andrei Tikhonov, a man who, even six years after Oleg Romantsev had declined his services, was still a firm favourite with Spartak Moscow's fans. As one unofficial Spartak site put it: 'When we say Spartak, we imply Tikhonov, and when we say Tikhonov, we imply Spartak.'

Khimki have their sports camp at one of many former Olympic training centres scattered around the Moscow region. Although Khimki were a side on the move, they could not yet hope to afford the facilities enjoyed by the top Moscow sides. The Olympic complex was a fine building, yet it had seen wear and tear, and everywhere there was the sound of hammering and scraping as workmen carried out repairs.

I met Vladimir Beschastnykh in his room at the camp. It was an incongruous sight. Having spent the previous months being awed by the facilities available to Premier League sides, I was a touch taken aback to see one of Russia's most capped players slouching on a downright uncomfortable mattress watching a repeat of a recent Zenit–Torpedo Moscow match on a flickering Soviet-made TV. He looked glum. Were the first 's' in his name a 'z', Beschastnykh, funnily enough, would translate as, 'he without happiness'.

How did Beschastnykh find life in the First Division?

He crinkled up his nose, eyes still trained on the football. 'It's tough, yeah, of course, fu – . . . all those . . . flights, y'know?'

Having only just met me, Vladimir was obviously trying to stem the flow of obscenities that usually flow from a professional footballer's mouth, and only partially succeeding. There is a Russian saying about swearing, or *mat*, that 'We don't cuss in *mat*, we converse in it.'

It is a received wisdom in Russia that fixed matches, *dogovorniki*, are a lot more common in the First Division. While I wasn't expecting Beschastnykh to open up and confess to having taken part in such things, I posed the question as to their existence anyway, reminding him that, not long before the interview, the president of the Russian Football Federation had claimed there were only four or five honest teams in Russia.

The ex-Spartak Moscow forward sighed, as if I had touched upon a subject deeply painful for him, but one that, nevertheless, deserved to be discussed. 'I can't count the teams, but it's a fact that there is corruption in Russian football. Still, it's getting cleaner, even in the First Division. After all, football isn't show business; you can't fake it all the time. What you gonna do, buy two or three games? And then what? Buy the Championship? And then? What's the point? It's only now that people are beginning to understand this. That it's not worth it. Still, if they started to battle against corruption like the Italians, I don't know what would happen. Something awful, that's for sure.'

Beschastnykh was a lot more open on the topic than the other players I had spoken to. Maybe it was something to do with the fact that he was approaching the end of his career, or that he was irritated with life in the First Division, or possibly he was just bored and wanted a chat. Taking advantage of his frankness, I asked if he had ever been involved in, or seen anything confirming the existence of fixed games.

He hesitated, and then replied, 'Personally, I've been lucky. No one has ever said to me that "You have to play badly in this match so that the other team wins". As I said, I've just been fortunate. I don't want to make myself out to be a hero or anything, but I've never done that. On the other hand, though, I've played matches where we've won, and then after the game found out that the other team had concrete instructions to throw the match.'

Was it, I wondered, possible to sense this, to become aware during the game that the other team was letting you score, that they were making no effort to win?

'I've never thrown a match in my life,' Beschastnykh repeated, 'but playing against teams who I've later found out threw the game, well, you just don't think about it. I mean, you score, and you want to think that it's because you are a good forward, not 'cos they let you.'

The hammering on the lower floor reached a crescendo, and we were silent for a few moments.

'But, you know,' he said, possibly sensing that he had given away too much, revealed too many trade secrets, 'it was never official. Everything I've told you is, well, hypothetical. It's what I think. I've just been lucky that I played for Spartak Moscow for many years. And that kind of thing just isn't practised at Spartak.'

In 2002, Beschastnykh went to England for a trial with Bolton Wanderers. He was, or so the Lancashire side believed, a free agent. Once in England, the former Spartak striker did well enough for the side to begin to make enquiries into his purchase. However, whilst negotiating with the player's agent, another agent turned up on the scene, claiming that Beschastnykh was still under contract with Spartak, and that the Moscow side would be due money in the event of a sale. Eventually, Bolton became frustrated with all the complications involved, and Beschastnykh was signed by the Turkish side, Fenerbahce.

Spartak continued to insist on a fee. The Turks were not willing to pay and, in January 2003, two Spartak representatives allegedly arrived at Beschastnykh's hotel room and told him to come with them to the mid-winter camp near Istanbul where the Moscow side were, conveniently, training. Beschastnykh did so, and then Spartak produced a copy of an agreement showing that the player had signed an extension to his contract until 2004, and that Spartak were owed $800,000. Beschastnykh subsequently confirmed this, claiming that he had 'forgotten' signing the extension. Whatever the truth of the matter, the Turks paid up.

'I went to England for a trial right after my holidays. I wasn't in any condition and they rejected me,' was Beschastnykh's version of events as to why he had been turned down by Bolton.

And what about the Spartak agents, about the Turkish adventure?

'There was some trouble, some confusion with agents, yeah.'

Whether Beschastnykh was being reluctant to speak on the matter, or indeed was as much in the dark as anyone else, it was hard to tell. What was clear was that it was just one more example of the sinister side of Russian football. Confusion reigns, threats are commonplace. I suddenly felt glad I wasn't a Russian footballer.

Andrei Tikhonov, 'Khimki's star', as Boris had introduced me to him, claimed, like so many before him, that foreigners were ruining the Russian game. 'Not high-quality players, you understand, but those guys who just come here to earn cash. It's no secret now that Russian teams, even in the First Division, pay pretty competitive wages. I mean, it really is like a business trip for them. I don't really think that anyone gets a great deal of pleasure out of flying the length of Russia, playing a match, training, flying off again, etc., etc.'

A no-nonsense kind of player, Tikhonov was one of the few footballers I spoke to who had served in the Russian Army. In Russia, military duty is compulsory, but the majority of young men either pay a fine, fake illness or study in order to avoid being shipped off to Chechnya, or beaten in the brutal hazing so common in the Russian armed forces. Had it not been possible for Tikhonov to get out of this? He grimaced, obviously not enjoying the memory of his time spent defending Mother Russia. 'I had problems,' he said.

What kind of problems?

'Problems. The usual kind.'

'The usual kind' in Russia involves not having the money to pay a bribe, or being faced with a particularly vigilant conscripting department. Back then, Tikhonov was an unknown, and I assume he had lacked the resources, both financial and otherwise, to dodge military duty.

'I did my time,' he said. 'No football for two years. Just drills, parades and weapon training.'

Both Tikhonov and Beschastnykh expressed the desire to become managers after hanging up their boots. Beschastnykh was, typically, more forthright about the problems. 'It's not that simple to become a manager in Russia, especially in the First Division, 'cos there are too many club presidents who interfere, and who won't let a new manager learn from his own mistakes.'

Tikhonov said he wanted to become a manager to pass on his experience, and the thought struck me that one good thing about the money being pumped into Russian football was that, aside from the top players it could potentially lure to the Russian Premier League, Russian players were no longer streaming out of the country. The player drain had been plugged. Veterans of the Russian game were remaining in the country to pass on what they had learned. That, surely, was a good thing.

On 2 November 2006, Khimki had the chance to gain promotion to the Russian Premier League for the first time in their, admittedly short, history. A victory against Fakel Voronezh would do it. The tiny stadium in Khimki was packed out. 'We are building a new one, for the future,' Boris had told me. If they went up, in order to accommodate the fans who were sure to flock to games against CSKA and Spartak, they would need it.

While everyone at Khimki had been good to me, I was still in two minds as to who to support. The fact was that their opponents came from Voronezh, a city where I had spent a happy summer studying Russian in 1998, meeting my future wife, Tanya, there.

Fakel were faced with relegation to the semi-professional third tier of Russian football. For the Voronezh side, three points could be the difference between the humiliation of having to play village teams, and retaining some respect amongst their ever-dwindling army of fans.

Voronezh has a population of just under a million, and is an eleven-hour train ride to the south of Moscow. It is famous for being the place where Peter the Great built the first Russian fleet, and where potatoes were first planted in Russia.

Its name derives from the Russian word *Voron*, meaning crow, although there aren't any more crows there than anywhere else in the country. Crows in Russia are huge vicious-looking things, with evil pointed beaks, and I have always been a touch wary of them, especially after one went crazy once and launched an attack on me like something out of Hitchcock's *The Birds*.

Like the majority of cities in the provinces, the standard of living in Voronezh lags way behind that of Moscow's. Little of Russia's oil money trickles down this far, and the area is plagued by high unemployment and alcoholism. It is also famed throughout Russia for its fertile 'Black Earth' soil. However, in recent years the land has been poisoned by heavy metals, making mushroom picking, for example, extremely hazardous. I had recently read a report that said that around one hundred people had died the year before as a result of eating toxic mushrooms, ones that should, by rights, have been safe for human consumption.

Despite the fact that Voronezh is quite a large city, it has never enjoyed any footballing success whatsoever. Although the team has existed since 1954, its highest ever position is thirteenth in the Premier League. Being a native of Bristol, another town never to have tasted much glory on the football field, I immediately felt a deep and lasting spiritual connection with the city.

Immediately after the conclusion of the 2006 World Cup in Germany, Fakel Voronezh's official website had this question for the club's fans.

'Which of the following teams do you think is closest to Fakel's style of play?'

There then followed a list of all the participating countries. Plus two extra options. 'Fakel's style is unrepeatable', and 'Fakel have no style'.

The latter came out on top, with 40 per cent, while the former, whether intended as sarcasm or not, came in second with 24 per cent. Of all the teams, Togo was judged to have the most in common with Fakel, gaining 7 per cent. No one saw any similarities at all between Fakel and the new world champions, Italy, although an eagle-eyed 2 per cent had noted some parallels between a side staring relegation to the third echelon of Russian football straight in the face and the five-times conquerors of the world, Brazil.

I took my place in the crowd at the promotion/relegation decider. Perhaps, the thought suddenly occurred to me, I was getting too close to the Russian game? Had I lost all perspective? Why, when it came down to it, was I so interested in a game between two Russian First Division sides? True, I still believed that 'football reflects society, and society football', yet what possible significance could the Khimki game have?

The answer, I guess, is that in Russia nothing is quite so simple as it seems. The corresponding fixture in England would be of interest, in all likelihood, merely to fans of the two teams. However, in Russia, where things are not so clear-cut, where social change takes place in the blinking of an eye, there are layers and layers of meaning around each event, sporting or otherwise. Here we had one team from the Moscow region, an up-and-coming town, its football team packed with ex-Spartak stars, the wealth behind the team apparent to all. And, on the other hand, we had a side from the Russian provinces, from the lost lands of the New Russia. The team, accordingly, lacked finances, and its fate had matched its economic circumstances. The Fakel players looked paler, less physically prepared for the match.

The Russian and English regions are two very different things. In Russia, the provinces are, with the exception of a few oil-rich areas, far, far poorer. Their residents are not welcome in the capital, and if they do venture to Moscow they face regular harassment from the police. Until recently, a non-Muscovite was only entitled to be in the capital of his own country for three days. This law has now been changed to three months, but this is, in reality, merely a cosmetic change. Both psychologically and physically, the Russian guest to the capital will feel exceedingly uncomfortable as he wanders across Red Square. Moscow has always been different from the rest of Russia, a law unto itself, but now, in the New Russia, the difference was becoming more and more pronounced.

Vladimir Kazachenok, Khimki's manager, recalled with horror the side's visit to Voronezh for the away fixture. 'We went there in March, and I got the impression that no one had cleared any snow away the whole winter. Everywhere there were mounds of dirty, melting snow. The roads were full of craters. It looked as if the city had just been liberated from Nazi occupation after a long battle.'

Khimki needed a point from their final two matches to guarantee promotion to the Premier League. The tiny 'Navigator' stadium was packed out. There was, in reality, little doubt that Khimki would succeed in getting the point they needed. Despite the obvious difference in class between sides at opposite ends of the division, I had also heard the rumour that, once more, the match had been fixed, and that Fakel would simply roll over. After all, as one Moscow sports journalist commented, 'They have ordered the fireworks, the roads have been cleared for a parade. The show must, and will, go on!' As ever, the bookmakers were a reliable indication of the truth of the rumours. No Russian bookmaker, despite displaying odds for the game, would accept a bet. 'The bookmakers have their guys in all of the teams,' the same journalist told me, 'they have to in this business. If they are not members of the actual side, then they are close to the team – relatives, agents, etc.'

Suspicions had been voiced that Khimki had reached the top of the league by less than honest methods, supposed proof of this being the fact that this Moscow-region side had been awarded more penalties than anyone else that season.

Vladimir Beschastnykh waved away such accusations. 'No one is going to spend a load of cash to bribe officials just get into the Premier League and be disgraced there. It doesn't make sense. All of the penalties were fairly given. Examine each case in detail and you'll see that.'

Whatever the truth of the matter, Khimki soon took charge, the ex-army veteran Andrei Tikhonov finding the net early on. Two more goals followed, and the scene was set for the party. Personally, taking into account all I had learned since beginning my book, I was willing to consider the rumours that Khimki had ensured victory in their penultimate match by less than honest means, but even if this were so, the side they had assembled was undoubtedly worthy of promotion.

Still, football is unpredictable, and perhaps, just perhaps, someone had decided not to leave things to chance, to make 100 per cent sure that Premier League football would be coming to Khimki. After all, as Boris had told me, the side had big plans: a stadium was being built, and investors and sponsors were actively being sought.

The match ended and the fireworks were let off. Russians are inordinately fond of fireworks, and this crowd was no exception. The tiny contingent of Fakel fans that had made the journey appeared to have had no doubts about the result of the match either, unfurling a home-made congratulatory banner at the final whistle that read, 'Good Luck in the Top Flight!'

However, for all the know-how and skill that Khimki had demonstrated in earning their promotion, if they were to survive in the intrigue-riddled world of top-level Russian football, even the grace of Lady Fortune, I feared, might not be sufficient.

In the event, Khimki's first season amongst the elite of Russian football saw them cement themselves as a mid-season side, notable results including a 3–0 home win over Spartak Moscow. Despite the fix rumours that had tarnished their promotion to the big time, the club's debut Premier League season was scandal free, Khimki even winning an award from the *Novaya Gazeta* newspaper for 'the most honest team in the Premier League in 2007'.

CHAPTER FOURTEEN

A most unlikely comeback

'Russia needs victory!'

Vladimir Putin

'A Russian revival,' intones the Sky TV commentator, as Russia pin back England in their own half, Guus Hiddink's men seeking a second goal to give them a famous and unexpected victory at the Luzhniki Stadium in Moscow.

A few seconds later, the word 'Progress', flashes up on the stadium's advertising hoardings, followed shortly by 'Eastern Promises', the respective ads for the Russian gas giant Gazprom and the new David Cronenberg film perfectly summing up the way the game is going.

A furious Russian attack culminates with Alexei Berezutsky letting loose a vicious shot from just outside the penalty area. In the England goal Paul Robinson leaps to his left, but can only parry the ball, pushing it out in front of him, where Spartak Moscow's Roman Pavlyuchenko, reacting quickest, evades the attentions of the English defence to prod the ball home. The 80,000 crowd goes predictably mental.

A little over fifteen minutes later, the final whistle blows and the Russian commentator, his voice by now hoarse with emotion, rasps, 'Can it really be? Can it? We have beaten England!'

Russia has lived through many illusions, its entire society at one time based around an economic and political self-delusion, but football, immune to doctored facts and statistics, to propaganda and distortion, does not lie, and the truth was there on the scoreboard for all to see.

'Russia 2 England 1.'

Moscow's political elite heralded the result as proof of the country's imminent superpower status, evidence that Russia had recovered from the trials and tribulations of the 1990s.

'The world should get used to Russian victories – and not only in sport,' said Boris Gryzlov, speaker in the State Duma, Russia's lower house of parliament.

His words were echoed, less eloquently perhaps, but certainly with more feeling, by the Russian football fans who filled the squares and streets of the largest nation on Earth, chanting 'Russia – Forward, Russia – Ahead!' until dawn.

It is a strange and wonderful thing to lose yourself in another nation's culture, sporting or otherwise, and I had often wondered what my reaction would be were the country of my birth and my adopted homeland to face each other on the football field. I was curious to know how I would react. Would I feel an instinctive bond with England's overpaid, pampered stars, or would I root for Russia, for footballers I saw week in, week out? After more than a decade in Russia, the names of the heroes and villains of the Russian Premier League were as familiar to me as those of old friends.

In January 2006 my hypothetical dilemma became a reality, as England were drawn with Russia in Group E for Euro 2008's qualifying stage. At first, when quizzed as to with which side my sympathies would lie, I took the easy way out, saying that I wished both nations home victories. However, in truth, my affections had already begun to drift eastwards.

The build-up to the matches, the first in September 2007, the second a month later, brought home to me just how revered, rightly or wrongly, English football is the world over. I had become used to being quizzed on the beautiful game by Russians, but the weeks before the qualifiers saw the country engulfed in a frenzy of interest in the English national side.

While attending a compulsory physical and mental health check in order to receive a Russian work visa, the psychiatrist, upon noting my nationality, abandoned all pretence of an examination of my mental state and launched straight into a dissection of Russia's chances against England.

'I stopped believing in our team after the 2002 World Cup,' he told me. 'Our players just don't have the heart for it. They are only interested in the money. Your lot though . . . they are the real thing. English football has a passion that the Russian game lacks. You'll do us, home and away.'

'But what about Hiddink?' I asked. Hadn't he breathed new life into the national game? Hadn't he changed the mentality of the Russian players?

The doctor sighed, and popped a stick of gum into his mouth.

'That lot,' he said, 'are incurable. Simply incurable.'

'Who do you support by the way?' the doctor asked as I was leaving his office.

For a second I wondered if this was a trick question, if his judgement as to my sanity would rest on my answer.

'Nottingham Forest,' I replied.

He shrugged, and handed me my clean bill of mental health.

The worldwide respect enjoyed by English and, in as much as most people are able to grasp the distinction, British football is to a certain degree due to the fact that many countries owe, in one way or another, the origins of their national game to expat Britons.

Russia is no exception. Indeed, the 12 September Wembley match was due to be played on the 110th anniversary of the first ever game between teams from Moscow and St Petersburg, a de facto Russian–England fixture, as the St Petersburg side was entirely made up of Englishmen employed at the city's port.

That game, which the St Petersburg Englishmen won 2–0, did much to stir up interest in football in Russia, and two years later the English national amateur side, the then Olympic champions, came to St Petersburg for a series of encounters, winning the first 14–0. Despite the next two matches also seeing easy English victories, the Russian press noted, somewhat optimistically perhaps, that 'a few more training sessions and we'll be able to beat those Englishmen'.

A century on, and countless training sessions later, the autumn Euro 2008 qualifying fixtures would, oddly enough, be the first ever meetings between the originators of the modern game and post-Soviet Russia.

Much was expected of the Russian national team at Wembley. By now, the vast majority of Russians had been won over to the idea of a foreign coach, and the memory of 2004's drubbing in Portugal was receding with every passing match. Although results had not yet made the world sit up and pay attention, there was an optimism in Russian football that perfectly reflected the nation's overall political and economic resurgence.

Andrei Kanchelskis still had reservations, however, pointing out to me when I called him a few weeks before the England game that Russia had yet to be really tested, that they had yet to meet any of the world's top sides in a competitive fixture. 'We'll see,' he said, when I asked him if Hiddink had made a difference to Russia's national side.

Indeed, in a friendly against Holland in February of that year, Russia had gone down 4–1 in Amsterdam. Still, the score had been goalless at half-time, and both teams had used the second half to experiment, so it was perhaps unwise to draw too many conclusions from the rather meaningless friendly. Nevertheless, it was an unpleasant reminder that Russia still had work to do, that football greatness could not be bought, no matter how many petrodollars were pumped into the sport.

Expectations, however, were high as Russia flew to London in search of the three points that would do much to boost their Euro 2008 hopes. Victory in England would undoubtedly be heralded as a cause for national celebration, a sign that the country's national sport was keeping up with the breakneck changes transforming Russia's major cities.

A mere decade after the incompetence of the Yeltsin administration had brought the country to its knees, ever-rising oil prices had seen a sharp increase in living standards – foreign holidays, cars, flats, all of these things were now, for many people at least, obtainable. Life had ceased to be a daily struggle for survival.

True, there were still many problems – food prices, for example, were frozen temporarily in late 2007 to keep the cost of basic groceries within the means of the poorest members of society, yet the vast majority of Russians in the main population centres had never had it so good.

A few days before the Wembley fixture I spoke to Kostya Murzin, a football-mad political analyst, about the recent boom in the Russian game.

'Real football passion is usually found, and I'm speaking on a national scale here, in countries that are either extremely poor,' he began, 'and for whom football is an escape from the struggle of everyday existence, or in countries on the ascent, either politically or economically, for whom the game is seen as being a source of national pride. It's no coincidence that sides representing nations that have just gained independence tend to do well – look at Croatia in the 1998 World Cup for example. Russia is, without a doubt, on the ascent, and its football, as the national sport, is an integral part of that. It's one of the ways in which we can announce our imminent return to superpower status.'

But did he really think that Russia could pull off a victory at Wembley?

'To be honest, no,' Kostya said, frowning. 'But that doesn't mean I don't believe in it with all my heart.'

I watched the September match in a sports bar on the glimmering, casino-filled New Arbat in Moscow, as obvious a symbol of Russia's rebirth as you are likely to find. There were a few expat England fans in attendance, but they were determinedly low-key, dressed in shirts and jeans rather than draped in Union Jacks.

However, a day after Russia announced that it had created the world's most powerful non-nuclear weapon in the shape of the thermobaric bomb, it was England's own instrument of mass destruction, Michael Owen, who decided things, scoring twice in the first half.

The sports bar howled with disappointment as Rio Ferdinand stroked home England's third goal, putting the game beyond doubt. All around Moscow before the game, the match had been the main topic of conversation, and there had been an uncommon belief in the side, something that I had never really heard before. While Russians had previously supported the national team with an enviable passion, they had never expected it to win, their fanaticism tempered with a deeply ingrained fatalism.

The 3–0 defeat at Wembley was a blow to the self-image of Russia, but it was no killer punch. Russia was strong now, and could take such a setback.

Although the mood in Moscow following Russia's defeat was dark (was it really coincidence that President Putin dismissed his entire government less than 24 hours after the final whistle?), the Russia media was subdued in its sorrow. The usual quote for times of disaster, former prime minister Viktor Chernomyrdin's post-1998 financial-crisis quip that 'We hoped for something better, but things turned out like they always do' was notably absent.

The result, its absence seemed to say, was a setback, and that was all. Defeats were no longer all-defining catastrophes, but hitches, battles lost in the wider war. Indeed, there was an enviable maturity and confidence in Russia's reaction to England's victory.

'Russia were overawed at Wembley,' a Moscow journalist told me after the match, drowning his sorrows in a perhaps ironic pint of imported British ale. 'We have always had a great respect for the

English game, and it showed in the players' performance. There is still the return to come, though,' he said, smiling wryly, 'and that will be a completely different game.'

The English press had made much of the Luzhniki's plastic pitch, and Gary O'Connor, who had played there for Lokomotiv against Spartak, seemed to think that Russia would have an advantage, as their players would be more used to the surface. However, in truth, there were only two players in the side able to profess intimate knowledge with the pitch – Dmitri Torbinsky and Roman Pavlyuchenko – both members of Spartak Moscow, for whom the Luzhniki was home turf.

'The pitch certainly favours technical players,' Ruslan Nigmatulin, who had played on the artificial surface many times during his period as Russian national goalkeeper, told me when I called him the day before the game.

Whatever the truth of the matter, the English tabloids hyped up the surface as Russia's secret weapon, a devastating part of the former Soviet republic's arsenal in the new Cold War that was rapidly unfolding on and off the pitch. Just days before the match, the head of Russia's Federal Security Service claimed that Russia had discovered multiple cases of 'foreign spies' in Russia over the last few years, many of them in the pay of British intelligence services.

Indeed, the political subtext behind autumn's England–Russia double bill was something that, as the Russians say, '*tolko lenivii*' – 'only the lazy' – had failed to mention.

Russia was unashamedly flexing its new-found economic and military strength, and relations between Moscow and London were at their lowest since the Cold War had ended. In the autumn of 2007, Russia's air force launched long-range patrols of the world's oceans, and the sight of Russian bombers off the coast of Scotland was an unwelcome reminder for Westminster of the rapidly changing political and military reality.

The relationship between Russia and Britain was also soured by extradition squabbles and diplomatic expulsions over the 2006

London murder of the ex-KGB man Alexander Litvinenko, and in July of that year, President Putin snapped, 'Britain forgets it is no longer a colonial power and that Russia was never its colony.'

To add spice to the match, if any were needed, there were rumours before the game that Andrei Lugovoi, the man accused by British police of adding an unordered nuclear element to Litvinenko's sushi experience, was planning to attend the game. 'I have a ticket,' said Lugovoi, 'but I have yet to decide if I will go.'

Ruslan Nigmatulin was doubtful, however, that politics would play a large role in the forthcoming fixture, saying, 'Both teams are desperate to get to Euro 2008, and the pure sporting motivation far outweighs any political aspect to the match.'

Before I hung up, I asked the former Spartak keeper for a prediction. 'Two–one to Russia,' he said, confidently.

As Moscow geared up for the visit of the English national football team, posters that read – 'Putin's plan for Russia – Victory!' sprang up on advertising billboards all over the Russian capital. No one was quite sure if the enigmatic message from the increasingly unpredictable president referred to the upcoming game or not, yet the country's football fans, with equal measures of enthusiasm and irony, adopted the slogan as their own.

The match was set to be the biggest that the Russian national team had played since the split-up of the USSR, and the country's FA announced before the game that they had received more than 600,000 applications for tickets. The fixture also looked set to become a glittering high-level Moscow social event, government and business leaders planning to take time out to attend. Rumour even had it that President Putin would drop by to lend the team some moral support.

And if that wasn't enough to fill Gerrard and co with apprehension, the Russian Football Federation had ordered a collection of gigantic banners to be draped across the stadium. The 'largest ever to be seen at a football match', the biggest of these was said to measure 50 × 70 metres. The exact content of the banners was being kept secret until the day of the match, yet there were many who would have laid money on 'Putin's Plan for Russia – Victory', as featuring prominently.

As the date of the return fixture grew closer, thousands of fans queued for some 6,500 tickets placed on open sale in early October. Braving torrential rain, their numbers far outstripped the queues to see Russia's first president, Boris Yeltsin, lying in state at the Christ the Saviour Cathedral earlier that year.

There was anger, however, as rumours began to circulate that touts had managed to strike a deal with Luzhniki employees, severely curtailing the already-pitiful amount of tickets on offer.

'Humanity has yet to develop an effective weapon against touts,' said Vitali Mutko, in his third year as head of the Russian Football Federation, upon being questioned on the issue.

On 16 October I attended Steve McClaren and John Terry's press conference at the luxury Baltschug Kempinski hotel in the centre of Moscow, a couple of corner kicks or so away from Red Square.

John Terry was up first, and the English journalists present quizzed him relentlessly about his recent knee injury.

'Will you be able to play, John?' asked one of them.

'The knee is OK. I'm fit,' replied the Hero of Istanbul.

'If it hurt, would you tell us?'

'I would,' nodded Terry.

And so on, the English press displaying an obsessiveness bordering on the masochistic as far as John Terry's knee was concerned.

'Did it really hurt when you hurt it?'

'It did.'

'If it hurts during the game, will you ask to come off?'

'I will.'

This went on for a good twenty minutes, which is not a great period of time in relative terms, I agree, but in my opinion far too long to spend discussing a Chelsea player's knee.

'Any questions from the Russian press? In English, please,' said the English side's press-attaché after all possible combinations of 'pain-knee-match-John' had been exhausted.

The Russian journalists looked a touch put out. One of them bravely put forward a question in torturously constructed English, but Terry didn't seem to get the exact gist of it, and launched into meaningless football-speak for a few minutes instead.

I thought for a second. And then raised my hand. I had often wondered why footballers spoke in clichés, but now I knew why – they could only answer the questions they were posed, and these were singularly without humour, wit or originality.

During the year in which I had spent investigating Russia's national game, I had come to appreciate the bizarre nature of press conferences. World-famous people stood, or sat, before you, and you could ask them anything you wanted at all. Although a wide range of non sequiturs immediately sprang to my mind, I decided to stick to the upcoming game.

No one doubts the connection between politics and football, especially at international level, yet the players themselves are very rarely asked to express their opinions on the subject. Of course, this could have been, as Alexei Smertin had pointed out to me, that most footballers are perceived as being somewhat dim-witted, yet this was no reason not to try to raise the level of questions being posed to Captain Marvel.

The press attaché nodded at me. I considered for a second putting on a thick Russian accent, but then decided against it.

'Do you think the match's political subtext will get to the players?'

Terry looked baffled.

'Especially Wayne Rooney?' I added, slightly cruelly perhaps, immediately regretting it.

The press attaché leaned over and muttered something, maybe clarifying the meaning of the phrase 'political subtext'. Terry didn't seem to have an answer, and smiled broadly in place of a reply. Much as he had done, in fact, a few weeks earlier when asked by a *Sovetski-Sport* journalist to back up his statement that he 'respected Russia's players' by actually naming a couple.

'He probably thought political subtext was a match formation,' a passing journalist said, as we awaited the appearance of the England manager.

In truth, during my time in Russia, I had almost forgotten about the existence of men like Steve McClaren. Of course, I had seen him on TV, but to see him in the flesh somehow brought back odd memories of youth-club teams and men who filled their days shouting at teenagers to 'move the ball, move the ball', of towel flicking and dodgy haircuts and chunky gold jewellery, of a singular lack of imagination or curiosity about the outside world.

The Russians weren't overly impressed with McClaren either, one sports journalist writing the next day: 'It really was hard to believe that Mr McClaren was speaking the language of Shakespeare and Dickens. He seemed to only know around a dozen words of English, one of which – "confidence" – he repeated many times throughout the press conference.'

There was, in truth, a blankness about McClaren, a void that longed to be filled.

'It's great that we have the chance to make sure of qualification,' he said, smiling. 'And we are very confident we can do a good job.'

Russia's hooligans had been looking forward to England's visit since the draw for Euro 2008 had been made in Montreux, Switzerland in January 2006. A couple of days before kick-off, groups of England fans began to arrive in Moscow, buying up en masse traditional Russian-style fur hats. I wasn't sure if this was an attempt to mingle in, but it had the opposite effect of making the Three Lions fans stand out like, well, England fans in Moscow. No one under the age of seventy has worn such hats in the capital since long before perestroika, even more so when the mercury has yet to drop below zero.

As well as buying fur hats, the England supporters went on vodka-buying sprees; predictably, some of them were unable to hold their drink. Trouble kicked off the evening before the game, a Russian police spokesman telling the Interfax news agency that the England fans 'had gone straight from the airport to the bars, and were looking for trouble'. Although these pissed-up, fur-hat-buying men and women were by no means representative of England's notorious hardcore hooligan scene, some Russian 'firms' decided to test themselves against the 'Hooligan Kings' anyhow, launching, for the most part, unprovoked attacks on England fans.

'First English Blood', read a Russian newspaper the next day, along with news that four England supporters had been hospitalised. Still, I reasoned, it could have been worse – when the Republic of Ireland had visited in 2002, an Irish supporter had been killed as Russia fans went on frenzied rampages, sharpened razor blades stuck to their boots.

I spoke to 'Gosha', the fan who had so relished testing himself against England's hard core, but he was dismissive, and, I sensed, a little affronted by the feebleness of Albion's hools. 'They weren't real hooligans,' he told me after the match. 'Sure, we got into a few fights, but it was men against boys,' he said. 'Men against fucking boys.'

The match at the Luzhniki began with the two sides' respective anthems, or 'hymns' as the Russians say, more than seventy years of Communism having blurred the distinction between the secular and the spiritual. The cameras zoomed in on Guus Hiddink. The sixty-year-old trainer had apparently already learned enough Russian to make a stab at singing Russia's Soviet-era anthem, revived, albeit with different words, by President Putin in 2000.

I went in search of my seat in the press box, almost getting kicked out of the stadium by a nervy cop as I clambered over a low wall. I looked in vain to my right for my wife and our friends, but they were lost in the ever-swelling sea of fans.

Tanya had told me that she thought a lot of Russians, including herself, admired English football so much that a significant number of them would support England at the Luzhniki. Personally, I couldn't see much evidence of this, especially as even she herself seemed to already have forgotten her prediction, any love or passion for Owen and co wiped out in the thrill of match day.

The 'largest banner ever seen at a football match' was subsequently revealed, covering a quarter of the crowd with an extremely evil and aggressive-looking bear. Despite widespread predictions, there was no sign of 'Putin's Plan for Russia – Victory!'

Or, come to that, no sign of Putin himself, the president evidently having decided not to attend the match, sending the country's recently appointed prime minister, Viktor Zubkov, in his place.

It was not too hard to see the logic behind Putin's decision. There was no guarantee that England would follow the script demanding a Russian victory, and the risk of being for ever linked to a Russian humiliation was too great. What if Russia crumbled? What if Owen and Rooney turned on the style, and England ran out easy victors? It would not do for the leader of the resurgent Russian Federation to be associated with defeat in any form or fashion.

Zubkov, a one-time tax official plucked from obscurity by Putin a little over a month before the encounter, had a rambling and bizarre pre-match message for the Russian team, saying, 'They have eleven players, and we have eleven players. They have two arms and two hands and one head each, and we have the same. But do you know what the most important thing is? We, Russians, won World War Two. And we were the first in space. And so we have to do all we can [to win]. And, come on Russia, come on, come on.'

True, this 'pre-match statement' was only released an hour after the match, when the result was already being celebrated up and down the country, but that, I guess, is politics for you.

When Wayne Rooney hammered home a volley from the edge of the box to put England ahead, Putin's decision to stay away was starting to look like an extremely well-thought-out move by the ex-KGB man.

Half-time came and went, and Russian passes began to go astray. On top of this, the twelfth man of home support was beginning to lose its voice. England had twenty minutes to hold out to get the win that would take them to Euro 2008.

However, if twenty minutes is a long time to talk about John Terry's knee, then it is an eternity on the football field.

Russia, as Guus Hiddink was to explain later, had put two men on Joe Cole, pushing the Chelsea player back, making him 'play as a defender', and the men in red were suddenly tearing down England's flanks.

And then, before anyone knew what was happening, Wayne Rooney had somehow found himself the last man in England's crumbling defence, his push-and-shove routine bringing down Russia's Player of the Year, Konstantin Zyryanov. The Italian referee had no doubts. Penalty.

Steve McClaren would later claim that initial contact had been outside the box, but, as the Russians pointed out the next day, Zyryanov had had a perfectly good 'goal' ruled out at Wembley for handball, and not a single England player had protested the referee's decision to grant Russia the spot-kick.

'God returned his debt, and punished the English,' Zyryanov later told the Russian press.

Spartak Moscow's Pavlyuchenko, who had been brought on by Hiddink ten minutes earlier, stepped up to the spot. Paul Robinson frowned. Pavlyuchenko struck. 1–1. The Russian sub had put a hole in England's Euro 2008 dreams, and it was about to get wider.

Hiddink stood at the edge of the touchline, gesturing for Russia to keep up the pressure. For once, it was a Russian goal that was looking inevitable, for once fortune had defected to Russia's side, and the crowd and the players knew it.

A couple of days before the match, the Russian tabloids had run a story about a voodoo witchdoctor hired to put a curse on the England players, one that would 'hinder their ability to communicate with each other during the game and make their limbs slow and heavy'. The seventy-something Haitian hired by 'a group of Russian fans' had used Russian matryoshka dolls painted with images of Cole, Terry and Lampard instead of the more customary voodoo variety.

Despite the deviation from tradition, the curse seemed to have been more than effective: Terry's knee had given way almost straight after the press conference at the Baltschug Kempinski hotel, Cole was being run into the corner flag by the Russians and Lampard was sulking on the bench.

Russia came forward again, and the crowd inhaled as one; hoping, praying, cursing, and then exhaled, blowing the ball, with some help from the boot of Roman Pavlyuchenko, into the back of the England net.

If English football has had more than forty years of mere 'hurt', as the song puts it, then the Russian game had seen more than fifteen years of utter humiliation and self-destruction.

Pavlyuchenko's second goal was instant catharsis, wiping away all the disappointments, the false dawns, the anger and the accusations. Everything was forgiven. True, there were unpleasant things happening in Russia, and the result would be seized on by publicity-hungry politicians, but right then, none of that mattered.

The Spartak fan and journalist in the press box next to me beamed with joy.

'Pavlyuchenko – Spartak!' he said, pointing to his matching Spartak hat, scarf and bag.

England tried to go forward, but it was a token gesture, empty and unconvincing, and Russia played out the final fifteen minutes of the game to complete a most unlikely comeback.

'Some will say we got lucky, but it is the ones who deserve it and want it the most who get lucky. At two–one I was sure we would win. There was plenty of time left and the English poured forward, but I suddenly felt some kind of calm inside,' said an effusive Roman Pavlyuchenko, grinning from ear to ear, straight after the game.

The happiness was infectious. I called my mother-in-law to congratulate her on Russia's victory. No one had really believed I would support Russia, and she sounded a touch bemused by my joy at Russia's success. Back in England, won over by my enthusiasm and their many trips to the country, my parents and younger sister by now shared something of my passion for the Russian game, and my father later told me than when Pavlyuchenko scored his second goal he and my mother had leaped around the room cheering so much that 'the neighbours must have thought we were Russian'. My sister Siobhan expressed her joy in simpler terms, sending a brief but heartfelt text message – 'Hurray!'

Back in Moscow, the press centre was full of seasoned Russian journalists, some of them wiping away actual tears of joy, many of them already toasting their country's victory. And then, when the congratulations were over, the crowd hushed and waited for Hiddink, the Wise Foreign General to Russia's Brave Partisans to come out and speak of Victory.

Hiddink waited until the applause had died down, and then spoke quietly into the microphone. 'Russian players have a great deal of talent and creativity,' he began, 'but sometimes I'd like to see that transformed into more effectiveness.'

He could, I realised, have been talking about Russia as a whole, putting his finger on the root of the country's many problems with his incisive post-match analysis.

'Hiddink for president,' whispered a journalist next to me.

'But today, everything came together, and I'm proud of the players,' the Dutch trainer continued, as the hall burst into another round of applause.

An English journalist posed a question about England's tactics, but Hiddink refused to be drawn into any criticism of Steve McClaren.

'Russia is a huge country,' he said, 'and I'm Russia's trainer, not England's.'

The English journalists in the room let out a collective sigh of regret. Hiddink was everything that McClaren was not – erudite, astute and successful.

Perhaps, I thought, that was the real reason why the men at the FA had never got round to appointing him England manager after Sven-Goran Eriksson's departure. They would have felt threatened, would have loathed his refusal to stand on ceremony. Hiddink had shaken up the Russian game, reorganising the structure of the Russian Football Federation as he saw fit, and the result was there for all to see.

Although Hiddink had upset and offended a lot of people with his no-nonsense tactics and style, the Russian national team had benefited from his willingness to make changes, to stand on toes if necessary. Russians, however, are used to painful transition, to the overthrow of inept and dying regimes, and perhaps it was a little easier for them to accept such earth-shaking and revolutionary changes than it would have been for the conservative, anonymous figures in charge of the English game to come to terms with the Dutchman's inevitable surgical strikes on their HQ in Soho Square.

'I told the players, get your equaliser, and you will get another,' added Hiddink, diplomatic enough not to dwell on England's well-known tendency to wilt under pressure.

McClaren stormed into the press conference, all sulks and petulance.

'Questions in English only,' the press attaché announced. 'The Russian journalists will get a translation afterwards.'

'Russian journalists speak English too,' came an objection from the hall, followed by, in Russian this time, 'You are a cad, Mr McClaren.'

'The penalty was a disgrace,' said the one-time Middlesbrough manager.

'So it's all down to the ref, then?' said an angry English journalist. 'What about the second goal? A draw would have been enough.' The press dogs sensed weakness and blood.

McClaren's grilling lasted a good twenty minutes. His face began to get redder and redder as the merciless criticism and stinging sarcasm continued. There were, it seemed to me, also tears in the England manager's eyes.

The majority of Russian journalists had left the room in protest at McClaren's 'questions only in English', statement, but the ones who remained, and understood enough English to grasp what was going on, looked shocked. This very public and merciless humiliation was something right out of the pages of Russian literature: a soul stripped bare, all its faults and neuroses torn out for public mockery. It was not a pretty sight, and certainly not something that 'English gentlemen' were supposed to indulge in.

I suddenly felt sorry for McClaren. I put my hand up, hoping to give the condemned man some breathing space, an opportunity to make a timely withdrawal.

'Apart from the result, how did you like Moscow?' I asked.

McClaren gazed at me, half-startled, half-relieved by the question. Had he understood what I was trying to do? Was that gratefulness I saw beneath the pain?

'Uh, I can't really think about anything but the result right now,' he said.

The press attaché seized the moment, however, announcing an immediate end to the press conference, and McClaren made his retreat.

However, there was still the informal 'briefing' of the English press to come. McClaren had made his way to the corner of the hall where a pack of English journalists, their blood lust not yet sated, immediately surrounded him.

'No Russians,' announced a chubby FA official.

'I'm Israeli,' said a cameraman.

'No Israelis either. Only English.'

The official turned to look at me. 'Who are you?' he asked.

'Virgin Books?'

'You're not one of ours,' the FA man replied, after a slight pause in which he weighed me up. He placed an arm on my shoulder in a friendly, yet stern, manner.

'Off you go.'

'Not one of yours?' I thought, making my way out of the hall.

In a way, I suppose, he was right.

Much was made of Steve McClaren's refusal to allow questions in Russian at the post-match press conference, with one Moscow sports journalist calling the former England manager in print 'an empty shell of a human being'. It was not only McClaren who had needled the Russians, however.

'The Russian players were particularly angry after the match at Wembley,' Igor Rabiner, the bestselling author who had opened my eyes to the truth behind today's Spartak, told me.

'When they went to exchange shirts with the England team after the game,' he went on, 'the England "stars" didn't particularly seem to care about taking our guys' tops. They offered to give our players their shirts, but weren't bothered about swapping, saying, kind of, "well, take them if you want – here". I know a lot of players were very upset about that, and some of them later told me it had boosted the side's desire for revenge prior to the return match in Moscow.'

Russia, understandably, greeted the victory as a piece of history, the players who had overcome 'the land that gave the world football' making the most of their triumph.

'Russia have a compact group of players who don't have anywhere near as much money, but with far more hard workers on the field. That's the difference between the countries. That's why we are in a strong position and England have been left just hoping,' said Alexander Kerzhakov, the man who had been substituted to make way for Pavlyuchenko, destroyer of English dreams. His words were widely reported in the English media, and seemed to strike a chord with the nation's grieving fans.

The nation's political leaders continued to heap praise on the side, Konstantin Kosachyev, chairman of Russia's State Duma International Affairs committee, saying that the victory went 'beyond mere sporting success', and that 'It's been a long time since we have had a victory capable of lifting the national spirit, something we desperately need in order to achieve victory in many different spheres.'

President Putin however was oddly subdued, commenting only that 'The victory was a result of team spirit, the professionalism of the trainer, and the support of the entire nation'.

But then, with his annual televised question-and-answer session scheduled for the next day, and parliamentary elections that were being promoted as a referendum on his almost eight years in the Kremlin slated for early December, he may very well have had other things to think about.

After the euphoria of the England game had died down, Russia began to prepare for a trip to Israel, to a country where, as the Soviet-era singer/songwriter Vladimir Vysotsky had once sung, 'one in every four' people were of Russian or Soviet descent.

Victory over the Israelis would then leave Russia with only with the formality of a match in Andorra to ensure qualification for Euro 2008. The tiny principality of some 80,000 had lost its previous 29 European Championship matches, and was not expected to pose the largest nation on earth too many problems.

'Russia is on the verge of a return and that's why qualifying is so important for the national team,' said Guus Hiddink, as the Russian side left Moscow, where the first winter snows had already begun to fall, adding later that the match was 'like a World Cup Final for me'.

For the Israelis the encounter was essentially meaningless, however, and doubts quickly arose in both England and Russia that Israel would offer much resistance to Hiddink's side.

The *Sun* ran a story a few days before the game quoting, with horror, Israel's Russian-born goalkeeping trainer, Alexander Ubarov, as saying, 'I would like Russia to qualify for the Euros – and for them that means winning in Israel.'

'It's not over until the fat lady sings, but I'm afraid she is likely to sing in this case,' former England manager Graham Taylor told BBC Radio Five Live.

Chelsea owner Roman Abramovich's well-known connections to Israel were also touched upon. Abramovich had spent large amounts of money on building up Israeli football, and the English and the Russian press voiced suspicions, at times bordering on allegations, that the country's national team would go easy on Russia as a result.

Hiddink, however, wasn't buying it, and rejected claims that the game's result was a foregone conclusion, telling journalists, 'The less serious sections of the mass media have been writing garbage, but I don't give them much credence. We are going to face another tough game against Israel, who are traditionally very strong at home.'

Vitali Mutko paid an official Russia Football Federation visit to the side as they prepared for the tie in sunny Cyprus, warning the players that the 'fix' rumours were just that, and that Israel would 'give it everything'.

Which, unfortunately for Russia, they did, an injury-time winner by Omer Golan in Tel Aviv handing England an unexpected lifeline, and simultaneously turning the Israeli player into an English sporting hero. Dmitri Sychev had come close seconds before Israel's winner, his shot clipping the edge of the post, but that meant nothing now. From the seemingly hopeless position that the Moscow defeat had left them in, McClaren's men simply needed to avoid defeat at home to Croatia to pip Russia to a Euro 2008 spot.

The sports bar where I had been watching the game fell silent as the final whistle blew. There were no cries of despair, no cursing, just a long and deathly silence.

Although Russia had dominated the last 25 minutes, before that there had been a casualness to their play, their movements slack and unfocused. While the players would subsequently deny accusations that the team had relaxed after the England match and were guilty of taking victory in Israel for granted, it was hard not to suspect that they had, indeed, as the Russians say, 'made a hide from a still-living bear'.

And then a voice at the next table piped up, the words inevitable, the suggestion self-mocking, a parody of Russia and Russianness.

'So, vodka, anyone?'

Later on, trailing home through the snow, the cries – ironic, sarcastic, full of spite – rang out in the distance.

'Russia – ahead, Russia – forward!'

After the catastrophic defeat in Israel, it was tempting, although admittedly illogical and unfair, to add Hiddink to the long list of men who had promised to lead Russia to a brighter future and failed.

Lenin, Stalin, Yeltsin, Hiddink . . . the list had a certain ring to it. But Hiddink had, to give him credit, promised nothing. 'I'm no magician,' he had said, 'but we'll give it our best shot.'

It was a very Russian, a very Slavic defeat. From the euphoria of a month ago, all hope had seemingly vanished. All the talk of a 'Russian revival', of victory in 'many different spheres' now seemed like nothing but a cruel joke. In the next few days, the ratings of United Russia, the leading party in Russia's State Duma, dropped almost 10 per cent in opinion polls.

Oddly enough, however, the masses of Russian politicians who had queued up to praise the side following the victory against England at the Luzhniki were silent. There were no words of support, no expressions of sympathy. No one wanted to be for ever linked to the defeat, to the apparent death of a nation's dreams.

Or maybe, just maybe, I'm being too cynical here, and the politicians, like Russia itself, were simply in shock.

'I woke up this morning and still couldn't come to grips with it,' said Dima, a long-suffering fan of the national team.

The Tel Aviv disaster recalled the nature of other earlier defeats, but this one was crueller, because Russia were, in truth, a decent side, with young players and a quality trainer. They had all the potential to become a major European force.

'It's always like that with Russia,' a Moscow sports journalist told me, his self-pity spilling over. 'Other teams get away with missing chances, and still win. But not Russia. Not Russia . . .'

'We lack a winning spirit,' said Vitali Mutko. 'We are all to blame.'

The next day, in a masochistic exercise in self-criticism, Russia TV broadcast a two-and-a-half-hour inquest into the defeat, including a replay of the entire game against Israel.

'I am to blame for the defeat,' said Vladimir Gabulov, Russia's goalkeeper, clearly having taken Mutko's words to heart, the interview taking place in an appropriately dark corner of the team's hotel. His face crumpled. 'I should have done more,' he said.

'The outfield players missed chances,' said the interviewer, attempting to offer some support, but the young keeper was inconsolable.

'Russia lost that match because of the amount of fixed games that went on at the end of the 2007 domestic season,' Igor Rabiner told me.

'There were so many games where the results had been arranged beforehand, that the players got out of the habit of battling for points,' he said. 'Even though Hiddink and Mutko told them that the game in Tel Aviv had not been fixed, they are only human and, subconsciously, it affected their performance.'

However, despite Russia's failure to book an early place at Euro 2008, and the subsequent self-pity, the fairly widespread opinion seemed to be that the side had simply missed its chance, that footballing success was, despite the setback, inevitable in the long run.

'I've waited too long, believed in my team for too many years to give up now,' wrote Vasili Utkin (the journalist who had spoken to me of his belief in Hiddink) on the *Sport Segodnya* website. 'My side's day will come, I assure you.' It came a lot sooner than he, or anyone else, could have ever imagined.

'Let's offer money to the Croatian team!' said the TV presenter, his voice shaking with excitement. 'Why not? Let's get all our businessmen to donate cash, and then make an official announcement from the Russia Football Federation. If you beat England at Wembley, we'll give you such and such a sum.'

Guests on the show included Alexander Mostovoi, the former Russian international, and Gennadiy Khazanov, a well-known actor and football fan.

'Does it have to be official, this offer?' said Khazanov, frowning.

'Such things go on in Spain,' interrupted Mostovoi, who had played in the country for many years with Celta Vigo, 'and they do have an effect on players' performances, I can tell you.'

Khazanov spoke up again, the actor's voice deadpan. 'Anyway, I consider that England are just obliged to lose to Croatia. If they don't, it just proves that they have no respect whatsoever for Russia.'

Although there may have been other attempts to offer incentives to the Croatians, the only public announcement was made by the Spartak owner and LUKoil vice president Leonid Fedun, who pledged to present the four best Croatian players with Mercedes cars if the Balkan team could help Russia out.

'I am acting as a private individual and a fan of the national team,' he said, drawing a line between his business activities and his attempt to give the Croatian players an edge over England.

'And now he expects us to believe that Spartak never offer incentives to our opponents?' an indignant CSKA fan complained to me after the businessman's promise.

Indeed, for a man who had spent much of 2006 and 2007 accusing CSKA of cynically undermining the concept of fair play, it was, I had to agree, a touch hypocritical of the Spartak owner to suddenly decide that 'stimulation' was, after all, a perfectly valid tactic.

Unlike the Israel match, the sports bars were empty for Russia's game against Andorra. There was little talk of the game beforehand, and Russia settled down to watch Croatia's visit to London, hoping against hope for a miracle.

'There were some encouraging things,' Igor, a Russian fan who watched the game in the early hours of the morning in Chita, Siberia (some six hours ahead of Moscow), told me later.

'I mean, the Croats are also Slavs, and there were two of "our" guys in the team [Stipe Pletikosa, the Spartak Moscow goalkeeper, and Ivica Olic, ex-CSKA forward], but the first fifteen minutes just blew me away. I felt like I was watching Brazil. As if it were all a dream. Or a hallucination.'

Indeed, flicking between channels, watching Russia struggle against Andorra in front of some 200 fans at a dark and bumpy shoe-box of a stadium, while Croatia put England to the sword at a packed Wembley to take a 2–0 lead with less than a quarter of the game gone, I couldn't help feeling we had all, somehow, slipped into the Twilight Zone.

At half-time, with Croatia still 2–0 up, footage was shown all over Russia of a massive pro-Putin rally at the Luzhniki Stadium. Thousands of supporters, the majority of them too young to remember life in the Soviet Union, crammed into the Olympic arena as President Putin slammed the country's tiny opposition movement.

'There are still those people in our country who scavenge like jackals at foreign embassies, who count on the support of foreign funds and governments but not the support of their own people,' he said, as Soviet-era songs boomed out over the loudspeakers.

'There are those confronting us who do not want us to carry out our plans, because they have a different view of Russia. They need a weak and feeble state. They need a disorganised and disoriented society, a split society, so that they can carry out their dirty tricks behind its back.' Above him, a huge banner read, 'Victory for Putin is Victory for Russia!'

The president, despite his at times apparent indifference towards football, was picking his moments well. Support Putin, the message seemed to be, and victory is guaranteed. Stand against him, as England had done, and a calamity was inevitable.

Of course, it could have just been good luck. After all, there was no way the Russian president could have known what was going to happen at Wembley, was there?

'I feel like we've been playing Russian roulette,' said Hiddink, after Croatia's 3–2 win at Wembley combined with his team's narrow 1–0 victory over a side made up of shoe salesmen and insurance clerks had put Russia into Euro 2008.

'We had one bullet in the chamber, and put the gun to our heads,' he went on, as a film crew recorded him coming off the pitch in Andorra, pressing a finger to his temple, a little like De Niro in *The Deerhunter*, 'and pulled the trigger. But we are still standing.'

Hiddink then went and sent a text message to Slavan Bilic. 'I'm proud to know you,' it read.

'Yesterday,' said a smiling Dmitri Sychev, the man whose goal against Andorra had given Russia all three points, 'I felt like shit, but now, now I'm the happiest person in the world!' ('Shit' in Russian, for those of you who take an interest in foreign oaths and curses, is govno. Pronounced – 'gav*no*'. With the stress on the final syllable.)

In 1991, a member of the Russian intelligentsia, commenting on the collapse of the USSR, wrote that, 'God has smiled on Russia for the first time this century.'

Less than a decade into the twenty-first century, it was tempting, for the country's football fans at least, to suggest that he may have decided not to wait quite so long this time round.

'I have never, in the forty years I have been watching football, seen a team get a free lunch like that before,' said Leonid Fedun, after confirming his intention to keep his word and present the Croatian team, who were fast becoming Russian folk heroes, with four sparkling new Mercedes.

'I know two extremely fortunate and successful people,' he went on. 'The first is our President Putin, under whom Russia has been reborn, and the second, Hiddink. His sides always seem to get lucky.'

'It was just dumb luck,' Roma, a Russian fan with an odd fondness for the English side Dagenham and Redbridge, told me in a text message after the games had finished. 'We were lucky as hell, but believe me, that was the first time ever the Russian team had seen that kind of good fortune!'

In Siberia, it was already early morning by the time the game at Wembley finished.

'I'd stayed up all night,' Igor told me, 'and I was feeling a bit dizzy. I had to start work at nine a.m. and my head was pounding. I remember standing in front of the window as the game came to an end, the sky just lightening on the horizon, and, fuck, it sounds trite and idiotic now, thinking about it, but I couldn't help feeling that here was a new dawn – in more ways than one.'

He laughed. 'I get quite emotional when Russia win.'

The draw for the final stages of Euro 2008 took place in Switzerland on 2 December 2007. Hiddink and Russia were drawn with Spain, Greece and Sweden in Group D, a virtual repeat of Euro 2004, when the side faced Spain, Greece and Portugal.

Guus Hiddink was guarded after the draw, saying that Russia was a 'young team' that would 'gain experience' at the tournament. Former Russian international Igor Shalimov was more optimistic however, telling *Sport-Express* that, 'Under Hiddink, Russia could get out of its group for the first time.'

However, if Russia was to overcome its habitual difficulties at major tournaments and make progress at Euro 2008, it would have to do so, for the first two games at least, without its captain, Zenit forward Andrei Arshavin. The 2006 Russian Footballer of the Year had been sent off towards the end of Russia's final qualifying fixture against Andorra, lashing out after being needled and harassed by the Andorran defenders all night. Although Russia had subsequently sent a video to UEFA with 'proof' of the said 'provocation', the disciplinary committee ruled that Arshavin would miss the country's first two ties, against Spain and Greece. It was a bitter blow indeed, and one that looked to throw a spanner in Hiddink's preparations for Euro 2008.

Despite the setback, Russia, used to its teams imploding at major tournaments, waited and hoped that Hiddink would yet again live up to his reputation as a master tactician who gets lucky more often than is properly decent.

'I believe we can perform well,' said midfielder Zyryanov. 'All the teams are equal before the start of the tournament,' he added. His words, although typically uncommitted and throwaway, couldn't help but recall the unexpected success of Greece at Euro 2004. Perhaps Hiddink could lead Russia to a similar victory?

'Russia could become champions,' said Igor Dobrovolski, former

Soviet and Russian international, and the coach of Moldova's national side. 'I'm serious. No one considered the Greeks among the favourites, and the dark horses became champions. Why shouldn't Russia follow their lead? Hiddink knows what to expect from his team, how to build it, what to say,' the trainer told *Sovestki-Sport*.

The Dutch master Hiddink reiterated his desire to remain in Russia, to see the side through to the 2010 World Cup in South Africa, the tournament that many believed would see the team reach the height of its powers.

Russia, Hiddink repeated, had great potential, 'but there is still a lot of work ahead of us', the phrase rapidly becoming his personal mantra. With the country's political and economic resurgence gaining pace to the backdrop of deep-seated corruption and the ugly side of nationalism, it was tempting, and not for the first time, to attach a wider significance to Hiddink's words.

As below, so above.

Epilogue

The Russian Football Dynamo, powered by black gold and the political support of the Kremlin, moved into 2008 in better shape than ever before. As the New Year began, world oil prices hit $100 a barrel and gas prices were rising steadily, and for Russia's top clubs that could only mean good news. Zenit St Petersburg and Spartak Moscow, funded by LUKoil and Gazprom respectively, looked set to push for Champions League and UEFA Cup glory with budgets and facilities equalling, and in many cases outstripping, those of their European rivals.

The national team, for so long a source of anguish and shame, was on the rise too, Guus Hiddink's side displaying an uncommon self-belief and tactical know-how. The team, its young stars Arshavin, Pavlyuchenko, Zhirkov and more eagerly sought after by European clubs, were the representatives of the first generation of players too young to consciously remember much of Soviet life, and there were signs that the overmanagement and paralysing fear that had stricken earlier Russian teams was coming to a welcome end.

It was not only Russia's football star that was rising; in January 2008 the leading US private intelligence agency Stratfor stated in a report: 'The country is flush with petrodollars, its debt has vanished, the Chechen insurgency has been suppressed, the central government has all but eliminated domestic opposition, the regime is popular at home, and the US military is too locked down to make more than a token gesture to block any Russian advances.'

Both Russia and its football are currently forging ahead with real power and force. The motor could so easily, however, grind to a halt. From the national side's tendency to press the self-destruct button, to the country's yearning for a Supreme Leader, to the uncertainty over future oil prices, there are many factors that threaten this seemingly unstoppable progress.

'This is Russia,' is the usual throwaway phrase the Russians use to give voice to the capriciousness of life in Moscow and elsewhere, to explain away all uncertainties, and the phrase, while undoubtedly trite and oversimplistic, contains a certain truth. This, indeed, is Russia, and as history has proven time and time again, there really is little point in making guesses as to its future. The largest country on Earth may continue its push for superpower status, its football team may one day become world champions, defying in the process Pele's famous (in Russia at least) prediction that the Russian national side will win the World Cup only when Brazil become world champions in ice hockey.

But the truth is that no one knows for sure. World experts in Soviet affairs, learned and respected Kremlinologists, spectacularly failed to foresee the downfall of the USSR in 1991 and modern Russia remains no less problematic as far as predictions go. The only thing I can say for sure is that the 'people's game' will continue to reflect the reality of life in modern Russia – whatever its shape or form.

As for me, 'A joy shared is a joy doubled', they say (or rather, Goethe said), and while this may be true, it would be equally as valid to suggest that 'A secret shared is a joy halved'. While this book has tried to promote Russian football, I'm not going to be too upset if in this respect it is a failure, if the world's football fans do not flock to Moscow, to Cherkizovo and the Luzhniki, if the players and clubs of the Russian Premier League do not become over-familiar media superstars, their copyrighted images plastered on advertisements in every bar and supermarket across the globe.

In other words, I have found my corner of the beach and, while I may find it hard to resist the temptation to wax lyrical about it, I won't be too concerned if I am left here alone to enjoy the view, to seek wider meaning in championship title races and World Cup qualifiers, in disputed penalties and the most unlikely of comebacks.

'*Sudyu na milo!*'

References, acknowledgements and an incomplete list of random inspirations

Sport-Express: www.sportexpress.ru
Sovetski-Sport: www.sovsport.ru
Sport-Segodnya: www.sports.ru
Total Football: www.totalfootball.ru
RIA Novosti: www.rian.ru
Novaya Gazeta: www.novayagazeta.ru
Futbol magazine (Russia)
Sport Weekend: www.sport-weekend.ru
UEFA: www.uefa.com
The Exile: www.exile.ru
Stratfor: www.stratfor.com
Everything by Daniil Kharms
Kino and Viktor Tsoi
Fakel Voronezh
St Petersburg's Fish Fabrique (1997–2000)
Nottingham Forest, Brian Clough and Archie Gemmill
Kak Ubivali Spartak, Igor Rabiner (Sekret Firmi) 2006
Football against the Enemy, Simon Kuper (Orion) 1994

Motown
Nikolai Gogol and Fyodor Dostoevsky
2000AD and Tharg the Mighty
Soulseek MP3 file sharing program

Thanks and greetings

Tanya Nevinsksya for her love, encouragement and good humour. Siobhan 'Shivka' Bennetts for being a cool sister, innit. Tamara Nikolayevna for her interesting stories and great adjika. Daniel 'Lost Cosmonaut' Humphries for reading my stuff and passing on the world's best flat. James Wills at Watson and Little Ltd for his great patience and spot-on advice.

Ed Faulkner at Virgin Books for his interest and enthusiasm. Simon Kuper for his initial encouragement. Natasha Martin at Aurum Press. Sadie Smith, Kathryn Lane, Alexandra Farrell and all at DK Eyewitnesses. Davina Russell and Sarah Flint at Virgin Books.

Ruslan Dubov at Novaya Gazeta. Igor Rabiner and Vladimir Konstantinov at Sport-Express. Vasili Utkin. Pavel Baev. Nikolai Roganov at Total Football. Sirop from Flint's Crew. All the press attachés who helped me out. Many thanks also to all the footballers, managers, trainers, club owners, officials, hooligans, journalists and fans who agreed to be interviewed.

Even more greetings to Stanislav Tulovsky and family. Dmitri Dudenkov. Elke Klusmann. Irina Konovalova. Irina Kaumbaeva. Arslan Aisakadiyev. Yulia Vainzof. Alex Mitchell. Sergei Murzin. All my aunts, uncles, cousins, etc. Everyone on the English 'Web site' at RIA Novosti.

Thanks to Vitya for not scratching us so much of late. Chupka for president!

Russia has two main daily national sports papers – *Sovetski-Sport* and *Sport-Express*. Both papers are superbly written, and I owe much to both of them for introducing me to the world of Russian football.

All questions, comments, proposals and gift offers to the author at marcbennetts@yahoo.com.

And finally, to my parents again – for everything.

Index